SHAKESPEARE'S TRAGEDIES:
VIOLATION AND IDENTITY

ALEXANDER LEGGATT

CAMBRIDGE
UNIVERSITY PRESS

CAMBRIDGE UNIVERSITY PRESS

Cambridge, New York, Melbourne, Madrid, Cape Town, Singapore, São Paulo

Cambridge University Press
The Edinburgh Building, Cambridge CB2 2RU, UK

Published in the United States of America by Cambridge University Press, New York

www.cambridge.org
Information on this title: www.cambridge.org/9780521608633

First published 2005
Reprinted 2006

Printed in the United Kingdom at the University Press, Cambridge

A catalogue record for this book is available from the British Library

ISBN-13 978-0-521-84624-0 - hardback
ISBN-10 0-521-84624-2   - hardback
ISBN-13 978-0-521-60863-3 - paperback
ISBN-10 0-521-60863-5   - paperback

for Brian Parker

Contents

Acknowledgements

During the long gestation of this book, I was able to test my ideas in lectures delivered at the Folger Library, the British Institute Summer School at Stratford-upon-Avon, Trent University, the Stratford Festival of Canada and the Shakespeare Institute; in conference presentations at the Pacific Northwest Renaissance Conference in Vancouver and the International Association of University Professors of English in Copenhagen; and in seminars at meetings of the Shakespeare Association of America in Albuquerque, Los Angeles, Victoria and New Orleans. At the University of Toronto, I have presented parts of this work at University College, Victoria College, and at meetings of the English Students' Union, the Senior Alumni, and the Work in Progress in English Group. I am grateful to the University of Toronto for conference travel grants, to the organizers who made the occasions possible, and to the audiences for their questions, advice and reactions. I am also grateful to the University of Toronto for the sabbatical leave in which much of the writing was done.

I owe a special debt of gratitude to the students who have worked with me on Shakespeare over the years, especially the students in my graduate course in Shakespearean tragedy. Their challenging insights and fresh thinking have been invaluable. Alan Ackerman read an early version of the chapter on *Hamlet*; Karen Bamford, David Bevington, Brian Gibbons, Peter Holland and Alan Somerset read the entire manuscript at various stages, and I owe much to their criticism, advice and encouragement. Sarah Stanton has been, as always, a wise and patient editor. The follies and errors that remain are my own.

A note on the texts

References to Shakespeare are to the Arden editions, using Arden 3 when available. The principal texts are *Titus Andronicus*, ed. Jonathan Bate (London and New York: Routledge 1995); *Romeo and Juliet*, ed. Brian Gibbons (London and New York: Methuen 1980); *Hamlet*, ed. Harold Jenkins (London and New York: Methuen 1982); *Troilus and Cressida*, ed. David Bevington (Walton-on-Thames: Nelson 1998); *Othello*, ed. E. A. J. Honigmann (Walton-on-Thames: Nelson 1997); *King Lear*, ed. R. A. Foakes (Walton-on-Thames: Nelson 1997); *Macbeth*, ed. Kenneth Muir (London: Methuen; Cambridge, Mass.: Harvard University Press, revised 1962).

Introduction

Shakespeare's first tragedy, *Titus Andronicus*, centers on an act of violation. Titus' daughter Lavinia has been raped in the woods by the Goths Chiron and Demetrius. They cut out her tongue and cut off her hands, taking language away from her. Her uncle Marcus finds her and brings her back to Rome, and to her father. What follows is a moment whose implications resonate throughout this play, and through the plays that follow. Titus at first does not recognize her: "But who comes with our brother Marcus here?" Marcus presents her with the words: "This was thy daughter." Titus replies, "Why, Marcus, so she is" (III.i.63–64). The question is not, what has happened to her? but, who is she? Her body mutilated and her language gone, she seems to Marcus no longer Lavinia but a nameless thing that used to be Lavinia. But for Titus, she is still Lavinia.

Shakespeare's interest in the idea of violation has been examined by critics from a number of angles. To name only two, Linda Woodbridge sees it in cultural terms, in the light of what she calls "magical thinking"; Heather Dubrow relates it to invasions of domestic space.[1] I would like to trace the idea of violation and its implications through the working of the play text itself. *Titus Andronicus* is not just a cultural document but a play – an early, self-conscious play at that. My approach is going to involve a close reading of individual texts, rather against the current practice of reading plays as embedded in their culture and determined by it. The best of this work (as in the two critics I have singled out) has been valuable and illuminating; but there is always the danger that a thick reading of the culture will entail a thin reading of the plays. I have tried to absorb what I find useful in the culturally oriented criticism of the last twenty-five years, and it should be clear that I have found much of it (feminist criticism in particular) very useful indeed. But the engagements with criticism will be mostly in the notes. My main business is a close engagement with the plays themselves, trying to keep them free to do their own thinking. The underlying assumption, implicit throughout, is that this thinking was shaped by dramatic considerations and by the theatrical conditions in which Shakespeare worked. This is not going to be a work of stage history, much less an attempt to reconstruct the performances of Shakespeare's time, though practical stage considerations will surface throughout the discussion. But I want to begin not just by introducing the main themes that cluster around the idea of violation but by relating those themes to the theatrical circumstances in which the plays began.

The first of these themes, and one that will concern us throughout, is identity. Lavinia is the subject of a dialogue between two other characters, the point of which is to establish who she is. The violated woman is displayed, debated, interpreted. Inevitably, there is cultural work going on here: what values are in play if a woman who has been raped is thought to have lost her identity? But there is dramatic work going on as well. Who is this character, and how does she relate to the characters who are discussing her? The rape is offstage: the onstage business of the play is the interpretation, the dialogue in which the brothers debate Lavinia. In that debate she has a dual identity, Lavinia and not Lavinia. There is something here that relates to the theatrical occasion itself. The double identity of Lavinia, herself and a nameless other, is the condition of a character played by an actor, with a double identity of an equivalent kind. Thomas Kyd opens *The Spanish Tragedy*, one of the seminal plays of the Elizabethan theatre, with a figure striding on to the stage, crossing the border from the tiring house into the acting area, and addressing the audience with a speech that identifies him, and does not identify him:

> When this eternal substance of my soul
> Did live imprison'd in my wanton flesh,
> Each in their function serving other's need,
> I was a courtier in the Spanish court.
> My name was Don Andrea. . . . (I.i.1–5)[2]

If his name was Don Andrea, what is it now? He has, like Lavinia, a dual identity, one named and one nameless. He is a liminal figure, a boundary-breaker, who has crossed from the world of the dead to the world of the living, a move dramatized by his crossing from the tiring house to the stage. Addressing the audience, he crosses another boundary, between the fiction in which he is enclosed and the literal reality in which he is an actor on stage, speaking to us. All this goes with his liminal identity. In *Hamlet* Horatio describes the Ghost, another boundary-breaker, not as Hamlet's father but as "A figure like your father" (I.ii.198). Troilus, seeing Cressida in the Greek camp with her new lover Diomedes, declares, "This is and is not Cressid" (V.ii.152). Othello at the end of his play is "he that was Othello" (V.ii.281).

These dual identities within the fiction are the equivalent of the combination of actor and role in the performance. Contemporary evidence suggests that audience perceptions, then as now, moved back and forth between the character and the actor. Sometimes, jokingly, the actor shows through. Richard Corbet describes how "mine host," "full of ale and history," recounted the Battle of Bosworth: "For, when he would have sayd, King Richard dyed, / And call'd – A horse! A horse! – He, Burbidge cry'de."[3] This would not work as a joke, however, if the figure on stage were identified simply as the actor. That identification is always in play with another, that of the figure on stage as the character. This means taking the play seriously. An account of a 1610 performance of *Othello* by the King's Men at Oxford reports, "Desdemona, though always excellent, moved us especially in her death when, as she lay on her bed, her face itself implored the pity of the audience."[4] Desdemona, not Master so-and-so; she, not he. Yet the actor, whose name the reporter does not acknowledge, is at work creating the pathos that moves him. This is, and is not, Desdemona; and it is the actor, not just Desdemona, who is "excellent."

The doubleness of Lavinia's identity links with the doubleness of the act of atrocity that has broken her. To the question, what is this person? is added the question, what is this act? Lavinia is a Roman matron raped by Goths: the attack on her is an attack on a woman, and on a city. Preparing to murder Desdemona, Othello threatens to stain the sheets with blood (V.i.36); they are her wedding sheets. Her murder is also her wedding night. Romeo kills Tybalt the day he is to consummate his marriage with Juliet. Both acts are a shedding of Capulet blood, and a loss of innocence: the lovers' first sexual encounter, and Romeo's first killing. It is by killing Duncan that the Macbeths consummate their marriage, in an act they themselves have trouble naming. Lavinia's rape, we shall see, is not just a figurative attack on Rome; it has disconcerting links with her marriage, which involves rape of another kind. The name of the deed, like the name of the character, becomes unsettled.

As acts of violation become figuratively connected with other acts, including acts of love, the idea of violation spreads through characters' other relationships, tainting them, and relationship itself comes into question. Relationship is a way of fixing identity. Marcus does not say

"This was Lavinia" but "This was thy daughter" and for a moment that is what he and Titus debate. As Evelyn Gajowski puts it, "To be a full human being, Shakespeare intimates, is to be a relational, rather than an autonomous being; yet he gives unblinking attention to the excruciating vulnerability involved."[5] Relationship can inflict suffering. Lavinia suffers as herself, and as Titus' daughter; Titus suffers as her father. Locked in silence, Lavinia is in one sense alone; but she is never alone on stage. As soon as the rapists leave, Marcus enters; and for the rest of the play she is surrounded by her family, trying to talk to her, trying to read her, trying to find some way of dealing with her intolerable suffering. These efforts, we shall see, take on a dual nature as the rape does: they become a form of attack on her, a new dimension to her suffering. Relationship can bring healing; it can also bring more damage. In Edgar's tending of the blind Gloucester we are going to see a disturbing conflation of caregiving and torture.

This is bound up with the workings of theatre. Dialogue is the condition of drama, putting the actors into relationship. Shakespeare's company was unusually stable, a team of sharers who worked together year after year, and an important part of their skill would have been an instinctive teamwork that came with mutual familiarity. "J. Cocke" in his character sketch of "a common player," describes a bad actor as one who concentrates on his own performance at the expense of the teamwork: "When he doth hold conference upon the stage; and should looke directly into his fellows face; hee turnes about his voice into the assembly for applause-sake, like a Trumpeter in the fields, that shifts places to get an echo."[6] For all the star power of actors like Burbage and Alleyn, they were not just building a single powerful character; they were part of a group experience. The opening of *Richard III*, with Richard revealing himself in a long soliloquy, is unique in Shakespeare. Hamlet is introduced in cross-talk with Claudius, Othello with Iago. The teamwork of the actors functions when Lavinia's family tries to deal with her; it even functions in the aftermath of the rape, as the taunting voices of Chiron and Demetrius play off against Lavinia's silence.

Dialogue is relationship, but in Shakespearean tragedy relationship is frequently damage. Shakespeare explored what the closeness of one person to another can mean in a non-dramatic work, *Lucrece*, that shares many of the concerns of his tragedies. After the rape Lucrece and Tarquin part, never to meet again; but the narrator holds them together:

She bears the load of lust he left behind,
And he the burden of a guilty mind.

He like a thievish dog creeps sadly thence,
She like a wearied lamb lies panting there;
He scowls, and hates himself for his offence,
She desperate, with her nails her flesh doth tear. (734–39)

There is a dark relationship here, a terrible mutual understanding; they have been together somewhere that no one else in the poem has been. We shall see such relationships in the plays, Othello and Iago being a prime example.

One part of relationship is interpretation, and this too does damage. Desdemona, Cordelia and Cressida are stared at by the men of their plays, debated, and interpreted. And the act of interpretation leads to their destruction. Lavinia is destroyed, then interpreted, then destroyed again. Interpretation is what audiences do. Usually it is in comedy that the act of interpretation, and especially of misinterpretation, is brought self-consciously on to the stage. In inductions and intercut scenes, Jonson has onstage characters debate how they should take the play, with the author's spokesmen getting it right and the fools getting it wrong. The comedy gets an increasingly bitter edge later in Jonson's career, as his relations with the audience become more hostile. Beaumont's *The Knight of the Burning Pestle* shows an onstage audience going one step further: the citizens not only object to the play the company is performing, reading it against the grain by attacking its sympathetic characters; they break it apart by insisting on the insertion of a play of their own devising, with an actor, the apprentice Rafe, they provide themselves. Here we see that misreading can actually destroy a play, and Beaumont's joke blew up in his face when his own audience rejected the play itself. When in tragedy Shakespeare brings acts of interpretation and misinterpretation on to the stage, within the play proper, the comedy falls away: these misreadings are deadly. This is what happens when Othello misreads Desdemona, when Lear misreads Cordelia.

Such acts of interpretation imply boundaries: between character and commentator, between the main action and the heckling of eavesdroppers. Such a boundary was created on stage – and we can confirm this by watching performances at the Bankside Globe – by the pillars that were a permanent part of the set. They divide the space into a central acting area and a periphery; it is in the periphery, where characters comment on what they are watching, that interpretation takes place. The other division to which the Globe alerts us is one we have suspected all along, the boundary between stage and audience. The boundary is there: the stage floor is well above the pit floor, and the audience is not likely to climb on to it. We are aware of our space, and their space. At the same time, the actors address the audience across the boundary, and the audience responds by sending voluble reactions back to the stage. Everyone is in the same light, making boundary-crossings more natural than they are when a lit proscenium stage faces a darkened auditorium.

Shakespeare's tragedies are full of boundary-crossings, and these boundary-crossings are themselves acts of violation. The Goths enter Rome; Romeo enters Juliet's bedroom, then breaks into the Capulet tomb; the Ghost breaks out of his sepulcher; Othello enters Desdemona's bedchamber, Macbeth enters Duncan's; Lavinia and Lear cross from civilization into the wilderness. These boundary-crossings relate to the double nature of the actions that take place – as the boundary, for example, between love-making and killing breaks down. National space is violated by enemy invasions, even invasions that aim to restore order (doubleness again: what is rescue, and what is enemy action?) Plays end with traditional enemies in the citadel: Goths in Rome, Norwegians in Denmark, the English in Scotland. Cordelia comes to save her father at the head of a French army, and even Albany, whose cause is hers, feels bound to resist. The enemy within is sometimes personal: Othello never has to fight the Turks, but he has to kill the Turk in himself; Hamlet's internal enemy, by his own account, is his madness, a thing within him that is not him. (This is, and is not, Hamlet.)

In moments like these we are very much inside the story, even inside the character. But they relate to the initial doubleness of perception created when an actor walks on to the stage. Burbage is and is not Hamlet; the thing that killed Polonius is and is not Hamlet; the army that has come to restore order is and is not an enemy. The effect is not (or not simply) metatheatre. It is not that Shakespeare wrote "This is and is not Cressid" to remind us that we are in a theatre watching an actor in a play. He wrote "This is and is not Cressid" because he himself was a theatre artist, and this shaped the way he thought about what was happening in the story, and determined what Troilus would say to express his sense of betrayal. It drew him to thinking of characters and actions as having double identities, and to seeing acts of interpretation that tease out those double identities as part of the action of the play itself.

There is also, I suspect, something personal here, whose roots we can only guess at. Shakespeare's theatrical thinking links up with an experience that obviously disturbed and engaged his imagination. His early work in particular is filled with images of rape, and with displaced rape: the literal sexual assaults on Lavinia and Lucrece are at the centers of his first two attempts at tragedy, dramatic and non-dramatic. In *Venus and Adonis* the boar kills Adonis in what Venus imagines as a complex sexual assault involving sodomy and oral sex: "And nuzzling in his flank, the loving swine/Sheath'd unaware the tusk in his soft groin" (1115–16). This too, like the debate over Lavinia, is an act of interpretation: it is Venus who sees this as a love-death, a displaced climax to her own aggressive wooing. She gives a destructive twist to the Ovidian transformation that should bring new life, plucking the flower Adonis has become (killing as deflowering) to let it wither and die between her breasts. In *Henry VI Part One* John Talbot's death in his first battle as a "maiden youth" (IV.vii.150) is another drawing of first blood, another deflowering.[7] The theme continues to haunt Shakespeare's work, and I would like to show – again, rather against the current practice of seeing plays as culturally determined – that one play feeds on another as ideas are picked up, transformed, and arranged in new combinations. There is an author at work here. He responds to the conditions of his society, and to the demands of the theatre in which he works. But he also responds to his sources, constantly transforming them; and those sources include his own work.

I have selected for consideration seven of Shakespeare's tragedies: *Titus Andronicus, Romeo and Juliet, Hamlet, Troilus and Cressida, Othello, King Lear* and *Macbeth*. Here the ideas I am interested in seem especially pervasive, though they could be traced in other tragedies, notably *Julius Caesar* and *Coriolanus*. Violated identity, violated space, the damage that comes with interpretation and even with relationship itself, the double nature of characters and of the acts they commit – these will be the concerns of the discussion that follows. They will appear and reappear in different combinations. They will not always relate to each other in the same way. Each chapter will take as its starting point an act of violation that provides a focus for the discussion, an angle of vision from which to view the play. The constant factor is that each act, wherever it occurs in the story (and the placing varies) resonates through the rest of the work, often linking with other acts of violation, using the resources of theatre to question not just what we do to each other, but who we are. The last question, as we shall see, is increasingly asked not just of those who suffer violence, like Lavinia, but of those who inflict it.

CHAPTER I

Titus Andronicus: *This was thy daughter*

DEBATING LAVINIA

The assault on Lavinia that forms the central act of violation in *Titus Andronicus* takes place, like the acts of violence in Greek tragedy, offstage. Chiron and Demetrius rape her, cut off her hands, and cut out her tongue. What the audience, and Lavinia's family, have to confront is not the sight of the event but its significance. For Chiron and Demetrius it is simple: they have done what they wanted to do, and now they can gloat. As they taunt her in the aftermath of the rape, their voices work together easily, each taunt sliding into the next:

> DEMETRIUS So, now go tell, and if thy tongue can speak,
>   Who 'twas that cut thy tongue and ravished thee.
> CHIRON Write down thy mind, bewray thy meaning so,
>   And if thy stumps will let thee play the scribe. (II.iii.1–4)

They use language smoothly and confidently to tell Lavinia she will never use language again. But in silencing her they have inadvertently made her the most powerful character in the play. What the rape means for them is straightforward: an expression of their power. What it means for her is beyond language, beyond imagining. That is what her silence conveys to us, and from this point on that silence haunts the play.

Yet plays use words, and on her next appearance we see her again with two brothers, her father and her uncle, who try to read the thing she has become and, unlike Chiron and Demetrius, disagree. And plays use the presence of the actor, who in circumstances like this can dominate a scene without language, simply by standing there. Lavinia must be dealt with. When Marcus, having found her in the woods, brings her back to Rome, out of the wild place where the unimaginable has happened to her, and back to the city where everything should be familiar, Titus at first does not know who she is: "But who comes with our brother Marcus here?" (III.i.58). Marcus replies, "This was thy daughter." She is finished, a nameless thing, like the ghost who can only say "My name was Don Andrea." But Titus replies, "Why, Marcus, so she is" (III.i.63–64). His reply puts Lavinia back into relationship. At first this may sound as simple as the taunts of the rapists: whatever has happened she is still his daughter. But what it means to be his daughter in her new condition is something the rest of the play has to explore, and in the process their relationship becomes the most difficult, conflicted one in the play. The rape has put identity into crisis: what is Lavinia now? It has put language into crisis: what words can be used about her? Relationship has to be renegotiated: is she Titus's daughter, and what does this mean? As we sense these questions forming, we sense the significance of the rape expanding beyond the pain of one character to include the network of relationships that form the community of her family, and ultimately of Rome. As two brothers debate her, earlier scenes return in memory, transformed, haunting the present action. Before Aaron pointed out that they could both have her, Chiron and Demetrius argued over her as rival lovers, debating which had the right to claim her as Marcus and Titus now debate how to read her. Earlier in the action yet another pair of brothers, Saturninus and Bassianus, competed to marry her. Further back still, at the beginning of the play, the same brothers competed for the empery of Rome. Lavinia's rape does not come from nowhere; it haunts, and is haunted by, her marriage and the larger political action.

HAUNTED BY RAPE

One feature of the stage itself is implicated in what happens to Lavinia, as though to warn us of the way the significance of the act will spread. We do not see the rape; but we see the stage trap, which represents the pit in the wood where the assault will take place. Like Lavinia herself, it is interpreted in different ways by different characters. Trying to entice Aaron, Tamora calls it a pleasant place fit for love (II.ii.10–29). Setting up the murder of Bassianus and the rape of Lavinia, she describes it as a place of terror (II.ii.91–104). Even so the sexual act, the act of love, will become an act of horror. Aaron has already described the wood itself as "ruthless, dreadful, deaf and dull" (I.i.628), going in one line from abstract menace to a more disturbing atmosphere of deadened senses and enervation. When Lavinia's brothers approach the pit Quintus complains, "My sight is very dull" (II.ii.195) and when Martius falls into the pit Quintus lacks the strength to pull him out; instead he lets Martius pull him in. The pit seems to exert a malign force that dulls the senses and weakens the body.

Something of this atmosphere creeps into Marcus' long speech over the mutilated Lavinia. The first shock of realizing what has happened to her produces not sharp emotion but a trance-like border state, neither sleeping nor waking:

> If I do dream, would all my wealth would wake me;
> If I do wake, some planet strike me down
> That I may slumber an eternal sleep. (II.iii.13–15)

From that point his will seems suspended; he goes on talking but does nothing, and he even projects this state of suspension on to her attacker who, if he had heard the music Lavinia made "would have dropped his knife and fell asleep, / As Cerberus at the Thracian poet's feet" (II.ii.50–51). The atmosphere suggests falling asleep after love-making; except that what has happened is not love-making but a violent parody of it, and any such feeling would not be that of Lavinia (who is beyond exhaustion) but that of Chiron and Demetrius. As something of Tarquin remains with Lucrece, the eerie mood of sleepiness that hits the play at this point seems to trap us in the consciousness of the rapists.[1]

The pit is also a sexual image, anticipating Lear's "there's hell, there's darkness, there is the sulphurous pit" (IV.vi.123–24). To the horror of what it is, suggesting a recoil from sexuality itself, is added the horror of what has been symbolically done to it. Quintus gives a graphic close-up:

> What subtle hole is this,
> Whose mouth is covered with rude-growing briers
> Upon whose leaves are drops of new-shed blood
> As fresh as morning dew distilled on flowers? (II.ii.198–201)

Having invoked both menace ("subtle") and damage, the speech is capped by a grotesquely inappropriate lyricism that takes us back to Tamora's description of the setting as a place for love. The association of the pit with Lavinia makes for a grim pun in the action. Three men have entered her body: her husband Bassianus, then the Gothic brothers. Three men enter the pit: first Bassianus, then Quintus and Martius.[2] In this pattern her own brothers take the place of the rapists, and this happens during the attack itself. (They fall into the pit while the rape is happening offstage.) As the significance of the rape expands, the division between Lavinia's family and her assailants, between the civilized structures of Rome and the horror of the woods, is shaken. The tomb of the Andronici dominates the first act as the pit dominates the second. It ought to represent piety and order. Titus sees it as a final resting place for the family, and a final reward that confirms their worth (I.i.85–87). But like the pit (and the stage trap could serve for both) it is a dark hole that draws life into it.[3] Its offer of "silence and eternal sleep" (I.i.158) anticipates the silence of Lavinia and the sleepiness that hits the play when she is raped. Tamora's plea, "Andronicus, stain not thy tomb with blood" (I.i.119), makes the tomb like the pit, a blood-stained opening in the earth. The tomb, symbol of the Andronici and of a whole Roman world of piety and order, dissolves into the blood-drinking pit in the woods.

By the same token Lavinia's marriage, which in theory should be an affirmation of the family and of chaste, regulated sexuality, is staged as another kind of rape. (The name of the act is unsettled, like the name of the woman who suffers it.) When Saturninus, granted the empery by Titus, keeps the woman-city analogy going by claiming Lavinia as his bride (again with Titus' consent), Bassianus with the support of the rest of her family asserts his claim as her betrothed and carries her off. Saturninus calls this "rape" and while Bassianus protests, "'Rape' call you it, my lord, to seize my own, / My true betrothed love, and now my wife?" (I.i.409–11), his claim of betrothal and his appeal to love are mixed with the claim that he is seizing her as property. This is not so far away as it should be from what happens in the woods. The word "surprised," with military overtones, is used for both actions (I.i.288–89, IV.i.51); but the most significant link is the fact that through the long sequence in which Bassianus claims her and carries her off Lavinia is silent.[4] Her silence can be read as consent, even as defiance of her father (who has been too ready to transfer her to Saturninus);[5] but the point is that we *have* to read it, as we have to read her later, more dreadful silence after the second rape. She does not speak for herself. The debate is entirely between the men, and the issue is not her wishes but Bassianus' rights. How little Lavinia matters as Lavinia is conveyed in one startling moment: Titus demands that her brother Lucius restore her to the emperor, and Lucius replies, "Dead if you will, but not to be his wife" (I.i.302).

Whatever we may imagine about Lavinia's feelings for Bassianus, she expresses them only after his death: "Poor I was slain when Bassianus died" (II.ii.171). Even here we may wonder what is personal, and what is social: in Roman society she is what her husband makes her. But that line can also justify the playing of her relationship with Bassianus as a betrothal of lovers. The tomb is not really the pit, and Bassianus does not rape her as Chiron and Demetrius do. But to play this as a love affair may simply increase the disturbance. Chiron and Demetrius began by using conventional love-language – "To serve, and to deserve my mistress' grace"

(I.i.533); "She is Lavinia, therefore must be loved" (I.i.584); we see what this comes to. The moment when Bassianus abruptly asserts his rights follows hard upon the moment when his brother, just as abruptly, frees the Goths (I.i.278–80). As her lover (if that is Bassianus' role) seizes her, her rapists are released, and the set-up to her second rape begins. As the pit is a place of pleasure and a place of horror, two kinds of sexual relationship are conflated in the simple fact that the word "rape" has a double meaning.

The second rape is also an act of revenge by Tamora's family on Titus', and as so often happens in revenge tragedy, the revenge echoes the act it is avenging. Lavinia pleads with Tamora to save her from her sons; in the first scene Tamora pleaded with Titus to save her first-born Alarbus from *his* sons, who demanded his death. Alarbus is even more silent than Lavinia, having no lines at all. "Alarbus' limbs are lopped" (I.i.146) and so are Lavinia's. One act foreshadows the other. The echoing continues when Titus avenges his daughter. Chiron and Demetrius are silenced, like Lavinia: the command to stop their mouths is repeated for the ritual count of three (V.ii.161, 164, 167). Tamora rejected Lavinia's pleas; Titus rules out any plea the rapists can make, without giving them a chance to make it: "What would you say if I should let you speak? / Villains, for shame you could not plead for grace" (V.ii.178–79). Holding a basin Lavinia, who was forced to receive their semen, now receives their blood. Finally, as they entered her body, they enter their mother's, in a grotesque "inversion of childbirth."[6] Tamora becomes the pit as Titus makes her "Like to the earth swallow her own increase" (V.ii.191). Sex and eating will be linked by Apemantus in *Timon of Athens* when he claims that ladies "eat lords; so they come by great bellies" (I.i.206). Tamora's cannibalistic, incestuous eating of her own sons punishes her lust and theirs, and grotesquely re-enacts the rape Titus is avenging.

The atrocity committed on Lavinia echoes and re-echoes through the play, not just in the killing of Alarbus that triggers it but in the marriage and the family that should be images of the normal life it violates, and in the counter-action that should provide relief by avenging it. There is no escape from this atrocity; it also encloses the larger political action. At the start of the play Saturninus and Bassianus are outside the Capitol, trying to gain entrance. At the same time Bassianus sounds as though he is protecting Rome from rape:[7]

> Keep then this passage to the Capitol,
> And suffer not dishonour to approach
> The imperial seat, to virtue consecrate,
> To justice, continence and nobility. . . . (I.i.12–15)

Virtue that must be protected, a passage that must be guarded; Saturninus does not know until the end of the play what has been done to Lavinia, but from the beginning he is symbolically implicated in it. More insidiously, Titus himself brings the Gothic enemy into the citadel. He brings them as prisoners, but he brings them; and with Tamora's marriage to Saturninus they emerge as it were from the Trojan horse and start to take over. The Roman triumph in which Titus makes his first entrance, a train of prisoners in his wake, begins the action that will lead to the rape of his daughter. When Aaron plots the rape it sounds like the sack of a city: "revel in Lavinia's treasury" (I.i.536); it is Titus himself who has let in the enemy.

BREAKING BOUNDARIES

The pit in the wood, the tomb in Rome; Lavinia's marriage and Lavinia's rape – there ought to be a clear distinction between atrocity and order, family and other. But as the rape is mirrored in other actions of the play, such distinctions begin to dissolve. Lavinia's brothers enter the pit at the same time as the Gothic brothers assault her body. From the first entrance of the prisoners, the division between Roman and Goth is challenged. Pleading for Alarbus, Tamora addresses the Andronici as "Roman brethren" (I.i.107) and asks Titus to see the likeness: "And if thy sons were ever dear to thee, / O, think my son to be as dear to me" (I.i.110–11); "O, if to fight for king and commonweal / Were piety in thine, it is in these" (I.i.117–18). Titus takes no notice. Minutes later he finds that Tamora is no longer his prisoner but Empress of Rome, "incorporate in Rome, / A Roman now adopted happily" (I.i.467–68). In that word "incorporate," the distinction between Roman and Goth, a line Titus has spent ten years policing, dissolves.[8] Tamora is at first the beneficiary of this loss of distinction, and then its victim. When Lucius enters Rome at the end of the play to avenge his family and restore order, he enters with an army of Goths. Once again the enemy is in the citadel. This is not the only time in Shakespeare that a foreign, even an enemy, power restores order. Richmond comes with Breton soldiers, allowing Richard III to do a passable Henry V impersonation as he rouses his troops against the invader; Malcolm comes with an English army; Fortinbras is quite simply the enemy. For a sick kingdom, as for a sick soul or a sick body, the cure that comes from outside, whether divine grace or radical surgery, can feel like enemy action. In *Titus* it is one more instance of a barrier broken, a line crossed. That Lucius should enlist the Goths is Titus' own idea, which he states quite matter-of-factly: "Hie to the Goths and raise an army there" (III.i.286). The Goths claim they are coming "To be avenged on cursed Tamora" (V.i.16), enlisting themselves, again quite matter-of-factly, in the cause of the Andronici. The political dimension of the revenge on Lavinia's Gothic attackers is a successful Gothic invasion of Rome. Once again the revenge mirrors the initial atrocity.

A story that juxtaposes rape with enemy invasion is naturally concerned with the crossing of thresholds. Mutius assists the first rape of Lavinia by guarding the doorway through which she has been taken; his father kills him for it. Titus in turn guards the threshold of the tomb, refusing to let Mutius be buried in it, and yielding only to overwhelming family pressure. Titus later guards the entrance to his study, resenting the attempt of Tamora and her sons to break his privacy:

> Who doth molest my contemplation?
> Is it your trick to make me ope the door,
> That so my sad decrees may fly away
> And all my study be to no effect? (V.ii.9–12)

He is concerned to keep his thoughts in, and undesirables out.

But eventually he himself lets the enemy in – "Welcome, dread Fury, to my woeful house" (V.ii.82) – as he did in act I. (Given that he is plotting revenge, and Tamora is Revenge, she has been there all along.) He has already challenged the barriers that divide the cosmos in his mad (and sanely ironic) attempt to find justice by digging in the earth, fishing in the sea and firing arrows at the gods. Throughout the play barriers fall: "Rome is but a wilderness of tigers" (III.i.54), as though a wall dividing the city from the wood had vanished.[9] The extended laments of III.i are full of flood imagery: Titus stands "as one upon a rock, / Environed with a wilderness of sea" (III.i.94–95), watching helplessly as the sea encroaches and threatens to drown him. Then the distinction between the human and the elemental, like other distinctions in the play, dissolves: Titus declares, "I am the sea. Hark, how her sighs doth blow. / She is the weeping welkin, I the earth" (III.i.226–27).

In a sexual encounter, the difference between one body and another seems to melt away as lovers become one; Juliet will imagine love this way. But boundaries are restored when lovers part. In the parody of love that is Lavinia's rape, Titus sees a permanent breaking of distinction, as though, just as Tamora is "incorporate" in Rome and Lucrece's blood is stained black by Tarquin (1742–43), something of Chiron and Demetrius has entered Lavinia forever: "Here stands the spring whom you have

stained with mud, / This goodly summer with your winter mixed"
(V.ii.170–71). The dissolving of distinction forced on Lavinia is willingly
embraced by Tamora in her sexual encounters with Aaron. Here the line
that is crossed is what in modern terms would be called the color bar: in
the lead-in to the rape Bassianus and Lavinia subject Tamora to crude
taunts for having a black lover. Lavinia guards the citadel of white pride
and sexual purity, and it gives Tamora extra satisfaction to urge her sons
to break into that citadel.

Yet Tamora herself cannot face the consequences of her boundary-
crossing. When she produces a black baby she wants it instantly killed,
and she demands that Aaron kill it. There is nothing here of her feeling
for Alarbus; she is more like Titus killing Mutius in response to being
dishonored; once again the two adversaries mirror each other. But Aaron
refuses, and his feeling for the child – "Sweet blowze, you are a beauteous
blossom, sure" (IV.ii.74) – has a quality of natural, unguarded affection
we hear nowhere else in the play. For the nurse, and for Tamora's other
sons, the baby is hardly human – "as loathsome as a toad"; "I'll broach the
tadpole on my rapier's point" (IV.ii.69, 87) – but Aaron's counterattack is
acute: "He is your brother, lords, sensibly fed / Of that self blood that first
gave life to you" (IV.ii.124–25). The line between Aaron and the rest of the
cast is one of the most firmly drawn in the play; his difference in color
embodies it. And Aaron himself here declares that line meaningless. "He
is your brother, lords," though it anticipates the logo of the abolitionists –
a black man kneeling in chains, circled by the words, "Am I not a man
and a brother?" – is not so much a humanitarian plea as (like Shylock's
"Hath not a Jew eyes?") a challenge to his listeners to drop their smug
exclusiveness and see in themselves the evil they see in the Other.

Aaron, like Tamora, seems radically opposed to Titus, yet has a strange
affinity with him. For Aaron the play is not a tragedy but a comedy:

> I played the cheater for thy father's hand,
> And when I had it, drew myself apart
> And almost broke my heart with extreme laughter;
> I pried me through the crevice of a wall
> When for his hand he had his two sons' heads,
> Beheld his tears and laughed so heartily
> That both mine eyes were rainy like to his. . . . (V.i.111–17)

The wall that separates Aaron from the suffering he witnesses conveys his
role as outsider, his ironic detachment. Yet it is in the same scene
that Titus himself breaks into laughter – "I have not another tear to shed"
(III.i.267) – signaling the ending of grief and the beginning of a revenge

action in which Titus will show a grim wit to match Aaron's own. Aaron
himself appreciates this, applauding the wit of his adversary's threatening
messages to the court (IV.ii.26–30). At one point the two men come
physically close, an effect more striking in that it is the only dialogue they
ever have. Aaron helps Titus cut off his hand. However it is staged (and
for Titus to cut off his own hand without help, as sometimes happens, is
against the text) the two are for a moment as physically close as lovers.
Titus' punning offer, "Lend me thy hand and I will give thee mine"
(III.i.188), like the punning double rape of Lavinia, fuses relationship and
atrocity.

     Amid all this blurring of categories, to which he contributes, Aaron
nonetheless claims an integrity of his own. His defense of blackness is a
defense of fixity in a world of dissolution, a defense of something that will
not change or be mixed with anything else, something over which the sea
itself, that recurring threat in Titus' imagination, has no power:

> Coal-black is better than another hue
> In that it scorns to bear another hue;
> For all the water in the ocean
> Can never turn the swan's black legs to white,
> Although she lave them hourly in the flood. (IV.ii.101–5)

Amid the blurring of Goth and Roman, family and enemy, marriage
and rape, atrocity and counter-atrocity, we may be looking for something fixed and clear, something with unshaken integrity. We find it in
the blackness of the play's self-proclaimed villain. As we shall see, this is
not the only challenge Aaron mounts to the prevailing concepts of the
play.

QUESTIONING LAVINIA

The discussion so far, with its emphasis on the way the rape of Lavinia
reverberates everywhere, has the disadvantage of making *Titus Andronicus*
sound a neatly constructed play. What happens is terrible of course, but
from an aesthetic viewpoint, how neatly it all fits together! There is some
truth in that, but not enough. We cannot just see Lavinia as the center of a
pattern: the challenge she presents is too unsettling. By depriving her of
language Chiron and Demetrius give their crime a significance that runs
deeper even than the sexual shock, anticipating the modern understanding
that rape is not just a sex crime. They cut her off in mid-sentence, even
mid-line. Her last words are "Confusion fall–" and Chiron declares, "Nay

then, I'll stop your mouth" (II.ii.184).[10] Taunting her after the rape, they tell her to do things – normal things – she can no longer do: tell who attacked her, write, call for water, wash her hands (II.iii.1–8).[11] In depriving her of language they have deprived her of human contact and of normal life, taking not just her chastity and her speech but her humanity.

We return to the question: who, or what, is Lavinia now? That problem haunts the scenes after the rape, beginning with Marcus' "Who is this – my niece that flies away so fast? / Cousin, a word. Where is your husband?" (II.iii.11–12). The rapists gave her impossible commands; Marcus, after a split second when he does not recognize her at all, asks a question, the first of many, that she cannot answer. The horror is compounded by the fact that the question is so natural and casual, and the answer she cannot give – her husband lies in the pit, murdered – is so terrible. In his first glimpse Marcus has seen her and not seen her, seen the old Lavinia but not the new one. Titus' "But who comes with our brother Marcus here?" (III.i.58) is a similar moment of non-recognition; and again it is a question. The answer, we have seen, is divided: "This was thy daughter . . . Why, Marcus, so she is" (III.i.63–64). For Marcus she is finished, a polluted thing with no identity. For Titus she is still his daughter, to be recognized, accepted and cared for. She is not a thing, and she is not finished.[12] But Titus' acceptance of her as his daughter is complex. It involves more than just caring; it also means that her shame is his shame, and on those grounds he will kill her. What follows in the next few scenes is the family's struggle to find a way of relating to Lavinia, and it is a real struggle: it cannot be reduced to affectionate concern on the one hand or patriarchal appropriation on the other.

The problem begins with the blurring of Lavinia's social and sexual identities. In the aftermath of the first rape, Saturninus called her "that changing piece" (I.i.314), as though to be passed from man to man reflected her own shiftiness. (This issue will return with Cressida.) In the second rape she is now a wife, yet Tamora talks of her as both a virgin and a whore, making her a mass of contradictions: "let my spleenful sons this trull deflower" (II.ii.191).[13] Newly married, she has gone through the transition from daughter to wife; with the murder of Bassianus and her own return to Rome she is dragged back across the line, becoming a daughter again, returning to the family she should have left. Her rite of passage is aborted. In the conventional categories of the play's society (and Shakespeare's) she is everything a woman can be: daughter, wife, widow, virgin, whore. Each role carries agony, and the literal impossibility of the combination turns Lavinia into a thing that should not exist.[14]

Her own first impulse is to hide. She tries to run away from Marcus, and at the end of their encounter he has to tell her, "Do not draw back" (II.iii.56). Others try to hide from her. Her brother Lucius' first impulse is to drop to the ground and look away, and Titus rebukes him as though he had deserted in the middle of a battle: "Faint-hearted boy, arise and look upon her" (III.i.66). When she pursues Young Lucius, seeking his help, the boy flees in terror. This embodies a brutal psychological insight: in their sheer otherness, the afflicted are frightening. At the center of Young Lucius' fear is his inability to understand her: "Alas, sweet aunt, I know not what you mean" (IV.i.4). Though he later calms down and apologizes, he has fled from the most helpless character in the play; what terrifies him is that she is unknowable, uncanny.

Marcus' first attempt to find a reaction to Lavinia is a long, artificial speech that makes poetic language out of her injuries, as though poetry is the scar that forms over a wound. His excess of words seems a desperate attempt to fill in her silence, and the desperation shows when he fixes on each injury and romanticizes it, turning her into a love-object in a way that recalls the initial love-language of Chiron and Demetrius – except that Marcus is more eloquent. Her mutilated arms are "her two branches, those sweet ornaments / Whose circling shadows kings have thought to sleep in" (II.iii.18–19); the blood in her mouth "Doth rise and fall between thy rosed lips, / Coming and going with thy honey breath" (II.iii.24–25). "She is Lavinia, therefore must be loved" (I.i.584) was how Demetrius put it; the darkest view of Marcus' speech is that she is being raped all over again. When he asks, "Why dost not speak to me?" and then notices "the crimson river of warm blood" in her mouth (II.iii.21–22), one possible staging is that she releases the blood in response to his question.[15] Does this touch on the belief that (as in *Richard III*, I.ii) a corpse bleeds in the presence of the murderer? Desperate to understand and deal with what has happened to Lavinia, Marcus unwittingly re-enacts the offense, eroticizing her body and making her bleed. As her marriage foreshadowed the atrocity in the woods, the first person she encounters afterwards, her own uncle, repeats the atrocity in a different key.

In the anonymous chapbook *History of Titus Andronicus* Lavinia, on her own initiative, writes in the sand to tell what has happened to her. Concerned to get on with the story, the chapbook does not give Lavinia the long period of helplessness she has in the play, a period further protracted by the addition of a new scene, III.ii, in the Folio.[16] But in the play the helplessness is important, and it is not just Lavinia's. Marcus seeks his own relief through language: "O that I knew thy heart, and knew

the beast,/That I might rail at him to ease my mind!" (II.iii.34–35). Relief
in language is something Lavinia can no longer find, and the sheer length
of Marcus' speech suggests he is not finding it either.[17]

Just to ask her a question, as Marcus does when he first sees her –
"Where is your husband?" – and as Lucius does on her return to Rome –
"Speak, gentle sister: who hath martyred thee?" (III.i.82) – is an act of
cruelty. Every question is like the taunts of Chiron and Demetrius,
reminding her of what she cannot do. The cruelty of Marcus and Lucius
is inadvertent; but Titus, long after he knows she cannot reply, goes on
compulsively flinging questions at her as though he needs to keep testing
the silence to see if he can break it:

> Or shall we cut away our hands like thine?
> Or shall we bite our tongues and in dumb shows
> Pass the remainder of our hateful days?
> What shall we do? (III.i.131–34)

The last question gathers the others together into a single cry of frustration. There is nothing to do. The other questions propose that the family
imitate Lavinia's helplessness, mirroring her as Tamora tries to mirror
Titus, so that everywhere she looks she will see images of her own agony.
In a sense this has already happened. Titus and the others are as helpless as
she is: they can speak, but nothing they say is any use. They cannot even
talk *about* her. Marcus' grotesquely comic slip when he protests at Titus'
telling Lavinia to kill herself, "Teach her not thus to lay/Such violent
hands upon her tender life" (III.ii.21–22), shows that language is not just
helpless but tainted: the most ordinary turn of speech, offered with the
best of intentions, is an unintended cruelty.

READING LAVINIA

Desperate for dialogue, the family goes from questioning Lavinia to trying
to supply the answers she would give. This means reading her reactions,
and one of their first attempts shows the difficulty. Hearing that her
brothers have been condemned to death for the murder of her husband,
she weeps:

> MARCUS Perchance she weeps because they killed her husband,
>   Perchance because she knows them innocent.
> TITUS If they did kill thy husband, then be joyful,
>   Because the law hath ta'en revenge on them.
>   No, no, they would not do so foul a deed:
>   Witness the sorrow that their sister makes. (III.i.115–20)

Marcus offers alternatives, and cannot decide; Titus decides, gets it wrong, and corrects himself. From this point we realize that any reading of Lavinia (including our own) could be wrong. Titus later claims he can read her, but his reading is grotesquely overelaborate:

> Mark, Marcus, mark! I understand her signs:
> Had she a tongue to speak, now would she say
> That to her brother which I said to thee.
> Her napkin with his true tears all bewet
> Can do no service on her sorrowful cheeks.
> O, what a sympathy of woe is this;
> As far from help as limbo is from bliss. (III.i.144–50)

The claim of understanding is self-defeating in its flagrant overconfidence, in the fact that Titus imagines Lavinia simply repeating his own words, and in the way the final claim of sympathy collapses into an admission of hopelessness. In the added scene, III.ii, which may be a Shakespearean afterthought exploring the play's issues in greater depth, Titus makes an even stronger claim, with a more overt admission of the problem:

> Hark, Marcus, what she says:
> I can interpret all her martyred signs –
> She says she drinks no other drink but tears,
> Brewed with her sorrow, mashed upon her cheeks.
> Speechless complainer, I will learn thy thought.
> In thy dumb action will I be as perfect
> As begging hermits in their holy prayers.
> Thou shalt not sigh, nor hold thy stumps to heaven,
> Nor wink, nor nod, nor kneel, nor make a sign,
> But I of these will wrest an alphabet
> And by still practice learn to know thy meaning. (III.ii.35–45)

Having in the previous scene told Marcus simply to "mark," he now tells him to listen: he can reproduce Lavinia's voice. But of course it is his own voice, and once again the speech he attributes to her is impossibly detailed. This time he retreats, implicitly confessing his failure by promising that he *will* learn to read her, and admitting that even in that effort there will be some forcing: "wrest an alphabet" suggests not just difficulty but coercion.[18]

He has been almost literally putting words in her mouth. This may help us read one of the play's most grotesque moments, his command, "Bear thou my hand, sweet wench, between thy teeth" (III.i.283). In the general crisis of language, the endearment "sweet wench" is as jarring as

Macbeth's "dearest chuck" (III.ii.45). In the first scene Lavinia called for a normal, decorous social gesture from her father: "O bless me here with thy victorious hand" (I.i.166). Now the hand, severed, will be in her mouth, a gag (as though she needed one), an invasion of her body in a symbolic, displaced rape ("sweet wench" is love-language), another echo of what Chiron and Demetrius did.[19] Since her return to Rome Titus has struggled to read Lavinia, to give her a voice again. But in his very sympathy and concern there is something invasive, and the only voice he can give her is his own.

One of the implications of his sympathy is that he tries to make her agony his, insisting that what happened to Lavinia has happened to him. As language is in crisis, so is the whole idea of relationship; it becomes impossible to separate love from appropriation. (The modern cliché "I feel your pain" can produce any reaction from "Thank you, that helps" to "It's my pain and you can't feel it.") Inadvertently picking up the rapists' hunting imagery (II.i.25–26), Titus declares, "It was my deer, and he that wounded her/Hath hurt me more than had he killed me dead" (III.i.92–93). When he cuts off his own hand he comes closer to suffering as Lavinia does;[20] yet by a crudely literal measurement he is less than half way there, and when he later talks as though he and Lavinia are in the same plight – "O handle not the theme, to talk of hands, / Lest we remember still that we have none" (III.ii.29–30) – he is claiming an identity with her to which he is not fully entitled. She has no hands, he has one; and this crude external sign of incomplete identification may suggest a deeper way in which Titus' sharing of pain is bound to fall short: he cannot fully know the feelings of a woman who has been raped. Indeed, it is not until the fourth act that he knows about the rape at all. We cannot see Titus' attempt to take Lavinia's pain as his own as entirely selfish, or entirely selfless; what we can see is that like everything else he attempts in the middle scenes it is doomed to fail. If he could really dissolve the distinction between them, really take her pain on himself, another barrier would fall. But the barrier holds. Trying desperately to read Lavinia, Titus reads only himself.

LAVINIA REPLIES

Lavinia's helplessness, however, is not total, and step by step she recovers language, beginning with the language of gesture. Titus' words, "Gentle Lavinia, let me kiss thy lips / Or make some sign how I may do thee ease" (III.i.121–22) imply a kiss offered and withdrawn: either he has decided himself that she does not want her mouth touched, or she has turned away. But when he kneels in a futile prayer to the unhearing gods, she kneels with him (III.i.210). Unasked, on her own initiative, she mirrors his posture in a gesture of sympathy. She is trying to feel his pain as he is trying to feel hers. When his severed hand and his sons' heads are returned to him in mockery, she kisses him: another gesture of comfort, again freely offered, but this time getting no response – as though Titus has gone into a catatonic silence equivalent to her own.[21] As Marcus puts it, "that kiss is comfortless / As frozen water to a starved snake" (III.i.251–52). But at least she is coming back to life, no longer shrinking from contact, and her ruined mouth can still kiss. In offering a gesture that gets no response, she is once more mirroring Titus' experience as he tries to mirror hers.

Lavinia recovers language in a more obvious way when she uses writing, first Ovid's and then her own, to report that she has been raped. When Marcus first comes across her he hits on the truth – "But sure some Tereus hath deflowered thee" (II.iii.26) – but when he later asks, "Shall I speak for thee? Shall I say 'tis so?" (II.iii.33) the answer, ungiven but understood, seems to be no. Bringing her back to Rome, Marcus retreats to generalization, comparing her to a deer "That hath received some unrecuring wound" (III.i.91). He forgets or buries his insight that she has been raped, leaving Titus and the others to concentrate on her visible wounds. Lavinia must name the crime herself.

Recovering language, she recovers community. While Chiron recalls reading Horace in school, implying he has read nothing since (IV.ii.22–23), the Andronici are a bookish family and Lavinia tells her story through a book, the tale of Philomel as recounted by Ovid. When she writes the name of the crime on the ground it is in Latin: "*Stuprum – Chiron – Demetrius*" (IV.i.78). Like Caesar's "*Et tu, Brute*" at the moment of his death, this fixes and formalizes the accusation as a literary tag, weighting her personal voice with the voice of a whole culture. Even the wood in which she was violated becomes a cultural artifact, "Patterned by that the poet here describes" (IV.i.57) as though Ovid invented the wood and nature copied it. Nor is this just a male culture: the book itself was given to Young Lucius by his mother, and Marcus at first thinks Lavinia has picked it out "For love of her that's gone" (IV.i.43). Titus' wife is buried in oblivion (there is something grotesque in his claim that *he* had twenty-five sons) and there is one glancing reference to his mother (III.i.182); but in picking this book Lavinia enlists one of the family's forgotten women to help her tell her story.

Yet it is Titus' voice that reads what she has found in Ovid, and that reads what she has written in the sand. It is Marcus who (as though to compensate for the linguistic failure of his first long speech to her) teaches her to write for herself, and it is his staff she puts in her mouth,[22] a displaced sexual image like the taking of her father's hand. The rape haunts the very action that could begin Lavinia's recovery from it. To use words again is to bring herself back into relationship with others, and that includes Chiron and Demetrius. Two of the three words she writes are their names; the third is what they did to her.

This act of naming restores clarity. Her own name may have been temporarily unfixed ("This was thy daughter") and in the double meaning of "rape" and the replication of the deed in different forms, so was the act itself. In Demetrius' "She is Lavinia, therefore must be loved" (I.i.584), her name was apparently fixed, but "loved" lost its meaning, dissolving into horror, ultimately taking Lavinia with it. Now she fixes the name of the act, and the names of the doers. Yet in the physical act of writing she cannot recall the rape without re-enacting it; she cannot use language without symbolically violating her own body.[23] Titus will later write his revenge plans in blood, presumably his own. Through the long, painful middle sequence of the play Lavinia's family has tried to use language as a way of understanding and compensating for her wounds. In the end it is language itself that wounds.

REVENGE AND RESTORATION

The words Lavinia writes in the sand launch the final movement of the play, Titus' revenge. Titus determines to fix her words in permanent form:

> And come, I will go get a leaf of brass
> And with a gad of steel will write these words,
> And lay it by. The angry northern wind
> Will blow these sands like Sybil's leaves abroad,
> And where's our lesson then? (IV.i.102–6)

Female language (Lavinia's and the Sybil's) seems to him shifting and evanescent. He wants the words fixed in a harder medium, in his own handwriting. In the process he will take over Lavinia's words and make them his own, writing for her as he spoke for her. Language, which for so long has been the medium of questioning, and which has suffered its own damage as ordinary words like "hands" become unusable, recovers its declarative power. Titus has Chiron and Demetrius bound and gagged, and subjects them to a long description of their fate, at the end of which he cuts their throats. Language issues in reality; almost literally, he talks them to death. He continues the Philomel myth Lavinia used in her accusation, and turns it into action: "For worse than Philomel you used my daughter, / And worse than Progne I will be revenged" (V.ii.194–95). Lavinia's last, unfinished sentence, "Confusion fall –" is finished for her by Titus in his revenge on her assailants. We have already seen how the punishment mirrors the crime. Titus uses for revenge the same hunting language Chiron and Demetrius used for rape (II.i.25–26; IV.i.96, 101); and for good measure he avenges Quintus and Martius, who were not allowed to speak when dragged out of the pit, and whose severed heads are recalled when Titus specifies that he will make his cannibalistic banquet from the heads of Chiron and Demetrius.

When Titus sends his mad messages around the universe, Publius brings him word from Pluto that he cannot have Justice (who is otherwise occupied) but he can have Revenge. In V.ii Revenge comes to his house in the form of Tamora, fulfilling Pluto's promise. She brings with her Chiron and Demetrius as Rape and Murder; in those roles Titus kills them. They are killed because they are Chiron and Demetrius, and they are killed because they are Rape and Murder. Lavinia's identity was doubled: herself, and a nameless thing. Chiron and Demetrius are also doubled, but their alternate names are clear, fixed and fatal. She was reduced to something that could not be named and that Titus could not cope with. They are reduced to what they have done, it is named, and Titus knows exactly what to do with it.

Death by allegory: you are what you have done, and what you have done is your death. As Lavinia and Titus, evoking Ovid, have enlisted literary tradition, the final scenes enlist theatrical tradition: the allegory of Revenge, Rape and Murder recalls a morality play, and Titus echoes *The Spanish Tragedy*: Hieronimo's "Why then I'll fit you" (IV.i.70)[24] becomes Titus' "Lucius, I'll fit thee" (IV.i.114) and Hieronimo's punning offer to "play the murderer" (IV.i.133) in a court entertainment becomes Titus' "I'll play the cook" (V.ii.204). In a sense theatre itself has been threatened in the play: the questions hurled against silence (not only the questioning of Lavinia, but Titus talking to the tribunes and then to the stones) have been a denial of dialogue itself, the medium of drama. Lavinia deprived of language and Lavinia and Titus deprived of hand-gestures have been deprived of two instruments of the actor's art. Even when Lavinia casts her arms up twice the gesture sends no clear signal: Marcus is not sure whether she is giving the number of her attackers or pleading to heaven for revenge (IV.i.38–40); we cannot be sure either. In the clarity and neatness of Titus' revenge it is as though theatre itself, damaged in the middle scenes, is restored.

The revenge is followed by images of healing. Hands function once again, as Marcus' offer that the Andronici will commit mass suicide "hand in hand" (V.iii.131) is countered by Emillius: "Come, come thou reverend man of Rome, / And bring our emperor gently in thy hand" (V.iii. 136–37). The play's preoccupation with dismembered bodies, signaled in the first act by Marcus' request to Titus to "help to set a head on headless Rome" (I.i.189) ends in the words of the same speaker:

> O let me teach you how to knit again
> This scattered corn into one mutual sheaf,
> These broken limbs again into one body. (V.iii.69–71)

Titus' own body is ritually honored by the kisses of his family. Lucius, Marcus and the Boy kiss him on the lips, as though to cure the wounds the play has inflicted on language. Lucius feels he is kissing a dead man, getting, like Lavinia, no response: "O, take this warm kiss on thy pale cold lips" (V.iii.152). We sense one barrier that will never fall, the barrier between the dead and the living, and once again the speakers are addressing someone who cannot reply. Yet Marcus' words tease us with another possibility: "Tear for tear and loving kiss for kiss, / Thy brother Marcus tenders on thy lips" (V.iii.155–56). Behind the literal meaning, that his kisses match those of Lucius, is the suggestion that the kisses are reciprocal. The boy Lucius gives Titus the last kiss, the last human contact before he enters the grave, and as he does so Marcus and Lucius bring Titus before us alive again, in an aspect we have never seen. Lucius recalls the grandfather who used to tell the boy stories, language drawing the generations together; Marcus recalls a time when the boy's kisses could restore his grandfather: "How many thousand times hath these poor lips, / When they were living, warmed themselves on thine!" (V.iii.166–67). The mouth becomes again the seat of affection, and with its healing language is healed.

UNSETTLING THE ENDING

But as Titus' body is honored in this way, Lavinia's just lies there. This may be because Titus has dealt with her, and there is nothing more to say. Or so the characters may think; the audience, noticing the silent body the others are ignoring, may think otherwise. She has only two scenes after she writes in the ground, and they are the scenes in which she is most passive, hardest to read, no longer reacting or sending out signals; some performers have played her at this point as "catatonic, no longer really human."[25] There is a terrible irony here. Silence, we saw, gave her extraordinary power to command attention and concern. So long as that silence was unbroken, so too was the concentration of the family on her. When she recovers language they turn to avenging her, but in the process they also turn away from Lavinia herself, and she leaves the stage. This was thy daughter; now she is, more simply and straightforwardly, the thing to be avenged.[26] Titus, Marcus and the others have a number of scenes without her. She enters the last scene veiled, making her less readable than ever. As he is killing her, Titus makes his own motive clear, characteristically linking her condition with his: "Die, die, Lavinia, and thy shame with thee, / And with thy shame thy father's sorrow die" (V.iii.45–46). Like Chiron and Demetrius after the rape ("So now go tell . . . Write down thy mind") he issues commands, not questions. But what is in Lavinia's mind at this moment? Does she go consenting, to the death she begged for in the woods when she still could speak (II.ii.168–78)? Is this her idea, as it is in the chapbook version?[27] Or does Titus catch her by surprise, as he does everyone else on stage? Performance choices have ranged from a ritual in which Lavinia participates fully to a sudden, brutal snapping of her neck.[28] What we can say is that Lavinia has been absorbed into an action controlled by her father, and having given her life he gives her death. She is not after all completely neglected at the play's end: Lucius commands, "My father and Lavinia shall forthwith / Be closed in our household's monument" (V.iii.192–93). Is this a final vindication, a homecoming? Or a final entrapment? To be with Titus forever: does that fulfill her identity or deny it? For her family, the problem of what to do with Lavinia has been resolved. Kill her, then bury her. For the audience, the problem of how to read her – and particularly what it means to say that she is Titus' daughter – remains.

Her final enclosure contrasts with the fate of Tamora, thrown out of the city "to beasts and birds to prey" (V.iii.197), not where she eats but where she is eaten. Titus called Rome a wilderness of tigers; in expelling what he calls the "ravenous tiger, Tamora" (V.iii.194) Lucius may seem to be cleansing the city by ejecting the only tiger left. In an obvious way she has been Lavinia's opposite number, the evil, murderous adulteress against the chaste, innocent victim. When Lavinia appeals to her as woman to woman she gets nowhere. Yet when Lavinia taunts her, her voice becomes not unlike Tamora's, and their careers, Cynthia Marshall has pointed out, run in parallel: both claimed by Saturninus, married simultaneously, hunting in the same woods where one wants sex and the other has it forced on her.[29] Each presents a problem for Rome, and while Lavinia is absorbed into her father's story and enclosed in the family tomb and Tamora (like Marlowe's Barabas) is cast over the walls, the common factor is that neither can live as herself in Rome, which can accept neither sexual disgrace nor sexual desire in a woman. This may be why the pit in the woods, read as an image of female sexuality – Tamora's no less than Lavinia's – registers not just as a site of damage but as a place of horror. Tamora's fate in particular contrasts with that of Saturninus. At the beginning of the play he claimed the empery as his father's eldest son, and on those terms Titus gave it to him. At the end Lucius orders, of the man who killed his father and whom he killed in turn, "Some loving friends convey the emperor hence, / And give him burial in his father's grave" (V.iii.190–91). Saturninus' claim to consideration through his father is acknowledged again, and he is honored in death as Titus is. For a woman to be raped or to have adulterous sex with a black man sets Roman nerves jangling; for men to kill each other is business as usual, and leaves no residue of shock.

Aaron is another matter: "Set him breast-deep in earth and famish him; / There let him stand and rave and cry for food" (V.iii.178–79). He is to be not buried but half-buried, not fed but starved, not silenced but left to plead. Lucius, whose orders these are, says nothing of his actual death, and it is easy to imagine that what he would like is for Aaron, half-buried, to remain forever on the border of life and death, howling. It is his response to Aaron's own gleeful fantasy of tormenting Lucius in hell by talking at him endlessly (V.i.147–50). In the scene in which Lucius captures him Aaron does indeed (after an initial refusal) threaten to talk forever, relentlessly cataloguing his crimes, and Lucius has to give the play's characteristic order, "stop his mouth" (V.i.152). While Titus with his leaf of brass wants language fixed, permanent, written (and, like all writing, silent unless he chooses to give it voice) Aaron gets his sense of power from the free, moment-by-moment improvisation of speech. But he too has a use for writing:

> Oft have I digged up dead men from their graves
> And set them upright at their dear friends' door,
> Even when their sorrows almost was forgot,
> And on their skins, as on the barks of trees,
> Have with my knife carved in Roman letters,
> "Let not your sorrow die though I am dead." (V.i.135–40)

Two thresholds, those of a grave and a house, are violated, as a corpse returns and stands in a doorway. Titus' suffering included the fear that the nightmare would be endless: "When will this fearful slumber have an end?" (III.i.253). It is just this nightmare that Aaron wants to create: endless grief, centered on a mutilated body that cannot be disposed of in death. The persistence of his unsilenced voice, even in Lucius' order for his punishment, suggests a refusal of closure that pulls against the ending of the play.[30]

In one of the additions to *The Spanish Tragedy* Hieronimo declares, "there is no end: the end is death and madness" (Fourth Addition, 163), a terrifying variation on Kyd's ending, where Don Andrea gloats over the "endless tragedy" (IV.v.48) of his enemies in Hell. In the final revenge sequence, speech is resolved into action and action leads to closure. But in Lavinia, who cannot speak, and in Aaron, who will not be silent, disturbances remain that resist this closure. Aaron's unstoppable voice suggests a story that will never end. Lavinia's unreadable silence (which has given her a power to disturb even greater than Aaron's voice) is a problem that remains unresolved, a problem signaled on her return from the woods, when Marcus removes her identity without giving her another one. Identities, after all, draw boundaries: between Roman and Goth, between love and rape – and, in the scene with which we began, between Lavinia and not-Lavinia, the named and the nameless. To remove boundaries is to remove identities and to deny closure. The play itself in the end resists closure; the audience cannot leave it behind as something settled and finished. Normally, with the completion of a stage action, a boundary is created between the play and the life that resumes after it is over. At the end of *Titus Andronicus* that boundary, like so many others, is broken.

CHAPTER 2

Romeo and Juliet: *What's in a name?*

FROM HEALING TO BREAKING

Romeo's first meeting with Juliet seems designed not only to begin the love story of *Romeo and Juliet* but to heal the wounds of Lavinia in *Titus Andronicus.* Chiron and Demetrius raped Lavinia, cut off her hands, and cut out her tongue. Romeo's first words to Juliet are:

> If I profane with my unworthiest hand
> This holy shrine, the gentle sin is this:
> My lips, two blushing pilgrims, ready stand
> To smooth that rough touch with a tender kiss. (I.v.92–95)

Just to touch her could seem a violation; but he does touch her, and wants to kiss her, and the idea that this is an offense is absorbed into a game of language that excuses it. Asking for a kiss, he is apologizing for the profanity of one physical contact, touching her hand, by proposing a more intimate one that will heal it. The shyness and the frank desire are nicely balanced against each other, and come together in the rush of blood evoked by "blushing."

This time the woman feels the same desire and finds a playful way of returning it:

> JULIET Saints do not move, though grant for prayers' sake.
> ROMEO Then move not, while my prayer's effect I take.
> [*He kisses her.*]
> Thus from my lips, by thine, my sin is purg'd.
> JULIET Then have my lips the sin that they have took.
> ROMEO Sin from my lips? O trespass sweetly urg'd.
> Give me my sin again.
> JULIET   You kiss by th'book. (I.v.104–9)

The couplet that opens this passage closes the sonnet they have been sharing, completing the sonnet's argument with a kiss. Juliet at this moment seems passive, holding still while Romeo kisses her; the kiss seems given rather than shared, the "sin" printed on her as on a blank medium. Lavinia has seemed at times to be such a medium, and the effect will return in the kissing of Cressida. But Juliet is no blank. She continues the argument beyond the closure of the first kiss (and the closure of the sonnet), setting in motion a game of wit that leads to a second kiss in which she will be the active one, returning the sin to Romeo's lips. Kissing becomes a reciprocal act, and in the end Juliet adds a teasing note ("You kiss by th' book") that gives her an edge of control, suggesting this will be one of those Shakespearean love-relationships in which the woman is stronger and brighter than the man. Lavinia is denied language, as part of the complete denial of her will embodied in rape. Juliet uses language, playfully, to participate in a love-game in which she wins the last round. Hands and mouths are touched with love. We seem as far as we could be from the violation of Lavinia.

In the play's last scene, however, something like the violence of *Titus* returns. Paris has come to the Capulet tomb with flowers and sweet water, for a decorous ritual of mourning. Romeo comes with a set of burglary tools, not to mourn outside the tomb but to break into it. Paris thinks he has come, like Aaron, "To do some villainous shame / To the dead bodies" (V.iii.52–53). Up to a point Paris misreads Romeo, one of many misreadings to which the lovers are subjected in the course of the play. Yet Romeo's own mood picks up the language of *Titus*: he warns his boy Balthazar that if he returns to spy on him,

> By heaven I will tear thee joint by joint,
> And strew this hungry churchyard with thy limbs.
> The time and my intents are savage-wild,
> More fierce and more inexorable far
> Than empty tigers or the roaring sea. (V.iii.35–39)

Dismemberment, the sea, the tiger – ideas and images from *Titus* are breaking into the play, as Romeo breaks into the tomb. His action is the violation of a threshold, and as Titus kills Mutius on a threshold, so Romeo kills Paris. The Friar, coming on the scene, cries out,

> Alack, alack, what blood is this which stains
> The stony entrance of this sepulchre?
> What mean these masterless and gory swords
> To lie discolour'd by this place of peace? (V.ii.140–43)

We are back to the bloodstained pit of *Titus*, and as that image figured Lavinia's violated body, the bloodstained entrance of the tomb links back to the brusque determination with which Romeo began the journey that ends here: "Well, Juliet, I will lie with thee tonight" (V.i.34). Literally, the lovers' wedding night took place, decorously offstage, several scenes earlier. Now we are getting a delayed and unexpectedly graphic image of it as a violent break-in, and Juliet's loss of virginity seems, like the rape of Lavinia, an act of violation.

NAMES

How did we get here? How did the playful, tentative love-game of the first meeting lead to this final bloodshed? The process begins with another and more ironic reversal of *Titus*. The denial of Lavina's identity – "This was thy daughter" – is part of the horror of what has happened to her. She has been as it were unnamed. But the trouble for Romeo and Juliet comes not with unnaming but with naming. It is latent in Romeo's first line about her, which is a question: "What lady's that which doth enrich the hand / Of yonder knight?" (Who comes with our brother Marcus here?) A nameless servant replies, "I know not, sir" (I.v.41–42). Like the questions directed at Lavinia, this one goes unanswered. This time the result is to create a free space in which the lovers can meet with no identity other than the attraction they find in each other. It is the equivalent of Alice's wood where things have no names. (In Chapter 3 of *Through the Looking-Glass* Alice, not knowing her own name, wanders through the wood with a fawn, her arms loving clasped around it. When they come to the edge of the wood the fawn, discovering that it is a fawn and Alice is a human child, takes fright and runs away.) Romeo falls in love with Juliet, and she with him, when they have no names to go by, and the names, when they learn them, are fraught with disaster. In Lavinia's involvement with her family there was coercion and damage as well as attempted comfort. The names of the lovers bring their families into play, breaking into the private world of love their opening dialogue creates, and the result is another variation on the idea of relationship as damage.

They confront the problem at their next meeting. What is commonly called the balcony scene might better be called the orchard scene. The word "balcony" occurs nowhere in the play (and according to OED nowhere in the English language before 1618); our clearest indication of setting is that the scene takes place in the Capulets' orchard, with Juliet at a window above.[1] Lovers meet in woods in the comedies, an effect *Titus* grimly parodies. But this orchard is a social space, enclosed by a high wall, and within it the lovers are not joined but separated, Juliet inside and above, Romeo outside and below, a separation emblematic of the problem of names that divides them.[2] We imagine the orchard; but we see the spatial division, and as with the stage trap in *Titus,* the stage itself is making a statement.

Romeo has entered the Capulet house, then the Capulet orchard. He will eventually enter Juliet's bedroom. While film versions can take the camera into the room, the lovers' appearance together at the window is a simpler, more powerful way of signaling that the barrier has fallen and they have made love. Finally Romeo will break into the Capulet tomb. He is a boundary-breaker, and his crossing of thresholds is increasingly dangerous, daring and violent. Yet, in line with the apologetic quality of his first approach, when Romeo sees Juliet above him at the window he retreats to generalized romantic adoration, not narrowing the distance between them but increasing it:

> O speak again bright angel, for thou art
> As glorious to this night, being o'er my head,
> As is the winged messenger of heaven
> Unto the white-upturned wondering eyes
> Of mortals that fall back to gaze on him
> When he bestrides the lazy-puffing clouds
> And sails upon the bosom of the air. (II.ii.26–32)

The playful religious language of his first approach to her has become extravagant adoration. He is no longer touching the figure of a saint but gazing at an angel in the sky. In a way, he is still in the wood with no names. This speech could be addressed by any lover, to any mistress.

Juliet's response could be addressed only to him:

> O Romeo, Romeo, wherefore art thou Romeo?
> Deny thy father and refuse thy name.
> Or if thou wilt not, be but sworn my love
> And I'll no longer be a Capulet. (II.ii.33–36)

Not knowing he can hear (to that extent there is still a barrier between them) she speaks directly to him, imagining him not up in the sky but standing right in front of her. The context she speaks in is not religious or romantic but social and familial. In that context she makes an extraordinary demand: nothing less than the denial of the identity embodied in his name. No sooner has she made that demand than she imagines his refusal and leaps ahead to offer the denial of her own name. Names separate them, a separation figured by the distance between them imposed by the stage picture. Juliet proposes to annihilate those names, and talks to

Romeo as though the physical separation did not exist. When it comes to boundary-breaking, Juliet is swifter and more daring than he is.

Juliet's idea that they should doff their names would keep them forever in a private world of love in which they had no social identities, the wood with no names. But that would be a fantasy world, and they are in Verona. Even Coriolanus, Shakespeare's ultimate egotist, fails in his attempt to become "a kind of nothing, titleless" (V.i.13). Juliet has already caressed the very name she wants Romeo to throw away: "O Romeo, Romeo, wherefore art thou Romeo?" (II.ii.33), and when he offers to take up her challenge, there is a fast play back and forth between unnaming and naming. On her command, "Romeo, doff thy name," he bursts from hiding:

> ROMEO   I take thee at thy word.
>   Call me but love, and I'll be new baptis'd:
>   Henceforth I never will be Romeo.
> JULIET What man art thou that thus bescreen'd in night
>   So stumblest on my counsel?
> ROMEO   By a name
>   I know not how to tell thee who I am:
>   My name, dear saint, is hateful to myself
>   Because it is an enemy to thee.
>   Had I it written, I would tear the word.
> JULIET My ears have not yet drunk a hundred words
>   Of thy tongue's uttering, yet I know the sound.
>   Art thou not Romeo, and a Montague? (II.ii.49–60)

She speaks of his name as a piece of clothing to be removed; he speaks of it as a scribble on paper, to be torn up. They imagine names as something physical, external and easily disposed of. Yet Juliet's "What man art thou?" – overtly a quick retreat from everything she has said, an admission that she would not have said it had she known he was listening – carries another suggestion: if this man is, as he claims, no longer Romeo, then she does not know who he is. He *was* Romeo (this was thy daughter), but he never acquires a new name. "That which we call a rose / By any other word would smell as sweet" (II.ii.42–43) but she has no other word to call it. A rose is a rose, and Romeo is Romeo. She calls him not just "Romeo" but "a Montague" and she goes from that to "fair Montague" and "sweet Montague" (II.ii.98, 137). She accepts everything his name has to offer, trouble and danger included.

She has already laid the ground for this when she learns who it was that kissed her:

> My only love sprung from my only hate.
> Too early seen unknown, and known too late.
> Prodigious birth of love it is to me
> That I must love a loathed enemy. (I.v.137–40)

"Must" says it all. And as names identify family origins, her "only love" is sprung from her "only hate." It is born not in a wood with no names, a place that does not exist, but in Verona, where names and families are all too important. It was part of the unreality of Romeo's love for Rosaline that he took no notice of her being Capulet's niece (I.ii.70). It did not matter, because she did not matter. But it matters deeply that Juliet is Capulet's daughter. Juliet asked, "What's in a name?" (II.ii.43) and tried to answer "Nothing." But the answer they both have to face is "everything."

JULIET AND HER FAMILY

The lovers' names signal their involvement with the world around them, and that is an important step in the journey from the private game of love that begins their relationship, in which the violence of *Titus* seems healed, to the ending in which that violence returns. However, the inevitability of Romeo's being a Montague, and of Juliet's being a Capulet, plays off against the isolation of the lovers within their families. Closed in silence, Lavinia was unreachable, and the family's attempts at dialogue with her led only to the pain of unanswerable questions and baffled misreading. In Romeo's case the isolation begins with the solitude of the adolescent. His father worries about it, finding in it not just the sort of life-transition parents fret about when their children become adults and go into their own world, but a denial of life itself, a foretaste of death. Romeo is

> to himself so secret and so close,
> So far from sounding and discovery,
> As is the bud bit with an envious worm
> Ere he can spread his sweet leaves to the air
> Or dedicate his beauty to the sun. (I.i.147–51)

This belongs to Romeo's infatuation with Rosaline, but it is one of the terms of that infatuation that will take a deeper and more serious form in his affair with Juliet, in which the lovers are not just alone and at odds with the world, but at odds with life itself. Like Montague's worm-bitten bud they are death-marked, and their misunderstanding with the world is fatal.

After the early scenes Romeo's family falls away; his real problem, we shall see, is with his friends. Juliet's isolation from her family is more fully dramatized. In the play's first reference to her, Capulet describes Juliet as "a stranger in the world" (I.ii.8), meaning only that she has led the sheltered life of the daughter of a respectable family. But she will go on being a stranger in the world, and a stranger in the family, in deeper ways than this. In I.ii. Capulet calls her "my child" (8) and never names her. Through much of I.iii, her first scene, the Nurse and Lady Capulet discuss Juliet in the third person as though she were not there. As the action advances the estrangement deepens. Finding her (as he thinks) mourning Tybalt, Capulet indulges in an elaborate comparison of Juliet to a ship in a tempest (III.v.130–37), whose artificial language is even more grotesquely off the mark than that of Marcus' speech over the wounded Lavinia; he is using the wrong words to console her for the wrong grief.[3] Thinking to cheer her up for Tybalt's death, the family plans her marriage to Paris, and she cannot explain why this marriage is a horror; the most she can do is express herself "thankful even for hate that is meant love" (III.v.148). Paris, the husband her family has chosen for her, approaches her affectionately, but with a possessiveness Romeo never shows: "That face is mine, and thou hast slandered it" (IV. i.35). The last living kiss she gets is from him: "Till then, adieu, and keep this holy kiss" (IV.i.43). Asking for the first kiss, Romeo saw *her* as holy. When Paris kisses her she must feel that her mouth has been violated, and as soon as Paris leaves her alone with the Friar we see her at her most desperate: "O shut the door, and when thou hast done so, / Come weep with me, past hope, past cure, past help!"(IV.i.44–45). The family's laments over her seemingly dead body have some of the futility of the family laments over the silenced Lavinia. The artificial, extravagant language becomes increasingly grotesque, and the suspicion grows that the mourners are feeling sorry for themselves.[4] The estrangement is touched by grotesque comedy in that while Lavinia's family is trying, however inadequately, to grieve over a real agony, Juliet's family is mourning an unreal death. Finally, through the whole sequence of her aborted wedding the servants simply carry on doing their jobs, moving furniture and carrying wood, and for the musicians her death is just a professional opportunity to "tarry for the mourners, and stay dinner" (IV.v.140–41).

Lavinia's family are painfully aware of her isolation from them. The Capulets simply carry on as though family life, with its quarrels and reconciliations, is unfolding normally. It is Juliet herself who registers the isolation. And while Lavinia for the most part is silent, helpless and unreadable, her will suspended, her sense of herself unknown, Juliet is articulate, self-assertive and very much in command. Lavinia, passed from Bassianus to Saturninus and back again, says nothing, remaining a pawn in a power game played by the men; Juliet, in defiance of all convention, takes the initiative in proposing marriage to Romeo (II.ii.143–48). (It is a sign of what love has done for him that he utters not a word of protest against this usurpation of a male prerogative.) We can guess, but do not know, what Lavinia feels about being given to Saturninus; Juliet is fiercely articulate about marrying Paris. With Romeo gone and her family against her she turns to the Friar, but is already thinking beyond him: "If all else fail, myself have power to die" (III.v.242) – precisely the power Lavinia was denied.

What's in a name? In I.iii, just before her first entrance, Juliet stands as it were stubbornly in the tiring house as the nurse calls, "What, lamb. What, ladybird. / God forbid. Where's this girl," entering only when the Nurse drops the childish endearments and calls her properly by her name, the first time it is spoken in the play: "What, Juliet!" (I.iii.3–4). She caps the Nurse's "falling backward' story by adding to its punchline, "It stinted, and said 'Ay,'" a punchline and a pun of her own: "And stint thou too, I pray thee, Nurse, say I" (I.iii.57–58). There is definitely an "I" here. Even when she returns to the pun as the nurse's inarticulate report makes her think Romeo is dead – "I am not I if there be such an 'I'" (III. ii.48) – her absorption of her identity in Romeo's, so that his death wipes out her life, is very much her decision, indicated by the hammering repetition of "I." As her life falls apart she holds to her command of language, and of herself.

Until she learns to write, Lavinia has only silence, and gestures that can be read more than one way. Juliet is unreadable when she chooses to be unreadable. She tells Lady Capulet what she feels about the man who killed her cousin:

> O, how my heart abhors
> To hear him nam'd, and cannot come to him
> To wreak the love I bore my cousin
> Upon his body that hath slaughter'd him. (III.v.99–102)

The speech has one meaning for Lady Capulet, another for Juliet and the audience. Her command of language is matched by her daring in telling her mother, knowing she cannot read the signal, that what she feels for Tybalt's killer is aching desire.

LOVE AND THE WORLD

In the scenes with her family, Juliet is going through a drama of her own that her family does not know how to read; they do not even know how ignorant they are. This is part of the lovers' general isolation: they do not think as the world does. Montague is bemused by the artificial darkness, the day–night reversal, in which Romeo lives:

> Away from light steals home my heavy son
> And private in his chamber pens himself,
> Shuts up his windows, locks fair daylight out
> And makes himself an artificial night. (I.i.135–38)

This is another case in which Romeo's fantasizing over Rosaline is a preparation for his relationship with Juliet. There too light and dark will be reversed, and Romeo will create a new cosmos with a new center, in which day can break in the middle of the night: "But soft, what light through yonder window breaks? / It is the east and Juliet is the sun!" (II. ii.2–3). Time operates differently for the lovers. The Nurse can ramble on about how long ago Juliet was born (I.iii.10–17); Capulet and his cousin can bicker about how long it was since they last were in a masque (I.v.30–40). Past events can be located by other past events: the earthquake, the nuptial of Lucentio. But for Romeo and Juliet the future is what matters. It has no landmarks, and it does not operate by clock-time but by their feelings. It is "twenty year" (II.ii.169) till tomorrow, and as Romeo goes into exile "in a minute there are many days" (III.v.45).

The contrasts between the private world of the lovers and the outside world can be abrasive. Bodies are more roughly handled in the latter, and language is tougher. A gentle touch of hands starts a love affair; out in the streets, Sampson bites his thumb to start a fight, and Mercutio expresses a rough physical affection for Romeo: "I will bite thee by the ear for that jest" (II.iv.78). Even fantasies are more coarse-grained. In Mercutio's Queen Mab speech the body is not touched with love but teased and tickled: Mab triggers dreams by driving over courtiers' knees, lawyers' fingers, a parson's nose and a soldier's neck (I.iv.72–83). She is particularly rough on lovers, driving

> O'er ladies' lips, who straight on kisses dream,
> Which oft the angry Mab with blisters plagues
> Because their breaths with sweetmeats tainted are. (I.iv.74–76)

Romeo will treat a lady's lips more gently than this. He interrupts the speech just as Mercutio is turning Mab into a female incubus who starts

off girls' sex lives with a lesbian encounter: "This is the hag, when maids
lie on their backs, / That presses them and learns them first to bear" (I.
iv.92–93). The Nurse will turn the joke back to heterosexual experience –
"you shall bear the burden soon at night" (II.v.77) – and elsewhere in the
play sex is hitting the mark, opening a lap, raising a spirit in a circle,
hiding a bauble in a hole (I.i.205, 212; II.i.24; II.iv.92–93). The Nurse sees
Juliet as a good material match in two senses: "he that can lay hold of
her / Shall have the chinks" (I.v.115–16). The difference between this sort
of talk and Juliet's "Give me my Romeo; and when I shall die / Take him
and cut him out in little stars" (III.ii.21–22) is the difference between a
leap of erotic imagination and a plumbing manual.

At first the gentleness of the lovers is contrasted with the violence of the
bawdry and the violence of the feud. The lovers touch hands; in the feud,
"civil blood makes civil hands unclean" (Prologue.4). In the opening
banter of Sampson and Gregory, our first glimpse of the feud mentality,
blades become sexual as one kind of manhood blurs with another: "To
move is to stir, and to be valiant is to stand" leads naturally to "Draw thy
tool" and "My naked weapon is out" (I.i.8, 30, 32). Romeo approached
Juliet by touching her hand; Sampson boasts that having fought the men
he will deflower the women: "Me they shall feel while I am able to stand,
and 'tis known I am a pretty piece of flesh" (I.i.27–28). All this suggests a
radical contrast between the shared feeling of the lovers and the aggressive
violence in the streets.

Yet as their names link the lovers to the feud, the wordplay makes us
think of love and the feud together. At first the link is through contrast.
But the effect runs deeper than that: as the narrator of *Lucrece* insists on
keeping Lucrece and Tarquin together, as Lavinia's rape echoes her
marriage, something of the feud infiltrates the love affair, as though borne
by the names the lovers cannot discard. It enters in Juliet's acknowledgement that her only love is sprung from her only hate. Even before the
action begins, the Chorus proclaims the link as the basic condition of the
story, and of the lovers' very existence:

> From forth the fatal loins of these two foes
> A pair of star-cross'd lovers take their life,
> Whose misadventured piteous overthrows
> Doth with their death bury their parents' strife. (Prologue.5–8)

At the end of her life Lavinia takes her death from Titus. Romeo and
Juliet took their deaths from their parents when they were born – another
prodigious birth, from "fatal loins." As Lavinia is buried with Titus, the

feud seems to be buried with them. Behind the ostensible meaning that the feud ends with their lives is the suggestion that as the feud was with them at birth it is with them forever in death. It is with them when they meet, though they do not yet know it: the sonnet form they use for their opening dialogue has been heard once before, in the Prologue that announces their fate.

It is Romeo's first tribute to Juliet's beauty ("O, she doth teach the torches to burn bright" [I.v.43]) that sets Tybalt to work: "This by his voice should be a Montague" (I.v.53). Tybalt is at his most frightening here. He has evidently not heard Romeo's words (or his reaction would be even stronger); he simply recognizes, at some distance, a Montague voice. He can smell them in the dark. He reacts to the sound of Romeo as powerfully as Romeo reacts to the sight of Juliet, and when Capulet restrains him his frustration has a physical charge that matches the erotic excitement of the lovers: "Patience perforce with wilful choler meeting / Makes my flesh tremble in their different greeting" (I.v.88–89). This is followed immediately by the lovers' first dialogue, their first touch of hands, and their first kiss. Romeo's affair with Juliet and his affair with Tybalt begin together, love born from hate and hate born from love.

The day Romeo marries Juliet is the day he kills Tybalt; the act of violence comes between the ceremony and the consummation. The Friar orders the lovers to the altar with the admonition, "by your leaves, you shall not stay alone / Till holy church incorporate two in one" – in effect, I've seen the way you look at each other and I'm getting you married right now before anything happens.[5] In the next words we hear, Benvolio sets the atmosphere of the fatal street scene:

> I pray thee, good Mercutio, let's retire;
> The day is hot, the Capels are abroad,
> And if we meet we shall not 'scape a brawl,
> For now these hot days is the mad blood stirring.
> (II.vi.36–III.i.4)

The wedding and the fight are not just contrasted but linked: in these hot days there are two kinds of mad blood stirring.[6]

ROMEO'S NAME

Yet love and the feud are still at odds, in that Romeo's killing of Tybalt is a betrayal of Juliet. The speed with which he drops Rosaline may suggest to a cynical eye that he will drop Juliet before long, and she herself plays briefly with the fear that Romeo will be unfaithful: "if thou swear'st, / Thou mayst prove false" (II.ii.91–92). This fear is in one sense groundless: the tragedy springs from the lovers' total commitment to each other. Yet Romeo does betray Juliet, not with another woman but with his fellow men. He has two natures, lover and killer, and his duality is signaled when he enters Friar Laurence's cell on the words, "Within the infant rind of this weak flower / Poison hath residence, and medicine power" (II.iii.19–20).[7] The medicine and the poison, like the two kinds of hot blood, correspond to his relationship with Juliet and his relationship with his friends. Both have claims on him. Though once he is at the Capulets' feast he seems alone with Juliet, he has entered with his friends, and their entrance has a macho swagger: Romeo cries, "On, lusty gentlemen," Benvolio commands, "Strike, drum" and *They march about the stage* (I.iv.113–I.v.sd). For Mercutio, Romeo is himself only when he is one of the boys, and to make that point he fixes as Juliet does on Romeo's name. After engaging Romeo in banter that seems to snap him out of his love-melancholy, Mercutio crows in triumph, "Now art thou sociable, now art thou Romeo" (II.iv.89).

For Romeo to be "sociable" in Mercutio's sense has more dangerous implications than either of them realizes. In Mercutio's scheme of things, Romeo cannot be himself (that is, Mercutio's friend), cannot truly be a man, if he is a lover. Though Romeo complains of getting nowhere with Rosaline, it suits Mercutio to imagine he is spending his manhood in sex with her, leaving him "Without his roe, like a dried herring" (II.iv.38). He has lost not just his manhood but half his name. He is only fully "Romeo" when he is sociable, Mercutio's friend. More ominously, he is disabled as a fighter: "stabbed with a white wench's black eye, run through the ear with a love song, the very pin of his heart cleft with the blind bow-boy's butt-shaft. And is he a man to encounter Tybalt?" (II.iv.13–17). Yet when the challenge comes, Mercutio expects Romeo to meet it (III.i.55–58) and he is outraged when Romeo fails the test, softened by a love of which Mercutio has no inkling.

The opening banter between Sampson and Gregory is a series of challenges to Sampson's manhood, which Gregory pointedly doubts. In retrospect, this comic scene is as ominous as the Prologue: Romeo will be challenged as Sampson is. Sampson's first line, "we'll not carry coals [put up with injuries]" (I.i.1) introduces the issue of the Romeo–Tybalt confrontation, where Tybalt will not bear insult but Romeo (at first) will. At this point Romeo and his friends enact a drama of misunderstanding like that of Juliet and her family. The other men do not recognize as we do what is holding Romeo back from a conventional display of manhood, what is stopping him from being the Romeo they think they know. They misread him, and language fails him. Words that fit the world of love seem hopelessly inarticulate in the street. Romeo tries to make peace in the language of the orchard scene, calling Tybalt "good Capulet" (III.i.70) as Juliet called him "fair Montague"; but such language has no currency here. With the death of Mercutio the pressure on Romeo to conform, to be sociable, becomes unbearable, and he has no words to defend himself. All he can say to the dying Mercutio is "I thought all for the best" and while in theory there is a weight of meaning behind that line, what registers at the moment is its terrible feebleness. Mercutio responds by refusing to acknowledge that Romeo even exists: "Help me into some house, Benvolio, / Or I shall faint" (III.i.106–8). No longer sociable, no longer Romeo, he is not even there. That icy dismissal is what drives Romeo to his next decision.

Mercutio's appearance in the sources is brief but striking: at the Capulet feast he is the equivalent of "yonder knight" Romeo sees dancing with Juliet, and his hands are ice-cold.[8] Shakespeare may have remembered that detail without using it overtly, when he made Mercutio the character who brings death into the play. He is not, as in the source, a potential rival with Romeo for Juliet; he is, without knowing it, Juliet's rival for Romeo. The pressure his death puts on Romeo is the pressure of relationship, of his role in a society of men, and it turns Romeo against Juliet:

> This gentleman, the Prince's near ally,
> My very friend, hath got this mortal hurt
> In my behalf – my reputation stain'd
> With Tybalt's slander – Tybalt that an hour
> Hath been my cousin. O sweet Juliet,
> Thy beauty hath made me effeminate
> And in my temper softened valour's steel. (III.i.111–17)

He is forced, as Coppélia Kahn puts it, to a "tragic choice" between "two conflicting definitions of manhood,"[9] a choice he himself sees as between manhood and effeminacy. We might see it as a choice between two ideas of what it means to be Romeo. Taking up Mercutio's cause, he accepts the idea behind Mercutio's jokes, that love has unmanned him. As in the opening banter of Sampson and Gregory, weapons are sexualized, and his weapon has gone soft. He has to show his capacity for violence, proving his manhood not by making love to Juliet but by killing her cousin. This is the moment when he betrays her, and himself, buying into the violence from which their love had seemed so isolated.

As he has turned – briefly, but long enough to cause disaster – against Juliet, she, just as briefly, turns against him. Like him she is torn between loyalties, "My dearest cousin and my dearer lord" (III.ii.66). The balance tilts towards Tybalt, as she sees Romeo's beauty masking an ugly reality:

> O serpent heart, hid with a flowering face.
> Did ever dragon keep so fair a cave?
> Beautiful tyrant, fiend angelical,
> Dove-feather'd raven, wolvish-ravening lamb! (III.ii.73–76)

The similarity to the mechanical paradoxes of Romeo's early love-language ("Feather of lead, bright smoke" [I.I.178]) is no accident: Juliet is betraying herself here, and her language is inauthentic.[10] Romeo's betrayal of Juliet was serious and believable, stemming from demands whose power we could recognize. Juliet's betrayal of Romeo is temporary, superficial, and soon over.

She and Romeo deal with the crisis by turning again to Romeo's name. There is heavy irony when Juliet greets the Nurse's entrance, "every tongue that speaks / But Romeo's name speaks heavenly eloquence" (III.ii.32–33), and when the Nurse echoes Juliet's first line in the orchard scene: "O Romeo, Romeo, / Whoever would have thought it? Romeo!" (III.ii.41–42). For Juliet, as for Mercutio, Romeo's name embodies her delight in their relationship; she loves the sound of it. For the Nurse, Romeo has betrayed his name. In his scene with the Friar, Romeo goes further, seeing his name as embodying the new, terrible thing he has become, not Juliet's husband but the man who killed her cousin. Earlier, he took up Juliet's challenge by offering to tear his name; now he wants to kill it by killing himself, because it has already killed Juliet. The name itself has become lethal:

> As if that name,
> Shot from the deadly level of a gun,
> Did murder her, as that name's cursed hand
> Murder'd her kinsman. O, tell me, Friar, tell me,
> In what vile part of this anatomy
> Doth my name lodge? Tell me that I may sack
> The hateful mansion. (III.iii.101–7)

In *Titus Andronicus* the political enemy was within. Now that threat becomes personal: the internal enemy is oneself, an effect to which Shakespeare will return in later tragedies. Romeo takes seriously the implications of Juliet's "'Tis but thy name that is my enemy" (II.ii.38), adding that it is his enemy too. He cannot doff his name as though it were a garment, or tear it as though it were written on paper; he can only kill it, by killing the enemy within who is himself.

But Juliet has already accepted his name. She could accept him as a Montague, because he was Romeo; she can accept him as Tybalt's killer, because he is still Romeo. His name has not hurt her, she has hurt it, and she tries to make amends: "Ah, poor my lord, what tongue shall smooth thy name / When I thy three-hours wife have mangled it?" (III.ii.98–99). As the word "wife" steadies her, the word "husband" helps her turn her loyalties around, rejecting Tybalt's word for Romeo ("villain") and substituting her own: "But wherefore, villain, didst thou kill my cousin? / That villain cousin would have kill'd my husband" (III.ii.100–1). As the word "villain" travels back from Romeo to Tybalt, Juliet does as much as she can to undo the damage Romeo did to her, and to himself.

SHEDDING CAPULET BLOOD

This is Juliet's way of working out the conflict between the two kinds of hot blood; but as I have suggested, there is a link as well as a conflict between them. In Brooke's *Tragicall Historye*, Romeo kills Tybalt only after three months of wedded happiness.[11] In Shakespeare, Romeo kills Tybalt on his wedding day, and this sets up a double action that recalls the double rape of Lavinia. If it is true that "a man who has never killed is a virgin"[12] Romeo loses his virginity in the street with Tybalt before he loses it in bed with Juliet.[13] Beginning with the jokes of Sampson and Gregory, a metaphorical connection between sex and violence runs through the play, and Sampson's threat to cut off "the heads of the maids, or their maidenheads" (I.i.24) is particularly apposite here.[14] There are two ways of shedding blood, as Romeo himself suggests:

> Doth she not think me an old murderer
> Now I have stain'd the childhood of our joy
> With blood remov'd but little from her own? (III.iii.93–95)

"Old murderer" suggests a speedy, unnatural growing up, and his spoiling of Juliet's happiness and his own is embodied in the shedding of blood, Tybalt's and Juliet's. "Remov'd but little" keeps a certain distance: killing Tybalt is not the same thing as taking Juliet's virginity. But the ideas come close enough together to suggest the element of violence in love-making: the loss of innocence the lovers both desire is not just fulfillment but damage, and it too means shedding blood. We are getting closer to the final violence of the tomb.

After the death of Tybalt we see Juliet eager for her wedding night, and there is more than an obvious irony of plotting in the juxtaposition of scenes:

> Gallop apace, you fiery-footed steeds,
> towards Phoebus' lodging. Such a waggoner
> As Phaeton would whip you to the west
> And bring in cloudy night immediately.
> Spread thy close curtain, love-performing night,
> That runaway's eyes may wink, and Romeo
> Leap to these arms untalk'd-of and unseen. (III.ii.1–7)

Gallop, whip, leap – the speech has the speed and excitement of the action in the streets, and just a touch of that action's violence. The Phaeton image carries a charge of disaster. Juliet is facing a new experience, and her eagerness is touched with fear: "till strange love grow bold, / Think true love acted simple modesty" (III.ii.15–16). Going into new territory, she is determined to make it familiar; but she feels its strangeness, and knows she will not overcome that strangeness all at once. The speed of Juliet's imagination seems to pick up the speed of the killing: Benvolio's narrative of the Mercutio–Tybalt fight is slow and detailed, but Romeo and Tybalt go to it "like lightning" and Romeo kills his man before Benvolio can draw to part them (III.i.160–77). Juliet's sense that she is going into strange new territory may recall the moment when Romeo, having killed Tybalt, stands in a daze, not knowing what he has done. Tybalt is dead, Juliet hopes to "die" (III.ii.21); as in the double rape of Lavinia, a single word with a double meaning draws disparate experiences together, joining with the sexual language of weaponry to link love and killing. Romeo has had, and Juliet is anticipating, a rite of passage in which love and death are imaginatively joined.

ON THE BORDER

Having taken us this close to the shock of the final scene, the play retreats. In the aubade that follows the lovers' wedding night, there is no hint of violence. If it was part of their love-making, it was dispelled by being acted out. Gentle and quiet, the aubade suggests that as Juliet has healed Romeo's name the play, having healed the wounds of *Titus Andronicus*, has now healed its own. The aubade picks up, and transforms, the problem of division between the lovers: the physical separation of the orchard scene, the way the death of Tybalt drove them briefly apart. It also picks up and transforms the division between the lovers and the

world. It translates their disagreement with each other, and their disagreement with the world, into lyrical, contemplative language. In that way the
aubade is like Marcus' attempt to transform Lavinia's suffering through
distance and stylization. But it is far more natural, far more subtle, and for
a while at least it succeeds.

In the debate between the lark and the nightingale, between day and
night, Romeo and Juliet find themselves poised on a border between their
world and the rest of life, debating which side they are on, caught in a
moment of transition. In *Titus Andronicus*, beginning with the killing of
Mutius, thresholds were sites of violence. Romeo and Juliet have found on
the threshold between night and day a place of stillness from which they
can look in either direction:

> JULIET Wilt thou be gone? It is not yet near day.
>   It was the nightingale and not the lark
>   That pierc'd the fearful hollow of thine ear.
>   Nightly she sings on yond pomegranate tree.
>   Believe me, love, it was the nightingale.
> ROMEO It was the lark, the herald of the morn,
>   No nightingale. Look, love, what envious streaks
>   Do lace the severing clouds in yonder east.
>   Night's candles are burnt out, and jocund day
>   Stands tiptoe on the misty mountain tops.
>   I must be gone and live, or stay and die. (III.v.1–11)

In the poise and balance of the voices, we hear everything we need to
know of the harmony they have won by making love. Though they are
formally debating, their voices work together as never before, just as by
appearing together at the window they are physically united as never
before. The quiet tone suggests fulfillment, more peaceful than the sleepy
exhaustion that overtakes *Titus Andronicus* after the rape of Lavinia. The
naturalness of Romeo's "Let's talk" (III.v.25) evokes a couple lying in bed
after making love. Juliet's equally natural detail about the nightingale,
"Nightly she sings on yond pomegranate tree," suggests she is letting
Romeo into the familiar routines of her life. They have absorbed even the
grief of parting into the general harmony, and their love seems deeper
because it includes the knowledge of that parting, just as Juliet has
deepened her love for Romeo by accepting everything his name means
– a Montague, and Tybalt's killer. They are debating; but in the manner
of their dialogue everything that troubles their love is for a moment
acknowledged, accepted, and absorbed. And the opposition between the
private world of their love and the world outside that threatens it is

reduced and distanced, even turned lyrical, in the rival notes of the nightingale and the lark.

Such a delicate balance cannot last; they cannot stay forever on the threshold. As they change sides the debate gets sharper:

> ROMEO . . . Come death, and welcome. Juliet wills it so.
> How is't, my soul? Let's talk. It is not day.
> JULIET It is, it is. Hie hence, begone, away. (III.v.24–26)

As he decides to stay and she commands him to leave, the quiet (still there for a moment in "Let's talk") falls away. They are no longer poised on the border of light and dark but standing on the side of light, which to them is darkness: Juliet declares, "O now be gone, more light and light it grows" and Romeo at last agrees, "More light and light: more dark and dark our woes" (III.v.35–36). Only by debating could they hold the balance, and now the debate is over. As Romeo prepares to leave there is a characteristic reversal of the values of the normal world: day brings grief, and Juliet sees a double movement across the threshold: "Then, window, let day in and let life out" (III.v.41).

Romeo stands again below the window, and once more a gap opens between them as he expresses an empty optimism:

> JULIET O think'st thou we shall ever meet again?
> ROMEO I doubt it not, and all these woes shall serve
> For sweet discourses in our times to come.
> JULIET O God, I have an ill-divining soul!
> Methinks I see thee, now thou art so low,
> As one dead in the bottom of a tomb. (III.v.51–56)

Poised between day and night, they seemed for a while to be in a state of suspended time. But time moves on, and the scene opens out to evoke both past and future. As in II.ii, Romeo is standing below her window, looking up; but this time the focus is on her view of him, not his of her, and what she sees is the ending of the play.

The return to the stage picture of the orchard scene is ominous. The aubade, in which disagreement became harmony, held them together. In its more somber way it was a game they shared, like the first, playful debate that kept their voices working closely together and led to a pair of kisses. Now, in the aftermath of consummation, as close as they will ever be, they have achieved their fullest harmony. But when Romeo descends to the main stage, leaving Juliet behind, this repeats the move from their first encounter to the orchard scene, a move from closeness to distance. In the orchard scene distance made their language, while still playful, more extravagant, even a little desperate. Now division has become separation, and in the following scenes, as the gulf widens and they try to reach back across it, that desperation will turn violent and the link between sex and killing will return.

From the beginning this has been, as the Prologue calls it, a "death-mark'd love" (9). In Juliet's first wedding night, the violence that is metaphorically connected with sex disappears in the harmony of fulfilled love. But as Lavinia undergoes two kinds of rape, Juliet has two wedding nights. The second one takes place in the tomb. The language of the play has persistently connected love and death, and in the end that connection is fulfilled. Romeo uses the argument of the procreation sonnets on Rosaline, insisting she pass her beauty on to posterity by having a child (I.i.217–18). But he sees in Juliet "Beauty too rich for use, for earth too dear" (I.v.46) and in their affair there is never a suggestion of Benedick's excuse for love, that the world must be peopled. In the standard pun, orgasm means not fertility but death. Juliet's "Give me my Romeo; and when I shall die / Take him and cut him out in little stars" (III.ii.21–22), making no distinction between her climax and his, not only suggests the blending of identities in perfect love-making but goes straight from sex to death. Heroes become stars when they die. There are the same overtones when Romeo, asking for a kiss, addresses Juliet as a saint: saints are people who have died, and their shrines are monuments to the dead.[15] Sex and death are connected to fertility only in a grotesque way: Juliet's reference to 'shrieks like mandrakes torn out of the earth' (IV.iii.47) may recall the legend that mandrakes grow from the semen of hanged men.

As their love begins, Juliet fears its brevity even as she hopes for natural fulfillment through time:

> It is too rash, too unadvis'd, too sudden,
> Too like the lightning, which doth cease to be
> Ere one can say 'It lightens'. Sweet, good night.
> This bud of love, by summer's ripening breath,
> May prove a beauteous flower when next we meet. (II.ii.118–22)

In the event their love is more like the lightning, the brilliant flash in the dark, than the slowly opening flower. It is Juliet herself who forces the pace: moments after this speech she calls Romeo back and proposes marriage. Preparing for the wedding, the Friar also thinks of the future, but Romeo retorts,

> Do thou but close our hands with holy words,
> Then love-devouring death do what he dare:
> It is enough I may but call her mine. (II.vi.6–8)

It is as though he wants his love to be brief so that he can feel it more intensely.

Connecting love and death, both lovers seem to have an instinct for disaster. Juliet's concern about Romeo's identity leaps ahead to the end of the play: "Go ask his name. If he be married, / My grave is like to be my wedding bed" (I.v.133–34). After the killing of Tybalt she seems prepared to take death as her first lover: "I'll to my wedding bed, / And death, not Romeo take my maidenhead" (III.ii.136–37). It takes the combined efforts of the Friar and the Nurse to make sure Romeo gets there first. Throughout this sequence the bawdry of the nurse – "he is even in my mistress' case" – "For Juliet's sake, for her sake, rise and stand" (III.iii.84, 89) – is a way of keeping life going for two lovers who seem temporarily more eager for death than for each other.

The connection between love and death is initially a trick of language fascinating to the lovers as a condition of their sexual excitement; in the second half of the play it gets closer to literal reality. The double action of Tybalt's death and the wedding night is the turning point. From then on, the "ill-divining soul" that lets them see each other dead at the end of their last meeting begins to operate powerfully. Romeo complains that while he will be exiled from Juliet, even

> carrion flies . . . may seize
> On the white wonder of dear Juliet's hand
> And steal immortal blessing from her lips. (III.iii.35–37)

Not just flies but carrion flies: he is imagining her dead. As the flies seize the hands and lips he gently touched, "seize" (strikingly odd, for the action of a fly) has overtones of rape. He asked for blessing, and she granted it; they steal it, while she is helpless to respond. The action of his love on the body of the living Juliet is parodied in the flies' action on her corpse. Romeo goes on to anticipate the lovers' actual suicides, demanding of the Friar, "Hast thou no poison mix'd, no sharp-ground knife" (III.iii.44); and later he recalls that he first thought of the apothecary as a means of death before he knew he would need him (V.i.49–52). The motif of the enemy within returns as the Friar offers Juliet, and Romeo demands from the Apothecary, drugs that will invade the lovers' bodies and turn them respectively into the image and the reality of death: "presently through all thy veins shall run / A cold and drowsy humour"

(IV.i.95–96); "such soon-speeding gear / As will disperse itself through all the veins" (V.i.60–61). (Old Hamlet will describe the invasion of his body by poison in very similar terms.) Juliet's response to the threat is "Give me, give me! O tell not me of fear" (IV.i.121). It is not so much that she trusts the Friar's plan; in her soliloquy before taking the potion she imagines all the terrible things that could happen, but not the possibility that the plan will work. Rather, she seems as eager to confront death as Romeo is in his scene with the apothecary.

In the later scenes, as the lovers become fixated on death, their estrangement from the world deepens. The plot machinery that delays the Friar's letter involves more than just bad luck: Friar John is locked in a plague-house, cannot deliver the letter himself, and can find no one else to take it, "So fearful were they of infection" (V.ii.16). Plague ("a plague o' both your houses"), enclosure and a letter no one will touch: the lovers, infected, are cut off from the world, and the symbolism may count for more than the plot machinery. In the drama of misunderstanding enacted by Juliet and her family, there is more than just estrangement. As Lavinia's rape resonates through the whole of *Titus Andronicus*, the lovers' impulse towards death begins to infect the world. After the death of Tybalt life goes on, and the effect is as incongruous as in the opening scenes of *Hamlet*. Capulet dismisses Tybalt, "Well, we were born to die" (III.iv.4), and sets about planning Juliet's wedding to Paris. But the preparations turn awry as the bride is taken, with all the pomp planned for her nuptial, not to her new husband's house but to the Capulet tomb. A rite of passage is aborted as, like Lavinia, the bride returns to her family. As the loins that gave her life were fatal, she returns to her family by entering the tomb.

The tomb of the Andronici is a looming presence, but we remain outside it. Whatever its other associations, Titus describes it as a place of peace (I.i.153–59). We enter the Capulet tomb through Juliet's imagination before she is literally there (once again, entering her experience as we cannot enter Lavinia's), and it is a place of horror. In the ultimate torture chamber in Orwell's *1984* the victims confront the worst thing in the world, the phobia peculiar to each individual, the one thing they cannot stand. For Winston Smith it is rats. For Juliet, as for the hero of Poe's "The Premature Burial," it is burial alive. Listing all the things she is prepared to do rather than marry Paris, she gets stuck on that one, and dwells on it with horrified fascination, suggesting that her eagerness for the grave and her fear of it are bound together (IV.i.80–88). This is the sex–death connection, with the fear of death turned uppermost.

As the killing of Tybalt is both a betrayal of her love and symbolically connected with its fulfillment, the tomb where she will die one last time with Romeo is associated with everything that menaces love. In the tomb she will be oppressed with the dead weight of the ancestral past,[16] the family and the feud, with Tybalt not as her beloved cousin but as the latest manifestation of that past and the sharpest image of its corruption:

> Where for this many hundred years the bones
> Of all my buried ancestors are pack'd,
> Where bloody Tybalt yet but green in earth
> Lies festering in his shroud.. . . (IV.iii.40–43)

The dead still have power to kill: Juliet imagines a symbolically appropriate death for herself, dashing out her brains "With some great kinsman's bone" (IV.iii.53). In the tomb the feud goes on in ghostly form, as Juliet imagines Tybalt seeking out Romeo for revenge. As the speech ends and she takes the potion, she calls out to both men as though she were already in the tomb with them. The three figures – Juliet, Tybalt, Romeo – form a group that dramatizes Romeo's fatal choice in III.i, and her own briefly divided loyalties.

Her final cry, "Romeo, Romeo, Romeo" (IV.iii.58), also shows how desperately she feels their separation, the separation we saw growing at the end of the aubade. While they moved through strongly paralleled laments after the death of Tybalt, they are going through very different experiences now, driven apart as never before. While Juliet confronts horror, Romeo reports a dream of ghostly, unreal happiness (V.i.1–11): his fantasy that Juliet will find him dead and kiss him to life is like, and terribly unlike, what actually happens. While Juliet imagines horror in the grave, the family packed around her and the feud going on forever, Romeo imagines only love. Hearing of her death, he confronts a death-world of his own in his description of the apothecary's shop crammed with "musty seeds" and "old cakes of roses" (V.i.46–47). But these dry plants (the apothecary, whom he first saw "culling of simples" [V.i.40], is the dark side of Friar Laurence) suggest natural death; what Juliet imagines in the tomb is dead people unnaturally alive.

While Juliet is carried in procession to the ultimate family reunion, Romeo increasingly cuts himself off from society. In "Is it e'en so? Then I defy you, stars!" (V.i.24) he takes his fate into his own hands and from here on thinks and acts like a criminal. Buying poison from the apothecary, he involves them both in an illegal act, which could end in the apothecary's death as well as his own. He urges the apothecary to think as he does: "The world is not thy friend, nor the world's law; . . . / Then be not poor, but break it, and take this" (V.i.72–74). Killing Tybalt, Romeo broke the law in a temporary burst of rage, under tremendous pressure; now his lawbreaking seems principled and endemic. This is the Romeo who comes to break into the tomb, and stains the entrance with Paris's blood – a blood that like Tybalt's becomes imaginatively conflated with Juliet's.

What now separates Romeo from Juliet is a barrier that can be crossed only by violence; and Romeo now seems violent as never before. At one point he even sounds like Tybalt, firing Tybalt's taunt, "boy" (V.iii.70), at Paris. Yet there are lingering touches of the old, courteous Romeo, whom even Capulet saw as "a virtuous and well-govern'd youth" (I.v.67); he gives Balthasar a letter for his father, a last acknowledgement of the family ties he has defied. Having killed Paris he apologizes, realizing who his victim is and remembering that Paris was to have married Juliet: "O, give me thy hand, / One writ with me in sour misfortune's book" (V.iii.81–82). There is a brotherhood, a mirroring, between the killer and the man he kills, an idea to which Shakespeare will return in *Hamlet*. When he enters the tomb the old Romeo who first saw Juliet returns in full force, except that he has the courtesy to share the sight, at least in his imagination, with Paris:

> A grave? O no, a lantern, slaughter'd youth.
> For here lies Juliet, and her beauty makes
> This vault a feasting presence, full of light. (V.iii.84–86)

But like the touches of his old courtesy, this echo of his first sight of Juliet teaching the torches to burn bright at the Capulet feast shows how far Romeo and the play have traveled. Granting Paris' request to lay him with Juliet, he drags a dead man across the threshold with him, a reminder that since he first saw Juliet he has killed two people and let revenge break the private world of love. If the tomb is Juliet's bedchamber, Paris is the last man she would want to see in it. Once Romeo begins to speak to Juliet, Paris is forgotten, like the knight he first saw holding her hand; but in the lovers' last scene the audience will still see him lying there, an image of the manly world of violence, and of the conventional marriage Capulet wanted, dragged by Romeo himself into Juliet's bedchamber. Through Romeo's own act, their last moments are haunted by the world. It is part of the violation the Friar sees when he describes the bloodstained entry of the tomb. That description evokes the physical reality of a sexual initi- ation.[17] Something that was suggested earlier but held back in the aubade

now returns: the acknowledgement that Romeo shed Juliet's blood as he
shed Tybalt's. The touch is no longer gentle.

Shakespeare keeps the effect in balance; Romeo is not Chiron and
Demetrius revisited. His death speech, like his first address to Juliet, is
gentle, even playful – "Here, here will I remain / With worms that are thy
chambermaids" (V.iii.108–9) – and ends, as their sonnet-exchange did, on
a kiss. And Juliet, determined to the end, is not Lavinia. She takes the final
violence on herself. Guiding the dagger – "This is thy sheath. There rust,
and let me die" (V.iii.169) – she dies on an image of violent penetration
and orgasm. As Juliet accepted her cousin's killer as her lover, it is Juliet,
not Romeo, who enacts most graphically the violence of their love-
making. As she proposed marriage, she now guides the dagger. Whether
the dagger is literally hers or Romeo's, she is enacting his penetration of
her as something she does herself, an act of her own will, recalling the way
she fused his orgasm with hers. We have gone from the symbolism of their
appearance at the window together to a more explicit image of the
wedding night itself: for the first time we see them lying together.[18] The
Friar's "Thy husband in thy bosom there lies dead" (V.iii.155) implies
Romeo is not just with her but on her. In Juliet's wedding-night speech
we could feel her sexual excitement, and in the aubade the peace of its
consummation. Now we are observers, even voyeurs, looking at the lovers
from a distance, and the effect is colder.

This time their voices do not work together at all. Throughout the last
scene, as Romeo speaks to Paris and Juliet, and Juliet speaks to Romeo,
they are doing what Lavinia's family spends so much time doing, speaking
to someone who cannot respond. As Titus may misread Lavinia, as Juliet's
family misread her, and as Romeo's friends misread him, now Romeo
terribly misreads Juliet:

> Thou art not conquer'd. Beauty's ensign yet
> Is crimson in thy lips and in thy cheeks,
> And Death's pale flag is not advanced there. (V.iii.94–96)

Juliet, like Lavinia, is contested ground; this time it is a battle between
beauty and death. So far Romeo has it right; but – in an ironic replay of
the day-night debate in the aubade – what he sees as beauty's last stand in
the face of death's inevitable victory is really beauty's return for death's
impending defeat. There is a complementary effect when Juliet gives
Romeo her last kiss: "Thy lips are warm!" (V.iii.167). They come this
close to being alive together again. As each kisses the other's unresponding
lips (recalling the honoring of the dead Titus) the barrier between life and

death is paper-thin. Some productions relent, giving them a few moments of shared consciousness for a last, reciprocal embrace, a last kiss they both can feel. But in the play the barrier holds. In this final image of consummation, they are more together than ever before, and more apart.

HAUNTED BY THE LOVERS

The beginning, middle and end of the play are punctuated by a recurring theatrical effect: the stage fills rapidly and symmetrically with Capulets and Montagues, and the Prince takes center stage. When the community crowds into the final scene they represent in parody form guests crowding into the bridal chamber to encourage the new couple.[19] This time the symmetry of the stage picture is damaged by the death of Lady Montague; more important, the renewal of life that marriage represents has been reversed: Montague complains to his son, "O thou untaught! What manners is in this, / To press before thy father to a grave?" (V.iii.213–14). The gold statues the fathers promise have the same futility as Marcus' attempt to turn the mutilated Lavinia into poetry, and they parody the bargaining over marriage portions that fathers would undertake in a normal wedding.[20]

In the incongruity of the statues and in the way the Friar's lengthy account reduces the lovers' experience to a plot summary, the lovers, though their story is now known, seem as distant from the world as ever. But we have also seen ways in which they are bound to the world: the names they cannot shed (and do not want to shed), the symbolic linking of their wedding night with the killing of Tybalt. Moments before the aubade we hear Capulet tell Paris, "Afore me, it is so very late that we / May call it early by and by. Good night" (III.iv.34–35). Though to be on the border between light and dark has a significance for the lovers it does not have for Capulet, they are all on the same border, and he provides the time-signal that introduces their most moving scene. For the most part, as we have seen, it is something of the world that invades the privacy of love. But in the fathers' handclasp that puts the seal of public approval on the lovers' marriage – "O brother Montague, give me thy hand. / This is my daughter's jointure" (V.iii.295–96) – something of the lovers, their first taking of hands, enters the world.[21] More than the Friar's narrative, certainly more than the statues, it brings a memory of them to life.

Something else of the lovers survives that is not so consoling. Throughout the last scene they have characteristically reversed life and death, in Romeo's pun, "O true apothecary, / Thy drugs are quick" (V.iii.119–20), and in Juliet's attempt to take death from Romeo's lips: "Haply some poison yet doth hang on them / To make me die with a restorative" (V. iii.165–66). This recalls their play-long tendency to reverse day and night, light and dark, as in the aubade: "O now be gone, more light and light it grows. . . . More light and light: more dark and dark our woes" (III.v.35–36). In the Prince's last speech this reversal now touches the external reality of Verona, as a sunless day dawns: "A glooming peace this morning with it brings: / The sun for sorrow will not show his head" (V.iii.304–5). On a winter afternoon in an Elizabethan playhouse, this darkness would also touch the external reality of the performance. In this image of a day that brings darkness, Juliet's second wedding night is touched by a memory of the aubade that concluded her first. The love affair began with gentle touching, and ended in separation and violence. The fathers' handclasp recalls the initial touch, and offers some consolation. But in the conclusion what escapes into Verona from the private world of love, with its recurring play of light and darkness, is the darkness.

The initial gentleness of the lovers, the first tentative touch of hands, turned violent through their involvement in the world, an involvement signaled by their names. Their consummation participated in the violence of the streets, as Romeo, twice on the same day, shed Capulet blood. In the final scene, Juliet's second wedding night, love itself becomes directly violent, expressed through acts of violation that are also acts of love. Violence parts the lovers; in the end, only violence can bring them together, united in death. As their love cannot be separated from the feuding families that gave them life along with their fatal names, their fathers' attempt at healing cannot be separated from their children's deaths. And the children are buried, like Lavinia with Titus, in an ancestral tomb.

CHAPTER 3

Hamlet: *A figure like your father*

WHO'S THERE?

Hamlet's father returns from the grave, as Lavinia returns from the woods, in a "questionable shape" (I.iv.43). In both cases something strange and silent, familiar and unfamiliar, comes on to the stage, posing a problem of interpretation like that of the ghost in *The Spanish Tragedy*: "My name was Don Andrea." The *Hamlet* Ghost, in full armor, looks imposing and powerful, a male figure to command respect as well as fear – in that sense the opposite of the mutilated Lavinia. But it too has a dislocated identity, and when in I.v it describes its own death, we learn that beneath the armor is another violated body.

Lavinia is bombarded with questions; so is the Ghost, and again the questions break against silence. Like Marcus' "This was thy daughter," the wording of Horatio's question shows how problematic the Ghost's identity is:

> What art thou that usurp'st this time of night,
> Together with that fair and warlike form
> In which the majesty of buried Denmark
> Did sometimes march? (I.i.49-52)

He asks not "Who art thou?" but "What art thou?" – seeing the Ghost not as the late King Hamlet but as a nameless thing that has usurped (the word is unsettling applied to something that looks like a king) the form of the late King Hamlet. The first reference to the Ghost is to "this thing" (I.i.24), and throughout the dialogue it is not "he" but "it." Over and over we are told how much it is *like* the King (I.i.44, 46, 61). Horatio calls it "a figure like your father" (I.ii.198) and his image for the resemblance is revealing: "These hands are not more like" (I.ii.212). One's hands are indeed like each other but they are reverse images, mirror-opposites; and the persistent use of "like" implies a final difference beneath the apparent identity.[1] Though when he is alone Hamlet seems prepared to seal the gap

– "My father's spirit – in arms!" (I.ii.255) – when he is with his friends he catches their way of speaking: "If it assume my noble father's person" (I.ii.244).

Even as the late King Hamlet, the Ghost poses a problem of interpretation. The noble, idealized king of Hamlet's memory is, as a ghost, "a guilty thing" (I.i.76) who by his own account died "in the blossoms" of his sin (I.v.76), a death Hamlet remembers when he wants Claudius's to replicate it: "A took my father grossly, full of bread, / With all his crimes broad blown, as fresh as May" (III.iii.80–81). The Ghost's own self-idealization is cut across by the memory of sin: even as it describes its marriage bed as "celestial"(I.v.56) it scents the morning air and speeds up its story, knowing it must return to the place where it is tormented for "the foul crimes done in my days of nature" (I.v.12). The idealized father and the tormented sinner are, like one's two hands, mirror-opposites, and Hamlet never tries to reconcile the two. Instead, in addressing the Ghost, he sets one against the other:

> Be thou a spirit of health or goblin damn'd,
> Bring with thee airs from heaven or blasts from hell,
> Be thy intents wicked or charitable. . . . (I.iv.40–42)

Later, Hamlet will entertain the thought that this thing may be a devil. That idea comes and goes at need, banished in the excitement of receiving the Ghost's command, revived when Hamlet needs to explain to himself why he is leaving the command unfulfilled. The identity of the Ghost, apparently settled when it addresses the prince, is unsettled again.

DISRUPTING NATURE

Claiming to come from Purgatory (information Hamlet never seems to absorb), the Ghost claims to come from a place that according to the official religion of Shakespeare's England does not exist. And it returns from the grave, from which no one returns. The tomb of the Andronici is a final resting place: in Titus' words, "How many sons hast thou of mine in store / That thou wilt never render to me more!" (I.i.97–98). The tomb of the Capulets is a closed space into which Romeo breaks by force, but once there he promises Juliet,

> I still will stay with thee
> And never from this palace of dim night
> Depart again. (V.iii.106–8)

But the Ghost has broken out of the grave, an action that in Hamlet's imagination has the same disruptive violence as Romeo's breaking into the Capulet tomb, and an even greater sense that the natural order has been violated:

> Let me not burst in ignorance, but tell
> Why thy canoniz'd bones, hearsed in death,
> Have burst their cerements, why the sepulchre
> Wherein we saw thee quietly inurn'd
> Hath op'd his ponderous and marble jaws
> To cast thee up again. What may this mean,
> That thou, dead corse, again in complete steel
> Revisits thus the glimpses of the moon,
> Making night hideous and we fools of nature
> So horridly to shake our disposition
> With thoughts beyond the reaches of our souls? (I.iv.46–56)

Hamlet's "thoughts beyond the reaches of our souls" introduce an issue to which we shall return: as Lavinia produces a crisis of language, the Ghost produces a crisis of meaning, in which Hamlet finds thought taking a wrenching leap into the unknown, the unthinkable.

The crisis, however, is not just metaphysical; it is physical. This Ghost is a solid presence, and the old photographic trick of double exposure will not do as a way of presenting it. It is not drifting ectoplasm but a walking corpse. It reverses the forward movement of time that seems normal to Claudius and Gertrude when in the first court scene they urge Hamlet to forget his father. Just as Richard II, uncrowning himself, ran the coronation ceremony backwards, the Ghost has produced "a kind of funeral in reverse."[2] Like the corpses dug up by Aaron to stand in the doorways of the bereaved, it prevents the mourning process from working through its natural course so that life can go on.[3] As though a fabric has been torn, the notion of interment has become meaningless, and from this point it seems impossible for anyone to get a decent burial in Elsinore. Polonius is interred in "hugger-mugger" (IV.v.84) after Hamlet has played hunt-the-corpse with his body; Ophelia is laid in the earth with "maimed rites" (V.i.213) as her brother argues with the priest and has a flaming row with her lover. With professional indifference, the Gravedigger scatters the bones of his former clients to make room for the new arrival. Fortinbras sees a violation of decorum in the bodies that litter the Danish court at the end of the play: "Such a sight as this / Becomes the field, but here shows much amiss." But he promises a proper funeral only to Hamlet, saying nothing of the King, the Queen and Laertes other than "Take up the bodies" (V.ii.406–7). At least we knew Tamora was to be thrown over the walls.[4]

The Ghost, having crossed the border between life and death in the wrong direction, has disrupted nature in a way that makes crossings in the usual direction problematic. This can be seen as a response to the unnaturalness of its own death. The late king was attacked, as Duncan will be, in his sleep. His body, like Lavinia's, was invaded: the poison "courses through / The natural gates and alleys of the body" (I.v.66-67) like an army entering a citadel – as Laertes' mob will later do, to the warning cry, "The doors are broke" (IV.v.111), and as Fortinbras' army does at the end of the play. The attack, the Ghost reports, came through "the porches of mine ears" (I.v.63) and the violation of this particular entry point to the body becomes obsessive in the play's language. Bernardo promises not just to tell his listeners about the Ghost but to "assail your ears" (I.i.34); elsewhere ears are abused (I.v.36–38), taken prisoner (II.ii.473), infected (IV.v.90–91). Gertrude tells her son, "These words like daggers enter in mine ears" (III.iv.95). Linda Woodbridge notes, "A long tradition links ear penetration with vaginal penetration"; the Virgin Mary was impregnated through the ear, and both openings are implicated in sexual slander.[5] The attack on the king was not so overtly sexual as the attack on Lavinia, but Hamlet cannot think about what Claudius did to his father's body without thinking about what he does to his mother's.[6] As the attack on Lavinia is replicated everywhere in *Titus Andronicus*, the attack on the old king's body reverberates throughout *Hamlet*.

In Hamlet's mind the murder of his father and his mother's second marriage are tangled together. Death and marriage, which ought to be opposites, come together for Romeo and Juliet as a sign of their mutual commitment. In *Hamlet* the link between death and marriage lies in the fact that both are disrupted and made unnatural. As the Ghost's appearance produces a disruption of identity, Gertrude's marriage, being incestuous, produces a scrambling of relationships in which words like brother and husband, wife and sister, fuse unnaturally. Hamlet, "A little more than kin" (I.ii.65), feels affected by this, referring bitterly to his "uncle-father and aunt-mother" (II.ii.372). Claudius' attempts to address Hamlet as his son are particularly galling (I.ii.64, 107–8), and when he says of the fencing match, "Our son shall win" (V.ii.290), we reflect that he is planning to kill his "son" as he killed his brother. Hamlet prefers to call him "mother"(IV.iii.52), since this highlights the obscenity. "Man and wife is one flesh" (IV.iii.55), out of context, is an attractive statement of the unity of two people in marriage; as Hamlet uses it, it is a protest against the reduction of distinct identities and family roles to a single undifferentiated mass, a lump of physical matter. In the case of the Ghost a single identity has become disturbingly detached from the figure that ought to bear it, and that identity comes into question. In the case of Gertrude's marriage the problem is not splitting but lumping, as words mingle and the whole idea of identity becomes meaningless.

DISRUPTING DRAMA

The revenge action of *Titus Andronicus* produced clarity and restoration of a kind. The question, "What is Lavinia?" was succeeded by growing knowledge, and the question of how to avenge her was decisively answered. But the idea that Hamlet's father was murdered depends on the word of a speaker whose identity and moral nature remain uncertain, and whose account of the deed is in one sense an impossibility: a dead man describing, with a wealth of detail, his own death. The puzzle of the Ghost grounds the main action of the play in uncertainty, and produces a disruption of it as drama equivalent to the disruptions of nature that follow from the murder, the Ghost's return, and the marriage.

Time is the medium of drama, and after an initial impression of orderliness – "twice before, and jump at this dead hour" (I.i.68) – the Ghost disrupts the characters' sense of time, and ours. Its habitual hour has been one (I.i.42); but it makes its third appearance only a minute or two in performance time after Bernardo gives the hour as twelve (I.i.6). Later the witnesses disagree over how long it stayed, and the second Ghost scene begins with a dispute over the time (I.iv.3–4). The Ghost exemplifies the temporal disorder of a kingdom in crisis, whose munitions workers labor day and night and treat Sunday as a weekday (I.i.73–81), and whose widowed queen remarried with unnatural speed: Hamlet's estimates shrink from two months to two hours (I.ii.138, III.ii.125). Hamlet's complaint, "The time is out of joint" (I.v.196) refers to the world in which he lives, to the Ghost he has just encountered, and to the effect the Ghost has on the play.

Being temporally disruptive, the Ghost is theatrically disruptive. Its early appearances, though anticipated, still come as surprises. Everyone sits to hear Bernardo talk about the Ghost (I.i.36–37); assuming it is not due for nearly an hour, we relax and prepare to listen to a story. But just as Bernardo is getting started the Ghost appears and cuts him off in mid-sentence, part way through a line. At least the Ghost's second entrance follows a completed thought (war preparations in the Folio, the omens around the death of Julius Caesar in the Second Quarto). But once again we have been lulled into a discursive mode (once more the watchers are sitting [I.i.73]), and we were not expecting the Ghost to make a second appearance. When the Ghost appears in I.iv it is while Hamlet is talking about something else – court revelry in the Folio, the fragility of reputation in the Second Quarto – and its appearance is again an expected event that comes as an interruption. Its final appearance in Gertrude's closet is a complete surprise, for which there is no preparation at all.

The Ghost, whose role is to start the main line of action, seems at times a digression. And as the unnaturalness of its death and reappearance affect the whole world of the play, so its digressiveness affects the play's dramatic movement – ironically, including digressions from the dramatic purpose it tries to introduce. The problem begins in Hamlet's response to the news that his father was murdered:

> Haste me to know't, that I with wings as swift
> As meditation or the thoughts of love
> May sweep to my revenge. (I.v.29–31)

The momentum of revenge is slowed down even in the words that express it, by a subordinate clause in which the key ideas, meditation and the thoughts of love, meant to express swiftness, actually delay the completion of the sentence.[7] They also anticipate two of the key factors that will distract Hamlet from the completion of his task. The play that follows is both an exciting drama of intrigue and revenge, plot and counterplot, and a work that challenges the whole idea of theatrical action in a manner so radical we have to wait for *Waiting for Godot* – whose first line is "Nothing to be done" – before we find its like.

The effect is strongest in the Second Quarto, probably the version closest to Shakespeare's manuscript, in which the play seems to move more and more slowly as it approaches its denouement, as though reluctant to end. Fortinbras and his attack on Poland, Ophelia's madness, the Gravedigger, Osric – all delay the ending. Even the plotting of Hamlet's death by Claudius and Laertes is extraordinarily long-winded. Much of this material is cut or trimmed in the Folio, quickening the pace. Even in the early scenes the Folio tends to cut digressions, like Horatio's discourse on Julius Caesar in I.i and Hamlet's lecture on the loss of reputation in I.v; but one could argue that digressions are the essence of this play. In individual speeches, and in the plotting of scenes, the current keeps turning awry. Waiting for the Ghost to appear, Hamlet digresses onto the court's drinking habits, and digresses from that onto the workings of reputation, so that when the Ghost enters we have almost forgotten it was coming. Polonius announces he has found the cause of Hamlet's madness, then insists Claudius hear the ambassadors first, then returns to the madness. His lecture on the subject is so full of verbal detours that Gertrude protests, at which point it gets worse (II.ii.85–107). Hamlet gets the evidence of Claudius' guilt, then detours from the revenge action to visit his mother, detours from that to watch Claudius at prayer and almost (but not quite) kills him, then returns to his mother, actually enters her closet, and is just getting down to business when he has to turn aside to kill Polonius, who lies there for the rest of the scene. Even as he is about to use a play to get at the truth, Hamlet takes several minutes to lecture the actors on the art of acting, including a rebuke to the clowns whose gags are liable to distract spectators from "some necessary question of the play" (III.ii.42–43). If drama is action, *Hamlet* is the most extraordinary combination of drama and anti-drama.

It all goes back to the Ghost. It is a condition of drama that we know who the actors are playing: the identification of performer with role is arguably what makes theatre. For the next two or three hours that figure represents Antigone, or Lear, or Willy Loman. But even in the theatre that purports to create illusion the spectators know they are watching actors, figures who are *like* the characters they play, but are not those characters. In *Hamlet* the figure who triggers the action is "like" the late king Hamlet, and this produces *within the play* that slight but crucial detachment from absolute belief that is normally the condition of the audience. It is no wonder that an action started in this manner has trouble fulfilling itself, and that the central character, who takes his own name from this figure who cannot be named with certainty, is an actor who seems unable to act.

AGAINST INTERPRETATION

The problem is not just one of action. Just as Titus' mad messages to an unresponding universe – digging the earth, fishing the sea, firing arrows at the gods – let the play open out to larger questions, so the violation of nature and the disruption of identity the Ghost (literally) embodies release a force of uncertainty into the play, to which the characters respond with desperate attempts to make sense of each other, and of the world.

The Ghost is not the only character who comes in "a questionable shape" (I.iv.43). Throughout the play characters are questioning, prying, trying to read each other. Rosencrantz and Guildenstern are hired to read

Hamlet. Polonius demands to know what Laertes and Ophelia have been talking about, and sends Reynaldo to spy on Laertes. Not trusting Gertrude to give an impartial account of her son (III.iii.30–33), he spies on their interview. Hamlet and Horatio watch Claudius as he watches the play. Private letters do not stay private. Polonius reads Hamlet's love-letters aloud to the King and Queen and Hamlet reads, with mounting interest, Claudius' private diplomatic correspondence with the King of England. As we prepare to watch Claudius and Polonius spying on Hamlet, we find we are spies ourselves when in an unexpected aside Claudius for the first time reveals his inner guilt (III.i.49–54). As audience, we would normally feel entitled to know everything; yet this sudden breaking of Claudius' privacy is almost embarrassing, making us feel like eavesdroppers.

The center of scrutiny is of course Hamlet, who is questioned more intensely even than the Ghost. Everyone has a reading of him, everyone has a theory. The seemingly endless proliferation of *Hamlet* criticism begins within the play itself. Ophelia, a romantic critic, sees him as a figure of pity, an ideal prince ruined by madness (III.i.152–63). Claudius, more pragmatic and materialist, doubts the madness and thinks of Hamlet as a political threat. Polonius clings with the stubbornness of a true academic to his theory of love-melancholy, whose stages he has carefully plotted out (II.ii.146–51). But we should credit him on one point at least: he has the grace to admit that his first theory, that Hamlet was merely trifling with Ophelia, was wrong, and to apologize for it (II.i.111–13).

Hamlet himself hates being interpreted. To Guildenstern's refusal to play the recorder, Hamlet retorts, "You would play upon me, you would seem to know my stops, you would pluck out the heart of my mystery" (III.ii.355–57). He has already warned Horatio and Marcellus against claiming they know what he is up to (I.v.181–87). He uses the antic disposition as a way of hiding. His own comments on it are deliberately unhelpful: "As I perchance hereafter shall think meet / To put an antic disposition on" (I.v.179–80), thrown in as a subordinate clause, makes the plan sound not deliberate but capricious and unpredictable. He is particularly unhelpful with Rosencrantz and Guildenstern: "I am but mad north-north-west. When the wind is southerly, I know a hawk from a handsaw" (II.ii.374–75). (Sometimes I'm mad, sometimes I'm sane, you figure it out.) Even in his first scene the clear signal sent by his wearing mourning is less clear by the time Hamlet has expounded on it. Taking "seems" as the key word in his mother's question, "Why seems it so particular with thee?" (for her the key word is "particular") he bridles at the suggestion of hypocrisy: "Seems, madam? Nay, it is. I know not 'seems'" (I.ii.75–76). Yet while claiming the outward signs are clues to his inward state, he also calls them "actions that a man might play" (I.ii.84), at once insisting on the truth of his performance and making that truth impossible to read with certainty.[8] The privacy and unreadability forced on Lavinia are conditions Hamlet, even more than Juliet, creates for himself.

Yet Hamlet is caught as it were in his own mousetrap: the antic disposition misfires when it gives Gertrude a reason not to take his accusations seriously, and he has to warn her, "Lay not that flattering unction to your soul, / That not your trespass but my madness speaks" (III.iv.147–48). In the "How all occasions" soliloquy he appears unreadable even to himself: asking, as generations of critics have asked after him, why he delays revenge, he is forced to conclude, "I do not know" (IV.iv.43). In the end he wants to be interpreted after all, anxious about how his actions will be read and demanding that Horatio tell his story: "O God, Horatio, what a wounded name, / Things standing thus unknown, shall I leave behind me" (V.ii.349–50). The general cry of "Treason! treason!" (V.ii.328) as he moves to kill the King shows he is right to worry. Nor does it seem likely that Horatio's report will be even close to adequate: his promise to speak "Of carnal, bloody, and unnatural acts, / Of accidental judgments, casual slaughters" (V.ii.386–87), suggests an account as externalized as Friar Laurence's summary of *Romeo and Juliet.*[9]

The problem of reading the Ghost, then, links with the problem of reading his namesake; indeed, the general problem of reading other people, and oneself. To the question, "what, is Horatio there?" Horatio replies enigmatically, "A piece of him" (I.i.21–22) and we have to be content with that. One reason for the play's digressiveness is the tendency for local problems to expand into general ones, and the problem of reading other people expands into a problem of reading the world. Playing games with other characters, Hamlet insists that it's all in the mind: "there is nothing either good or bad but thinking makes it so" (II.ii.249–50). This means not just one's own thoughts but the pressure of others' opinions: in a parody of the witnesses' attempts to identify the Ghost, Hamlet talks Polonius into agreeing that a cloud is like a camel, like a weasel, and very like a whale; he talks Osric into agreeing that the day is very cold, and very sultry.

In his first soliloquy Hamlet seems to have his own view of the world settled:

> How weary, stale, flat, and unprofitable
> Seem to me all the uses of this world!
> Fie on't, ah fie, 'tis an unweeded garden
> That grows to seed. . . . (I.ii.133–36)

We have to notice that insidious "Seem." It is followed by a plain statement – "'tis an unweeded garden" – but the doubt it creates lingers, to re-emerge in one of Hamlet's most extraordinary speeches:

it goes so heavily with my disposition that this goodly frame the earth seems to me a sterile promontory, this most excellent canopy the air, look you, this brave o'erhanging firmament, this majestical roof fretted with golden fire, why, it appeareth nothing to me but a foul and pestilent congregation of vapours. What a piece of work is a man, how noble in reason, how infinite in faculties, in form and moving how express and admirable, in action how like an angel, in apprehension how like a god: the beauty of the world, the paragon of animals – and yet, to me, what is this quintessence of dust? (II.ii.297–308)

He does not say, as we might expect, that he used to think the world was beautiful and man was noble but now he knows better. He says the world *is* beautiful and man *is* noble, yet *to him* they seem a foul and pestilent congregation of vapors and a quintessence of dust. The idealistic view is not a rejected opinion but an objective reality. On "look you" he can, standing on the stage of the Globe, point either to its painted roof or to the sky itself. He attributes his disillusionment to a mood that has hit him "of late, but wherefore I know not" (II.ii.295–96). Yet he asserts it as his view, the subjective in direct contradiction to the objective, each stated eloquently. Opposing what he knows to what he believes, Hamlet creates a radical problem in consciousness itself. (The paradox is compounded when we reflect that Hamlet's statement of objective reality is just that, Hamlet's statement; that he can illustrate reality by pointing to the painted roof of a stage; and as if that were not enough, that he is talking to Rosencrantz and Guildenstern, whom he enjoys teasing.) Through much of the play he resists interpretations of himself, while insisting on his own interpretation of the world around him. Here he calls his own role as interpreter into question.

UNKNOWING

The problem of reading the next world is if anything even more acute, and it too is a problem of consciousness. "To be or not to be" is perhaps the play's most notorious digression, falling across the action between Hamlet's plan to catch the conscience of the King and his springing of the trap,[10] seemingly irrelevant not only to the larger action but to the immediate business of III.i, which is the testing of Hamlet's relationship with Ophelia (who is onstage during the soliloquy as though to stress its irrelevance). Yet in that seeming irrelevance lies its relevance. Hamlet has been blocked from killing Claudius (so he claims) by uncertainty about the Ghost; we – he presents the speech as a general reflection of the human condition, not particular to himself – are blocked from suicide by not knowing what awaits us in the next world, what will happen to the consciousness after we die. Not knowing means not doing. In the end the subject expands beyond suicide to the way any thought can deflect any action:

> And enterprises of great pitch and moment
> With this regard their currents turn awry
> And lose the name of action. (III.i.86–88)

If in the placing of the speech the current of the play has turned awry, that simply reflects the human condition. It is not just that lack of knowledge leads to lack of action: the word "action" becomes detached from the enterprises it described, and in the process both the word and the enterprise seem to lose meaning in an act of unnaming.

Action can be stymied by belief as well as by doubt. Claudius attempting to pray, and Hamlet watching him kneeling, both accept for the moment an orthodox scheme of damnation and salvation, contradicting the uncertainty of the famous soliloquy. The result is that Claudius, knowing he does not meet the conditions for forgiveness, fails to pray, and Hamlet, thinking he does, fails to kill him. Each man enters the scene determined on an action, and does nothing. For Claudius it is again a problem of language: "My words fly up, my thoughts remain below. / Words without thoughts never to heaven go" (III.iii.97–98). When Polonius asks what he is reading Hamlet replies "Words, words, words" (II.ii.192), separating them from thought, draining them of meaning.

CAPTURING REALITY

Words seem helpless in *Titus* and dangerous in *Romeo*, where civil brawls are bred of an airy word and the names the lovers bear are fatal. In *Hamlet*, where so much is unknown or unknowable, words at times seem meaningless. Yet those unreliable instruments are all we have. Hamlet and Claudius both use words to declare the emptiness of words. In the first part of the "rogue and peasant slave" soliloquy Hamlet attacks himself not for doing nothing, but for saying nothing, as though words if he could use them properly would have some value after all (II.ii.564). Confronted with Fortinbras, he rebukes himself for saying the wrong thing: "I do not know / Why yet I live to say this thing's to do" (IV.iv.43–44). His offense is not just failing to do the deed, but saying he *will* do it, deferring it through speech. He questions not just his language but his life: why is he even alive, if that is all he can say? He has failed even to name the deed, calling it, as the watchers call the Ghost, "this thing." Yet it is language itself that conveys, with minute precision, all these failures; and "live to say" equates language with life itself. Death is silence: the silence of Yorick, the silence out of which the Ghost emerges and into which Hamlet departs.

The joke about the audience member who never realized *Hamlet* was so full of quotations is a comment on the play's style, which is full of gnomic aphorisms in which reality is caught in words, pinned like a dead butterfly: something is rotten in the state of Denmark, I shall not look upon his like again, frailty thy name is woman, neither a borrower nor a lender be. While Titus writes down the plan for a revenge action, Hamlet writes down a generalizing aphorism "That one may smile, and smile, and be a villain," adding, "So, uncle, there you are" (I.v.108–10), as though to find the right words for Claudius is to dispose of him, trapping him in a specimen bottle.

Writing the words down may fix not only the subject but the words themselves, helping them hold their meanings. Writing is also an aid to memory, a factor as critical for the characters as it is for the actors who play them. Ophelia calls Hamlet's love-tokens "remembrances" (III.i.93) and in her madness hands out rosemary for remembrance, adding, "pray you, love, remember" (IV.v.173–74). The Ghost's parting command to Hamlet is not "Avenge me" but "Remember me" (I.v.91).[11] Polonius equates memory with writing when he advises Laertes, "these few precepts in thy memory / Look thou character" (I.iii.58–59) and Hamlet, the Ghost's words ringing in his ears, makes the same equation:

> Remember thee?
> Yea, from the table of my memory
> I'll wipe away all trivial fond records,
> All saws of books, all forms, all pressures past
> That youth and observation copied there,
> And thy commandment all alone shall live
> Within the book and volume of my brain,
> Unmix'd with baser matter. Yes, by heaven!

O most pernicious woman!
O villain, villain, smiling, damned villain!
My tables. Meet it is I set it down
That one may smile, and smile, and be a villain – (I.v.97–108)

Desperate to remember, Hamlet immediately starts forgetting. The Ghost has told him to leave his mother alone, yet having wiped the slate of his memory clean the first thing Hamlet scribbles on it is not the Ghost's command but the thought of his mother. The next thought is in a way just as irrelevant: the Ghost has told Hamlet to kill Claudius, not to trap him in aphorisms. The discipline of fixing key ideas in words goes wrong as soon as Hamlet starts to practice it; the current turns awry.

Writing is one way to attempt to get a fix on reality. Looking – in this play, long, intense staring – is another. We remember Titus' urgent command to Lucius when he turns away from Lavinia: "look upon her" (III.i.66). In every scene in which Lavinia appears that is what the other characters, and the audience, have to do. Romeo looks long and intently at Juliet. Hamlet looks long and intently at Ophelia – "He falls to such perusal of my face / As a would draw it" (II.i.90–91) – but the gesture that accompanies this gaze is not Romeo's gentle touch of hands: "He took me by the wrist and held me hard" (II.i.88). It is a gesture of entrapment which Ophelia, held by the wrist, cannot turn into a mutual handclasp. Instead, as her detailed account of his appearance suggests, she stares at him as intently as he stares at her. As Claudius watches the play, Hamlet promises, "I mine eyes will rivet to his face" (III.ii.85). He awakens his mother's sense of shame by making her look, steadily and at length, at pictures of her two husbands. These pictures function as a mirror in which Gertrude sees herself, not just her face but her soul: "You go not till I set you up a glass / Where you may see the inmost part of you" (III.iv.18–19). Again the sense of entrapment; and by Gertrude's account the device works as intended:

> Thou turn'st mine eyes into my very soul,
> And there I see such black and grained spots
> As will not leave their tinct. (III.iv.89–91)

But later in the scene one of those husbands returns, and Hamlet and Gertrude, both staring at the same point on the stage, disagree (like Marcus and Titus looking at Lavinia) about what it is they are looking at. Hamlet sees his father, Gertrude sees nothing. We may be tempted to say that Hamlet sees truly; but he has just been deceived by the sight of Claudius on his knees. Eyesight does not always show the truth.[12]

Theatre itself is seeming, and the wording of the stage directions for the dumb show – "*makes show of protestation*"; "*seem to condole*"; "*seems harsh awhile*" (III.ii.133sd) – captures for the reader what the actors presumably capture for the audience: the display of false feelings by the actors reflects the display of false feelings by the court that watches them. Hamlet plans to use *The Murder of Gonzago* for one specific purpose, to catch the conscience of the King by re-enacting the murder. But characteristically Hamlet's thinking about theatre expands beyond this one very special use of it to the aphorism that the purpose of playing is to hold "the mirror up to nature" (III.ii.22). Words and pictures, the instruments of drama, are exposed as unreliable within the play. Yet the paradox of theatre is that, never claiming to tell the truth, dealing only in seeming, it conveys through deceptions images of reality.

Hamlet wants to use *The Murder of Gonzago* to fix one point of reality, Claudius' guilt. But as the action (and inaction) of *Hamlet* have already made it clear that this is not just a revenge play the point of which is to dispose of Claudius, so the inset play is a mirror more spacious than Hamlet seems to realize, and the reality it captures is wider. In its nagging insistence on the iniquity of second marriage, it seems designed, as Janet Adelman puts it, "to catch the conscience of the queen";[13] in that way it reflects Hamlet's disobedience to the Ghost's command to concentrate on Claudius and leave his mother alone. When the Player King declares "*Purpose is but the slave to memory, / Of violent birth but poor validity*" and "*What to ourselves in passion we propose, / The passion ending, doth the purpose lose*" (III.ii.183–84, 189–90) Hamlet himself, without seeming to realize it, is caught in the mirror, his failed purpose linked with his mother's failed grief. In the odd twist that the Player King is poisoned by his nephew, Claudius' murder and Hamlet's revenge are conflated, making crime and punishment seem similar acts, as they did in *Titus Andronicus*. And Hamlet's prediction that the nephew will marry his uncle's wife brings the Oedipal possibility of the incest theme as close to the surface as it ever gets.

All this goes beyond the immediate purpose of catching the conscience of the King; and there is some question as to how clearly that purpose is served. Once again the issue is interpretation, and Hamlet's reliability as an interpreter. Claudius cracks, not on the sight of the poisoning, but on Hamlet's line, "You shall see anon how the murderer gets the love of Gonzago's wife" (III.ii.257–58). It is as though he knows he is going to break, but has just enough control to time it on a reference to the second marriage, which is public knowledge, making it seem as though that is what offends him.[14] Hamlet, recalling the moment, rewrites it, claiming Claudius betrayed himself "Upon the talk of the poisoning" (III.ii.283). Either his memory is faulty (again) or more likely, in his excitement he saw what he expected to see. It is not what we saw.[15] The experiment in fixing reality is not so decisive as Hamlet imagines.

READING THE WOMEN

This is not the only lapse in concentration of which Hamlet as spectator is guilty. As in his response to the Ghost's command he splits his attention between Claudius and Gertrude, so in the play scene he splits his attention between Claudius and Ophelia. When he should be concentrating on Claudius, he seems to be not only having sex with Ophelia in his imagination but speaking his sexual fantasies out loud, going from the position – "That's a fair thought to lie between maid's legs" – to the consummation: "It would cost you a groaning to take off my edge" (III. ii.117, 244). It says much for Ophelia's self-control that she stays cool, if tense, under this attack. I have suggested that Hamlet cannot separate his concern with what Claudius did to his father's body from his concern with what he does to his mother's; and the latter concern is the more obsessive. It is perhaps for this reason that as the excitement of the revenge action mounts, so does Hamlet's erotic excitement, sex and killing twisting together in his mind. As he approaches the moment when he will see the attack on his father's body re-enacted, he mentally enacts his own attack on Ophelia's. What he imagines is nothing like Juliet's vision of a shared consummation: the woman is paying the price for the man's lust ("It would cost you"), and the man is acting not out of love but out of contempt.

The aphorism "Frailty, thy name is woman" (I.ii.146) allows him to include Ophelia in the misogyny centered on Gertrude. The long stare he gives her in her closet may be his way of looking for signs of Gertrude in her. He is compulsive about both women: the "nunnery" and closet scenes are marked by the same device, a series of false endings as Hamlet, seemingly finished with the woman, comes back and attacks her again. Whatever doubts he may have about the Ghost, he seems sure of Gertrude: her marriage is a betrayal of marriage itself, a deed that

> from the body of contraction plucks
> The very soul, and sweet religion makes
> A rhapsody of words. (III.iv.46–48)

The particular moves to the general: the very ideas of contract, religion itself, and finally language, are violated by what Gertrude has done. But the protest is not just at the level of ideas. There is a recurring, voyeuristic physical disgust as Hamlet imagines "the bloat King . . . paddling in your neck with his damn'd fingers" (III.iv.184, 187). This affects even his memory of Gertrude's grief – "Ere yet the salt of most unrighteous tears / Had left the flushing in her galled eyes" (I.ii.154–55) – and of her first marriage. Hamlet remembers his father as loving, benevolent, protective, and his mother as a parasitic growth:

> Why, she would hang on him
> As if increase of appetite had grown
> By what it fed on. . . . (I.ii.143–45)

Whatever the Ghost commands, Hamlet cannot keep his imagination off his mother, and his thoughts of her are driven by physical disgust. The play follows him far enough down this route, which from the viewpoint of the revenge story ought to be a digression, that the Ghost's final appearance in the closet scene seems itself the digression, not a call to return to the main line.

So far Gertrude has seemed subject to, and controlled by, the men's interpretation of her, with the Ghost and Hamlet agreeing about her guilt. But in the scene in which she is most sharply under attack Gertrude, like the silenced Lavinia, begins to exert a curious power. In Gertrude's space rather than the military space of act I the Ghost (in its nightgown, according to the First Quarto) seems weakened and attenuated, unable to appear to her as it did to the common soldiers. That its entrance cue is Hamlet's "A king of shreds and patches" (III.iv.103) seems to bring it down to the level of the despised Claudius. When it finally goes "out at the portal" (III.iv.138) it is crossing the threshold between two worlds for the last time, and we never see it again. Appearing to men (including its fellow soldiers) it has extraordinary power to frighten and fascinate; appearing with Gertrude, it fades and vanishes.[16]

As though to take over the Ghost's earlier role – and Lavinia's – Gertrude from this point becomes hard to read. The uncertainty that the Ghost has released into the play now includes her. Up till now she has seemed good-natured but morally obtuse, justifying Hamlet's view of her if not the extreme language in which he couches it. Her marriage is technically an offense, but we see enough of Claudius' charm to make it understandable at the personal level, and she may have bought into the argument implied in the King's first speech that she is assuring the continuity of the state. We may wonder if the Ghost reads her accurately. His command to leave her "to those thorns that in her bosom lodge / To prick and sting her" (I.v.87–88) suggests an inner torment of which we see no evidence till Hamlet himself awakens her conscience. It is from this point that the questions begin to multiply. Does her repentance last? Claudius' report that he has seen evidence in his own life of the fading of love (IV.vii.109–14) implies that he and Gertrude are drawing apart, but it is couched in general terms and may be contradicted by the physical courage she shows in protecting her husband from Laertes. When Gertrude claims Hamlet killed Polonius in madness, is she obeying his command to keep the secret that he is mad in craft, or does she really think he is mad?[17] When she drinks the poisoned cup, does she know what she is doing? Janet Adelman sees enough maternal protectiveness in her treatment of Hamlet in the last scene to create the possibility that she is saving him at the cost of her own life.[18] It can be staged that way. Yet Hamlet's words, "I dare not drink yet, madam – by and by" (V.ii.297), suggest that having drunk she offers him the cup. She does *not* know what she is doing, and very nearly kills him before Laertes does.

In the later scenes the focus is never so intently on Gertrude as it is on Lavinia or (in the early scenes) on the Ghost. Yet she has the same capacity to baffle and disturb, and the focus returns to her powerfully at the end. In the last scene what looks like an innocent sporting event, a court pastime, is nothing of the kind, and it is Gertrude's voice that calls out the truth: "No, no, the drink, the drink! O my dear Hamlet! / The drink, the drink! I am poison'd" (V.ii.315–16). The thought of her has always been able to pull Hamlet aside from the task of avenging his father, and his last words to Claudius as he kills him are not "Now is my father avenged" but "Follow my mother" (V.ii.332). That line is as cryptic as Gertrude herself has become. Is Hamlet consigning two miscreants to the same fate, suggesting they belong together? Is he avenging Gertrude? What do we make of the fact that having told Gertrude to stay away from Claudius, he is now putting them together? At the beginning of the play Hamlet's reading of Gertrude was clear and powerful, imposing itself on our own minds. But as the play goes on Gertrude escapes from that reading, if not into a fully realized dramatic life of her own, at least into an unreadability that makes all interpretations provisional.

Hamlet's initial reading of Gertrude as corrupt is, I have already noted, powerful enough that (given Hamlet's, and the play's, tendency to generalize) it expands to take in Ophelia. Whether Hamlet knows or merely suspects that he is being spied on in the "nunnery" scene, his sudden turn from echoing her family's advice, "we are arrant knaves all, believe none of us" to the seemingly irrelevant question, "Where's your father?" (Can I believe *you?*) (III.i.129–31) is a test she fails. We have our own questions, our own problem of reading Ophelia and her relations with Hamlet. When she hands back his love-tokens, declaring, "to the noble mind/Rich gifts wax poor when givers prove unkind" (III.i.100–1), she appears to be breaking with Hamlet on her own initiative, for her own reasons, not just following her father's orders. She declares the trouble began not with her but with Hamlet's unkindness, and using for herself the term she will later use for the unfallen Hamlet, "the noble mind," she asserts her self-respect. This is a stronger, more independent Ophelia than we might have expected; yet she does all this knowing Polonius is listening, and the possibility remains that she is carrying out his orders without betraying his involvement, putting the best face on it she can.

Hamlet's own reading of Ophelia is an unstable mixture of idealism and disgust. The disgust is involved with his feelings about his mother, but his recoil from the female body is even sharper when he thinks of Ophelia, presumably because his sexual interest in her is more direct. His image of a pregnant Ophelia is the sun breeding maggots in a dead dog (II.ii.181–86). Yet some of the disgust recoils on himself, since he is the one most likely to make her pregnant. He himself is too much in the sun, and his view of his own flesh (in the Second Quarto) as "sullied" (I.ii.129) is strongest when he is with her, as though something about her makes him feel dirty. (His appearance in her closet with fouled stockings may be a way of dramatizing this.) He is capable at times of setting his corruption against her purity. He comes out of the cloud of unknowing that is the "To be or not to be" soliloquy with a return to conventional belief centered on Ophelia's own faith and virtue: "The fair Ophelia! Nymph, in thy orisons / Be all my sins remember'd" (III.i.89–90). She seems able to do what Claudius cannot, talk effectively to heaven. The fact that the prayer book she carries is part of a deception contrived by Polonius creates an irony for us, but it is not clear that Hamlet is being ironic.

For the rest of the "nunnery" scene he alternates between attacking her (and all women) and attacking himself (and all men): "Get thee to a nunnery. Why, wouldst thou be a breeder of sinners? I am myself indifferent honest, but yet I could accuse me of such things that it were better my mother had not borne me. I am very proud, revengeful, ambitious. . . . What should such fellows as I do crawling between earth and heaven? We are arrant knaves all, believe none of us" (III.i.121–30). It is particularly revealing that when he contemplates her his mission of revenge seems sinful; we touch here on something like Romeo's dilemma. Ophelia's very presence calls the whole male ethos of violence into question; that may be one reason why he wants her out of his life and into a nunnery. She is too good for the world he has to live in, and makes him feel too strongly the emptiness and corruption of his own existence. His other way of dealing with this – and most of his energy in the scene goes in this direction – is to attack *her* corruption as a woman. Even here there is a reservation: "If thou dost marry, I'll give thee this plague for thy dowry: be thou as chaste as ice, as pure as snow, thou shalt not escape calumny" (III.i.136–38). As in 'what a piece of work is a man' there is an opposition between the slander he believes and the virtue he acknowledges.

Ophelia in her normal state creates a profound disturbance for Hamlet; mad, she creates a profound disturbance for the whole court. In the First Quarto stage direction she appears with her hair down, a violation of decorum like Hamlet's disordered clothing.[19] There is also something invasive about her. Her second entrance is preceded, like her brother's threatening return to the court, by "*A noise within*" (IV.v.152). Paradoxically, what she brings into the mad world of Elsinore is a sense of normality. In her songs, she imagines Polonius getting a decent burial after all: "*And on his grave rain'd many a tear.*"[20] Unlike the late King Hamlet "*He never will come again*" (IV.v.165, 191). In place of the queasy incestuous sexuality Hamlet imagines in the royal marriage, Ophelia's song of St. Valentine's day tells an ordinary story, its sheer familiarity conveyed by the ballad form: the boy promised the girl marriage, got her pregnant and abandoned her. It's sad, it's unfair, and it happens all the time. It also shows Ophelia internalizing the conventional pragmatic advice she had from her family. This is what Hamlet could have done to her; there may be some part of her that wishes he had. It is a sign of what Elsinore has become that these glimpses of normal death and ordinary sex are given by a mad voice that seems to come from another world.

In her sheer otherness Ophelia, like Lavinia, presents a problem of interpretation and control. Deprived of reason – "Without the which we are pictures, or mere beasts" (IV.v.86) – as Lavinia is deprived of speech (without which she too is a picture) Ophelia provokes others to fill in the blank with their own readings:

> Her speech is nothing,
> Yet the unshaped use of it doth move
> The hearers to collection. They aim at it,
> And botch the words up fit to their own thoughts. . . .
> (IV.v.7–10)

The thoughts in this case can be politically threatening, "Dangerous conjectures in ill-breeding minds" (IV.v.15). In the Folio, Ophelia is a silent presence in the first court scene; she gets a public role, and the world at large starts paying attention to her, only when she goes mad.[21] Like Marcus with Lavinia, Laertes tries to bring her under control through his own language, making her seem logical – "A document in madness; thoughts and remembrance fitted" (IV.v.176–77) – and, more incongruously, decorative: "Thought and affliction, passion, hell itself / She turns to favour and to prettiness" (IV.v.185–86). Like Hamlet, Laertes loves Ophelia, and finds her disturbing: he tries to control her madness as he tried to control her sexuality.

The challenge of reading Ophelia becomes a set of controversies over her death. Our questions about the manner of Lavinia's death were provoked by the silence of the text; here they are provoked by its contradictions. Through it all Ophelia herself is silenced; she has not the Ghost's privilege of giving her own account. Gertrude describes (and controls) her drowning in decorative language, recalling Marcus and Laertes; part of her speech's artifice is a narrative mode that belongs to fiction, not drama. (Otherwise we would ask, who saw all this and did nothing to help?) What she describes sounds like an accident: the branch on which Ophelia stood broke, she fell into the river, and the weight of her clothes pulled her down. Yet in the next scene the Gravedigger, with prosy chop-logic, describes a suicide. The Priest clearly sees her as a suicide, and protests that even maimed rites are more than she is entitled to.[22] In *Lucrece* the central character's suicide is followed by a grotesque outbreak of male competitiveness as her husband and her father debate who has the greater right to mourn her (1791–1806). There is an equally grotesque competition of grief between Hamlet and Laertes, and one possible staging is that they actually fight in her grave.[23] At least Paris and Romeo settled their dispute outside Juliet's tomb.

Gertrude, whose friendly wish that Ophelia's virtues might cure Hamlet (III.i.38-42) is the most encouraging speech Ophelia ever hears, is the only mourner who shows true respect for the dead:

> Sweets to the sweet. Farewell.
> I hop'd thou shouldst have been my Hamlet's wife:
> I thought thy bride-bed to have deck'd, sweet maid,
> And not have strew'd thy grave. (V.i.236–39)

Even in "Farewell" there is a decorum none of the men shows; leaping into her grave for a last embrace, Laertes cannot let his sister go in peace.[24]

Gertrude, evoking the marriage Ophelia's family said was impossible, recalls the linking of grave and bride-bed in *Romeo and Juliet*; but this time the emphasis is on the difference. There is no consummation here, only a lost opportunity to be lamented, and Hamlet's agonized cry, "I lov'd Ophelia" (V.i.264), comes far too late. Interpreted, misread and disputed, Ophelia is ultimately forgotten, far more thoroughly than Lavinia. The last scene, though it features a return bout between Hamlet and Laertes, contains no overt memory of her.

Like Tamora and Lavinia in Rome, Gertrude and Ophelia are disturbing presences in Elsinore. In their own way they are as disruptive as the Ghost; and like the Ghost they both provoke and resist attempts at interpretation. The transgressive sexuality of the one and the tragic ruin of the other leave their men shocked and uneasy, and this time there is some blending between the two. ("Frailty," like "rape," can have two meanings.) If man's work is to be done, the women, both in their corruption and in their suffering, need to be set aside, as Romeo has to set Juliet aside to avenge Mercutio.[25] That is one of the implications of the Ghost's demand that Hamlet should not concern himself with his mother; she will distract him, as indeed she does. The player's speech on the fall of Troy is "Aeneas' tale to Dido" (II.ii.442–43), recalling another man who had to abandon a woman in pursuit of his male destiny. Laertes and Hamlet both denigrate the woman in themselves. Laertes seems ashamed of his tears: "When these are gone, / The woman will be out" (IV.vii.187–88); weeping is exorcising the feminine. Hamlet dismisses the illness about his heart: "It is but foolery, but it is such a kind of gaingiving as would perhaps trouble a woman" (V.ii.211–12). Women are dangerous: "wise men know well enough what monsters you make of them" (III.i.140–41).[26] Even the grave, like the pit in *Titus*, has something feminine about it: as Hamlet imagines it, a politician, a courtier, and a lord are now "my Lady Worm's" (V.i.87).

Finally, and perhaps most dangerously, women are (to men) unreadable. As Lavinia's identity is blurred by her rape, Ophelia's is blurred by death. Hamlet and the Grave-digger play a verbal game about whose grave this is: not a man, not a woman, but one that was a woman (V.i.126–32). Yet the Ghost was similarly unreadable. And like a woman being raped – like Lucrece, in fact – he was attacked while lying prone and vulnerable, his body invaded. It is not so easy to separate male and female, and throw away the female. In the last movement of the play Hamlet looks for the clarity and steadiness that come, as he sees it, through bonding with his fellow men. But the play's women, and the disturbances they have set up, are not so easy to dismiss.

FIXING ON DEATH

The steadiness Hamlet seeks through the male code of action is late in coming. His killing of Polonius is up to a point like Romeo's killing of Tybalt: it is his initiation into violence, his loss of virginity. Tybalt's death shocks Juliet; Polonius' death shatters Ophelia. But Hamlet's act has nothing like the clarity and purpose of Romeo's. He runs his rapier through the arras, and then wonders who he has killed, even what he has done: "Nay, I know not. / Is it the King?" (III.iv.25–26). Learning the truth, he is at first irritated (Polonius again, always around when you don't want him) and sees his victim's fate as a comic punishment: "Thou wretched, rash, intruding fool, farewell. . . . Thou find'st to be too busy is some danger" (III.iv.31–33). Later he gives the act tragic dignity and significance:

> heaven hath pleas'd it so,
> To punish me with this and this with me,
> That I must be their scourge and minister. (III.iv.175–77)

Then Polonius becomes a problem in garbage disposal – "I'll lug the guts into the neighbour room" (III.iv.214) – and finally the butt of jokes: "A certain convocation of politic worms are e'en at him" (IV.iii.19–20). In all these shifting responses one thing Hamlet never remarks on is that he has killed Ophelia's father. Romeo saw the significance of his act more clearly than that.

Hamlet finds a clearer meaning for the deaths of Rosencrantz and Guildenstern – "their defeat / Does by their own insinuation grow" (V.ii.58–59) – but the event itself is distant, and Hamlet does not live to hear the punchline of the joke he played on them. At least the corpse of Polonius gives him a sense of the physical reality of death; he has to drag it about. And the new steadiness of manner he shows on his return from England appears first in the graveyard scene. To the question of what happens to the consciousness after death, there can be no answer in this world. But there can be a precise answer to the question, "How long will a man lie i'th' earth ere he rot?" Eight or nine years, nine for a tanner (V.i.158–66). The skull of Yorick is something Hamlet can hold in his hand. On the stage of a playhouse called the Globe, the grave (represented like the pit in *Titus* by the stage trap) can be the Grave: in the Gravedigger's language games it is his grave, Ophelia's, Hamlet's, and by extension everyone's (V.i.115–132). Romeo and Juliet were born of fatal loins; the day Hamlet was born, right at the beginning of the story, the Gravedigger started to work (V.i.138–43). Since he last appeared Hamlet has seen his own name on a death warrant. Death, having been the great uncertainty, is now the great certainty: "That's the end" (IV.iii.25). As with the Ghost's appearances, the timing is still in question, but the event is not: "If it be now, 'tis not to come; if it be not to come, it will be now; if it be not now, yet it will come. The readiness is all. Since no man, of aught he leaves, knows aught[27] what is't to leave betimes? Let be" (V.ii.216–220). It is life itself that is unknowable, and therefore it does not matter when we leave it; the undiscovered country is not the next world, but this one.

"Let be": Hamlet has stopped asking questions. He has also surrendered at least some part of his will: "There's a divinity that shapes our ends, / Rough-hew them how we will" (V.ii.10–11). He can now kill Claudius not only because he is no longer asking questions, but because he is no longer trying to kill Claudius, or at least no longer transfixed by the thought of his own responsibility. He can let it happen. When he does the deed he seems driven not just by his own will or decision but by the theatrical momentum of the scene. And the event seems less significant than we might have expected. In a passage added in the Folio, Hamlet finds the time no longer out of joint, merely short. Once Claudius hears the news from England, he will act: "It will be short. The interim is mine. / And a man's life no more than to say 'one'" (V.ii.73–74). It was on the stroke of "one" that the Ghost initially appeared, and the time it takes to say "one" is long enough for a man to die, with the suggestion that in that instant an entire life passes. It is not clear, and it does not matter, whether Hamlet means his own death or that of Claudius; in his present thinking they are equally short, equally insignificant. And so the killing of Claudius, when it finally comes, seems not the single climax to which the whole play was building but one more event in a busy scene.[28]

READING THE MEN

We have seen Hamlet steady himself after the emotional upheaval of the "nunnery" scene by fixing on the stoic calm of Horatio, enlisting him for the first time as an ally against Claudius (III.ii.54–8). Hamlet steadies himself for the final act not just by accepting the reality and insignificance of death and by surrendering to Providence, but also by seeking out other men with clearer identities and sharper wills, in whom he can find himself mirrored. It is in this spirit that in the Second Quarto (and only in that text) he responds to Fortinbras. In the "How all occasions" soliloquy Hamlet sets himself against Fortinbras as he set himself against the Player, and asks the same question: if this man is doing so much for a trivial cause (weeping for Hecuba, attacking a tiny patch of Poland) why am I doing so little for a great cause? In the earlier soliloquy there is a crucial turning point when Hamlet stops trying to emulate the Player's noisy passion and turns instead to practical action. But Hamlet's determination to emulate Fortinbras holds. He ends with what sounds like a decisive tag: "O, from this time forth / My thoughts be bloody or be nothing worth" (IV.iv.65–66). It sounds as though Hamlet, with the example of Fortinbras to steady him, will now be a determined avenger. But he can promise only bloody thoughts, not bloody deeds; as he delivers this speech he is on his way out of the country, under guard, and (though he does not yet know it) under sentence of death.

His identification with Fortinbras is even more problematic than that. The Norwegian Captain has emphasized – and Hamlet has clearly taken the point – the absurdity of fighting for a patch of ground that is not worth renting, not big enough either to fight the battle on or to bury the dead (IV.iv.20, 62–65). When Hamlet tries to take this as an example of honorable action, his own syntax shows the strain:

> Rightly to be great
> Is not to stir without great argument,
> But greatly to find quarrel in a straw
> When honour's at the stake. (IV.iv.53–56)

The logic requires "not not to stir"; Hamlet's actual words declare that great actions require great arguments, yet that is not what he intends to say. His own language is trying to tell him the truth, and he refuses to listen.

In the larger action Fortinbras is the national enemy. Refusing to accept Old Hamlet's victory over his father, he has tried to recapture by force, with a gang of "lawless resolutes," "by strong hand / And terms compulsatory" (I.i.101, 105–6) the land his father lost under the terms of "a seal'd compact / Well ratified by law and heraldry" (I.i.89–90). Old Hamlet won by force, but in a chivalric combat whose consequences were set by an elaborate legal agreement; Young Fortinbras seems by comparison a lawless thug. His uncle is now king (the configuration mirrors what has happened in Denmark, encouraging Hamlet's identification of himself with Fortinbras), and his way of restraining the young man, as reported in a diplomatic message to Claudius, can be decoded as follows: "I had no idea he was attacking Denmark (I haven't been well, you know); I've called him back and told him he's not to do it again, but since he has this army it seems a pity to waste it, so I've sent him to attack Poland, which he should have been doing in the first place, and do you mind if he marches over your land?" Claudius is satisfied; we may wonder if he should be. When Fortinbras enters Elsinore at the end of the play, he is strictly speaking on a detour after his Polish victory (another current turned awry), and his picking up the crown of Denmark is entirely fortuitous. But the staging of his entry in Kenneth Branagh's 1996 film as a deliberate invasion draws legitimately on suspicions aroused in the text.

Once again, as in *Titus Andronicus*, the enemy is within the gates, restoring order. But while the distinction between Goth and Roman was blurred, there is a sharper distinction between Dane and Norwegian, and a greater unease when the soldiers come marching in. The combat of the old kings began with the "emulate pride" (I.i.86) of Fortinbras' father, and his son has inherited his hot blood. At the end, having declared, "For me, with sorrow I embrace my fortune" (V.ii.393) (T. McAlindon notes the touch of Claudius)[29] he goes on, "I have some rights of memory in this kingdom / Which now to claim my vantage doth invite me" (V.ii.394–95). He never explains what those rights are, we have heard nothing of them, and it is hard to imagine what they could be. The key word is really "vantage." From the Danish side, Horatio quietly insists there is an electoral process to go through: "Of that I shall have also cause to speak, / And from his mouth whose voice will draw on more" (V.ii.396–97). Hamlet having voted for him, Fortinbras has a good chance of winning; but he never acknowledges Horatio's point, and we are left with a contrast of Danish legality and Norwegian force. We have already heard the sound of Fortinbras' artillery; he enters with pounding drums, shattering the mood of "the rest is silence" and "flights of angels sing thee to thy rest." In Horatio's "Why does the drum come hither?" (V.ii.363–66), we hear a note of protest.[30]

By cutting "How all occasions" the Folio plays down Hamlet's relationship with Fortinbras, and removes the absurdity of Hamlet's emulation of him. It adds a new passage that builds up Hamlet's relationship with Laertes:

> But I am very sorry, good Horatio,
> That to Laertes I forgot myself;
> For by the image of my cause I see
> The portraiture of his. (V.ii.75–78)

It is for just that cause, avenging a father's murder, that Laertes is already planning to kill Hamlet. As Fortinbras holds up a mirror in which Hamlet sees (but does not seem to appreciate) the absurdity of manly action, Laertes holds up a mirror in which Hamlet should see – and possibly does, given the misgivings about the duel he expresses to Horatio – not just his own cause but his own death. When Claudius places their hands together, the gesture of friendship is like Titus' embrace of Tamora (V.ii.221). When Hamlet addresses Laertes as his brother (V.ii.239–40, 249), we are reminded of the theme of fratricide, the first murder in the story of this play, and (Claudius himself makes the link [III.iii.36–38]) the first murder in the Book of Genesis. Two fencers facing each other create mirror images. If theatre holds the mirror up to nature, Hamlet and Laertes hold for each other the mirror up to death. Facing each other, each man sees a man who is like him, and the man who will kill him.

Identifying with Fortinbras' rage for action in one text, and with Laertes' particular cause in the other, Hamlet may seem to be strengthening his resolve and clarifying his purpose through the example of men he admires. Yet in each identification there is a disturbing irony. While the Folio removes the absurdity of Fortinbras' attack on Poland, it preserves a larger irony. Hamlet, giving his dying voice to the Norwegian prince, helps to let in the enemy, and finally undoes the achievement of the father he so admired. The larger story begins with Old Hamlet defeating Old Fortinbras and taking land from him; it ends with Young Fortinbras, with Young Hamlet's connivance, taking Denmark. In the story in which Laertes is (like Hamlet) the revenge hero, Hamlet becomes the equivalent of Claudius. In that sense he does not just let in the enemy; he becomes the enemy.

WHAT'S IN A NAME?

He is also his own enemy. Apologizing to Laertes for the murder of Polonius, Hamlet blames it on an enemy within, an enemy bearing his own name:

> Was't Hamlet wrong'd Laertes? Never Hamlet.
> If Hamlet from himself be ta'en away
> And when he's not himself does wrong Laertes,
> Then Hamlet does it not, Hamlet denies it.
> Who does it then? His madness. If't be so,
> Hamlet is of the faction that is wrong'd;
> His madness is poor Hamlet's enemy. (V.ii.229–35)

He tries to make it sound as simple as his advice to Gertrude when she told him he had cleft her heart in twain: "O throw away the worser part of it / And live the purer with the other half" (III.iv.159–60). There is Hamlet and there is Hamlet's madness, and he can dissociate himself from the latter. But again his syntax betrays him. As the sentence beginning "If Hamlet from himself be ta'en away" is constructed, there are in fact two Hamlets, one of whom has wronged Laertes, and one of whom has not. The Hamlet who wronged Laertes and the Hamlet who apologizes to him bear the same name. This is, and is not, Hamlet.

In this double use of his name Hamlet's identity breaks apart, and this takes us back to our starting point, back to the Ghost, whose identity was also fissured. Hamlet tries different ways of addressing it: "I'll call thee Hamlet, / King, father, royal Dane" (I.iv.44–45). He begins with his own name; as hands mirror each other, the name he projects on to the nameless thing is his own.[31] When he himself is first named in the play, it is as "young Hamlet" (I.i.175), his identity created by splitting himself off from his father; even so Hamlet goes on to split the Ghost off from himself ("King, father"). But the meeting point is the shared name, Hamlet. Like the names Romeo and Juliet try to discard, and cannot, it carries with it a fatal destiny. When the Ghost beckons the prince to go with it, and his friends try to hold them back, he fights them off with the words, "My fate cries out" (I.iv.81). The shared name creates a mirroring, and in that mirror, as with Laertes, Hamlet sees his own death.

Yet after its last appearance in Gertrude's closet even the memory of the Ghost seems to fade from the play.[32] It does not return, as revenge ghosts conventionally do, to gloat over the final carnage.[33] As Hamlet kills Claudius he calls him "murd'rous" (V.ii.330) but makes no specific reference to his father. He has executed his father's command, but only, it seems, after freeing himself from the memory of the figure who commanded it. This struggle with his father's memory begins early in the play. When the news is first brought to him that his father has appeared again, Hamlet for a moment fights it off. To Horatio's "My lord, I think I saw him yesternight" he replies, "Saw? Who?" (I.ii.189–90). As he questions the witnesses he seems to be looking for reasons to disbelieve them: "Then saw you not his face?" (I.ii.228). It is as though he does not want this to be his father, and we can understand why. "I shall not look upon his like again" (I.ii.188): he can safely idealize his father, seeing him as the epitome of human perfection and the standard by which to judge the corruption of the world, so long as his father stays dead. His return would force Hamlet to confront the ordinary sinful man that by the Ghost's own account he actually was. There is something in Hamlet that resents not only his mission – "The time is out of joint. O cursed spite, / That ever I was born to set it right" (I.v.196–97) – but the figure who gave it to him, the man who should have stayed dead; and who not incidentally was responsible for another of Hamlet's complaints, the fact that he was born at all. In his final silence about his father, and his gesture of giving Denmark to the son of his father's enemy, do we sense not just absent-mindedness but the workings of a buried hostility?

That he bears his father's name may be a clue to another case of the enemy within, and another way of seeing the relationship between father and son. According to Barbara Everett, "The Prince never does revenge his father; he does something more natural and perhaps more terrible, he becomes his father."[34] Hamlet's appearance in Ophelia's closet, pale, silent, staring, and looking "As if he had been loosed out of hell / To speak of horrors" (II.i.83–84), may recall the early appearances of the Ghost; it has the same power to create bewilderment and fear.[35] His disordered dress, as opposed to the Ghost's armor, keeps the identification less than absolute; he does not become his father, he is only a figure *like* his father. But the resemblance goes on developing. Returning to Denmark, Hamlet produces in Claudius something like the shock his father produces in him: someone who should have been dead has returned. Shakespeare risks an echo of Pyramus' "*Now am I dead, / Now am I fled*" (V.i.290–91), when Hamlet makes the literally impossible statement, "Horatio, I am dead" (V.ii.343). Like the Ghost, he is a dead man talking.[36] He ends where his father began: "The rest is silence" (V.ii.363). The father–daughter relationship in *Titus Andronicus* ends with Titus killing Lavinia, and the prospect of their burial together; Romeo and Juliet take their fatal names from their parents; by one reading, the father–son relationship in *Hamlet* ends with Hamlet absorbing the identity of a dead man, named like him and soon to be dead like him. At the end, a figure in armor stands over his body.[37]

To anyone who sees Hamlet as more fitted to a chair of philosophy than a royal throne, Fortinbras' final tribute must seem like another misinterpretation:

> Let four captains
> Bear Hamlet like a soldier to the stage,
> For he was likely, had he been put on,
> To have prov'd most royal. . . . (V.ii.400–3)

Fortinbras sees in Hamlet a mirror image of himself, soldier and king-in-waiting. The dead prince loses his own nature and is absorbed into the man who is speaking of him. Yet Fortinbras' words also identify Hamlet with his father; he too was a soldier and a king. The identification is not absolute: he is to be borne *like* a soldier; he could have been a king, but never was. But the identification of the Ghost was not absolute either: at the end of the play Hamlet has become what the Ghost was at the beginning, a figure like his father.

The Ghost's initial appearance brings on to the stage an image of violation, both in the late king's murder, and in this figure's bursting out of the grave. It raises, like Lavinia, a problem of identity which is also a problem of knowledge. Problems of knowledge, like Lavinia's rape, reverberate through the play, in tension with attempts to fix reality in words, pictures, and drama itself. Gertrude and Ophelia, unreadable and disturbing, are part of the problem; as Hamlet turns to revenge he tries to steady himself through contemplating other men. But he also steadies himself through contemplating the reality of death, and both these attempts implicitly call back the seemingly forgotten figure of the Ghost. As Lavinia will be buried with Titus, and Romeo and Juliet die in the Capulet tomb, Hamlet, who divides himself in two and senses an enemy within, finally takes on – almost – the identity of the father whose name he bears.

CHAPTER 4

Troilus and Cressida: *This is and is not Cressid*

The question asked of Lavinia and the Ghost – who or what is this? – is a question that in *Troilus and Cressida* is provoked by the play itself. What is this play? The Quarto title page calls it a history, in Elizabethan usage a loose term that can simply mean "story." The Quarto includes a prefatory letter praising Shakespeare as a master of comedy, and the play itself as a triumph of wit. Modern critics and editors sometimes group it as a "problem comedy" along with *All's Well That Ends Well* and *Measure for Measure*. The Folio groups it with the tragedies, a category somewhat destabilized by the inclusion of *Cymbeline*. (Could we call *Troilus* and *Cymbeline* "problem tragedies"?) Hector, the principal character who dies in *Troilus*, is not one of the title characters. That alone might seem to disqualify it as tragedy. There are many Greek tragedies, and at least one Elizabethan one, Marston's *Antonio's Revenge*, in which the title character does not die; but by the general practice of Shakespeare's time to keep the title characters alive at the end is an odd way to end a tragedy. On the other hand, Hector is sufficiently important, and his death sufficiently momentous, that by normal usage the play seems disqualified as a comedy. And this chapter will argue for a more positive link with the tragedies, based on the connected ideas of violation and identity.

Troilus and Cressida, then, breaks generic boundaries. In *Titus*, *Romeo* and *Hamlet* boundary-breaking is something the characters do – the Goths, Romeo, the Ghost; in *Troilus and Cressida* it is the play itself that crosses borders. With this in mind it is appropriate that this play's act of violation – equivalent to the rape of Lavinia, Romeo and Juliet's violent second wedding night, and Ghost's breaking out of the grave – is a kissing scene. Hardly the stuff of tragedy, we might think. Kissing is what lovers do to seal the relationships that end a comedy. At the end of *Much Ado*

About Nothing it is the only way Benedick can get Beatrice to stop talking (V.iv.97). The love story of *Romeo and Juliet* begins with a pair of kisses, whose gentleness contrasts with the ensuing violence. Yet when Cressida comes into the Greek camp, her situation bears a resemblance to Lavinia's from the murder of her husband to the offstage rape: she is alone, surrounded by enemies. In a reversal of the usual pattern in which kissing stops a woman from talking, she begins the scene in silence, and starts talking only after four men have kissed her – at which point the kissing stops, as she turns the kissing game into a game of wit. Whatever this is, it is not a love scene. The wit is edgy and acid; but what finally makes the effect more disturbing than comic is the way Cressida seems broken and re-made before our eyes through the pressure of relationship. We have seen her, not long before, vowing fidelity to Troilus and devastated by their parting when she was commanded to leave Troy. In the silence she maintains as Agamemnon, Nestor, Achilles and Patroclus kiss her she is in her own way as unreadable as Lavinia. Calculation, fear, sexual interest, catatonic stupor – what lies beneath that silence? And when she recovers her voice, stops kissing, and puts off Menelaus and Ulysses with banter, is this an access of confidence or a desperate holding action? These are questions to which we shall return.

Troilus does not witness any of this; but he watches Cressida betraying him – or so he sees it – with her new lover Diomedes, and he sees her as Marcus saw Lavinia, as Hamlet saw the Ghost: something that was Cressida, something like Cressida. As in Hamlet's attempt to divide himself, there is a crisis of identity: this is and is not Cressida. For Troilus as for Hamlet, the stakes are high: values are shattered and words seem to lose their meanings:

> This she? No, this is Diomed's Cressida.
> If beauty have a soul, this is not she;
> If souls guide vows, if vows be sanctimonies,
> If sanctimony be the gods' delight,
> If there be rule in unity itself,
> This is not she. O, madness of discourse,
> That cause sets up with and against itself!
> Bifold authority, where reason can revolt
> Without perdition, and loss assume all reason
> Without revolt! This is and is not Cressid. (V.ii.144–53)

He goes on to suggest that this sense of split reality produces, even reflects, a radical split in his own nature, as he sees a divided reality with a divided mind:

> Within my soul there doth conduce a fight
> Of this strange nature, that a thing inseparate
> Divides more wider than the sky and earth. . . . (V.ii.154–56)

What has happened is that a woman, having been in love with one man, is now it seems in love with another one. In the history of the human race such things have happened, and the stars have not been shaken in their courses. To see it that way is to see Cressida's behavior through the lens of realistic comedy, as the way of the world. Troilus' apocalyptic language by this reading is overinflated. Yet the kissing of Cressida – alone, outnumbered, unreadable both in silence and in speech – has had disturbing echoes of the rape of Lavinia, and suggests that what is at stake here may be, if not the breakup of the universe, the breakup of a human identity. It is violation of a less literal kind, but still violation; and it is momentous enough, if not to qualify the play simply as a tragedy, at least to give it a serious affinity with the unquestioned tragedies that precede and follow it.

WHO'S THERE?

As the rape of Lavinia haunts the world of *Titus Andronicus*, the breakup of Cressida's identity reverberates through the rest of the play. The problem Troilus has with Cressida brings into sharp focus a pervasive problem, the questionable nature of identity. The *Hamlet* question, "Who's there?," is asked over and over. When Hector comes to the Greek camp he is passed around, like Cressida, to be introduced one by one to the men he has been fighting; and in general introductions are necessary when Greeks and Trojans meet. Given that they are used to seeing each other armed and helmeted, this is not too surprising, but it plants the thought that these warriors are fighting enemies they know as reputations, as armored shapes, but not as faces or people. It is more surprising when Cressida asks "Who were those went by?" and her man Alexander replies, "Queen Hecuba and Helen" (I.ii.1). Even familiar identities need to be constantly checked. Similarly Pandarus has to identify for Cressida the parade of talent coming off the battlefield. He leads up to Troilus as the climax, then fails to recognize him when he appears. Cressida sets Pandarus up with the question, "What sneaking fellow comes yonder?" and Pandarus at first thinks it is Deiphobus (I.ii.218–19). Cressida's joke makes it clear that whether or not she recognizes the others she knows Troilus perfectly well, and doesn't think much of him. Or so she claims.

The anticlimax is typical. One reason why identities need to be constantly checked is that these great characters do not live up to their great reputations. Aeneas' question, when he comes to the Greek camp, "Which is that god in office, guiding men? / Which is the high and mighty Agamemnon?" (I.iii.231–32) is the same kind of calculated insult as Caesar's question on entering Cleopatra's monument, "Which is the Queen of Egypt?" (V.ii.111). Just before Helen's first and only appearance, Paris's servant builds her up as "the mortal Venus, the heart-blood of beauty, love's visible soul" (III.i.30–32) and Pandarus affects to believe he is describing Cressida. It is in Patroclus' caricatures that Achilles claims to recognize his fellow Greeks most clearly: "Excellent! 'Tis Agamemnon just"; "Excellent! 'Tis Nestor right!" (I.iii.164, 169–70). Not only is the reductive view the surest one, but the stage caricature – Patroclus is doing imitations – *is* the man himself. Even so, as we watch *Troilus and Cressida* we are seeing not the great Homeric characters but actors' impersonations of them, figures like them, and that is all we are going to see.

As Troilus watches Cressida with Diomedes, she seems to break apart. The intent gaze that in *Hamlet* was one way of trying to fix reality seems in this play to make the figure gazed at lose identity rather than gain it:

THERSITES Nay, look upon him.
ACHILLES So I do. What's the matter?
THERSITES Nay, but regard him well.
ACHILLES Well, why, I do so.
THERSITES But yet you look not well upon him; for, whomsoever you take him
        to be, he is Ajax.
ACHILLES I know that, fool.
THERSITES Ay, but that fool knows not himself. (II.i.57–64)

Besides the usual pun (Ajax is a jakes, and doesn't know it) there is a suggestion that Ajax is truly known neither to himself nor to the people who think they know him, and the harder one looks the less there is to see.

Sometimes those who are watched watch back. Achilles is disturbed when his fellow Greeks fail to greet him or even recognize him: "What mean these fellows? Know they not Achilles?" (III.iii.70). Ulysses warns him that his identity depends on how others see him: a man

> Cannot make boast to have that which he hath,
> Nor feels not what he owes, but by reflection;
> As when his virtues, shining upon others,
> Heat them, and they return that heat again
> To the first givers. (III.iii.99–103)

Achilles has already given himself the same caution:

> What the declined is
> He shall as soon read in the eyes of others
> As feel in his own fall. . . . (III.iii.76–78)

This seems one solution to the identity problem: a character is defined by that character's reflection in the eyes of others. (It is Troilus who says Cressida is no longer Cressida.) Yet in the case of Achilles the whole exercise is a fake. His fellow warriors' neglect of him is a contrived performance: he is the fighter they care about most, and they are anxious to get him fighting again. What he sees as evidence of his decline is in fact evidence that his reputation has never stood higher. The mirror deceives.

Or does it? We might think that the real Achilles would be revealed in action. If so, what we see when he finally acts is what he saw in the mirror of others' eyes: a hero in decline. Out of shape and unable to defeat Hector in single combat, he sets upon him when he is unarmed, gets his Myrmidons to kill him – "Strike, fellows, strike! This is the man I seek!" (V.ix.10) – then tells them to spread the word, "Achilles hath the mighty Hector slain!" (V.ix.14). However his fellow Greeks may take his achievement, the audience is likely to be as disillusioned as Troilus is with Cressida, and we could frame our disillusionment as he does: this is Achilles?

We could ask a similar question about Hector. The play's first detailed reference to the great Trojan hero is to Hector acting out of character:

> Hector, whose patience
> Is as a virtue fixed, today was moved.
> He chid Andromache and struck his armourer. . . . (I.ii.4–6)

In the Trojan council scene he makes an eloquent plea for the return of Helen, then concludes:

> Hector's opinion
> Is this in way of truth; yet, ne'ertheless,
> My sprightly brethren, I propend to you
> In resolution to keep Helen still. . . . (II.ii.188–91)

As Hamlet is split between declaring the world is beautiful and believing it is corrupt, Hector is split between the truth he believes and the opposing argument he agrees with. His reference to his brothers suggests that, like Cressida in the kissing scene, he is succumbing to the pressure of a group. The speed of his surrender is startling enough; even more so is his revelation that he has *already* sent a challenge to the Greeks, buying

into his brothers' view of the war as a matter of chivalric honor. Through-
out the scene he has been defending a position he has already abandoned.
If he betrays himself in this scene, on the day of his death he betrays Troy.
His father, wife and sister plead with him not to go into battle, and
Cassandra's last words to him are, "Thou dost thyself and all our Troy
deceive" (V.iii.90). He goes because he has promised the Greeks he will.
As Romeo briefly places Tybalt before Juliet, Hector's commitment to his
enemies outweighs his commitment to his city and his family. In that
sense, like Cressida, he goes over to the other side. No one ever says, this is
and is not Hector. But we see in him a divided will and a capacity for
betrayal that correspond to what Troilus sees in Cressida.

WAR AND LOVE

A similar division affects Troilus – and in the Folio version the play itself
– right from the beginning. But while Achilles and Hector fail to live up
to their roles, Troilus is unsure what role he is playing. In the casting
session in *A Midsummer Night's Dream* Bottom asks, "What is Pyramus?
A lover, or a tyrant?" (I.ii.19). The question here is, what is Troilus? A
lover, or a warrior? After a Prologue (in the Folio) that announces a play
about war, the first line of the play proper is Troilus' "Call hither my
varlet; I'll unarm again." He continues, "Why should I war without the
walls of Troy, / That find such cruel battle here within?" (I.i.1–3). The
sense of self-division he later projects on to Cressida begins in himself, in
his opening words. And like Achilles and Hector he defines himself and
decides what he what he wants through relationship, in the company of
others. He spends the bulk of the opening scene lamenting his frustrated
love, in the company of Pandarus; then at the end he goes off to war after
all, in the company of Aeneas. He is challenged, like Romeo, to decide
whether he is a lover or a fighter, and while under pressure Romeo makes
one fatal decision, regretting it too late, Troilus keeps slipping back and
forth.

In *Venus and Adonis* Adonis rejects the pleas of Venus and goes to his
death in the boar-hunt: "'I am,' quoth he, 'expected of my friends'" (718).
The demands of Mercutio's friendship make Romeo turn to the male
code of violence and reject Juliet, claiming she has unmanned him.
Hamlet and Laertes reject the woman in themselves and turn to the manly
action of killing. Troilus complains that his love for Cressida has made
him "weaker than a woman's tear" and "Less valiant than the virgin in the
night" (I.i.9–11). When Aeneas asks why he is not in the field, he replies,

"Because not there. This woman's answer sorts, / For womanish it is to be from thence" (I.i.102–3). When he goes off to battle with Aeneas, his "Come, go we then together" (I.i.112) echoes Hamlet's "Nay, come, let's go together" (I.v.198), registering the same need for male company. Paris' excuse for not going to war shows him unmanned in action and enervated in language: "I would fain have armed today, but my Nell will not have it so" (III.i.130–31). The official reason for Achilles' withdrawal from the war is his love for Priam's daughter Polyxena, and Ulysses asks him to imagine the feelings of his son Pyrrhus when the Greek girls sing ribald songs about his father's lack of manhood (III.iii.209–15).

Arguing for peace, Hector admits it is the woman in him who wants it:

> There is no lady of more softer bowels,
> More spongy to suck in the sense of fear,
> More ready to cry out, 'Who knows what follows?'
> Than Hector is. (II.ii.11–14)

In this view of his own pacifism there may be a fundamental discomfort that helps to explain his change of front later in the scene, when he joins his brothers. Like Troilus he is torn between the man and the woman in himself, and there is a violent reversion to his male side on the morning of his last battle. For the only time in the play there are two women on stage: Andromache and Cassandra, begging him to stay home and invoking the pleas of his mother Hecuba. (Hecuba never appears, but there are enough references to her in the final sequence to make her a voice crying from just outside the boundaries of the play.) Hector's refusal, which I have already suggested is a betrayal, is a choice of his fellow men: "I do stand engaged to many Greeks" (V.iii.68). The last words his wife hears from him before he dies are, "Andromache, I am offended with you. / Upon the love you bear me, get you in" (V.iii.77–78).

Sometimes the men are torn between male and female loyalties; but Troilus and Hector in particular are also torn between the man and the woman in themselves, suffering not just divided loyalties but, like Cressida, divided selves. One way of resolving the opposition is the chivalric convention of fighting *for* a woman. The challenge Hector sends to the Greeks proposes a combat whose participants will fight to prove the worth of their ladies, with the usual pun: "And dare avow her beauty and her worth / In other arms than hers" (I.iii.287–88). Agamemnon replies in kind: "may that soldier a mere recreant prove / That means not, hath not, or is not in love" (I.iii.271–72). But the play is full of soldiers who are recreant *because* they are in love, and the chivalric ideal comes into this gritty, disillusioned play with a certain archaic stiffness. In the actual combat of Hector and Ajax, the notion of knights fighting for their ladies is silently dropped.

The whole Trojan war is a combat for the sake of a woman, in which the chivalric ideal is both writ large and critically examined. The Trojans argue the matter back and forth, with Hector (for a while) claiming Helen is not worth a fraction of the men who have died for her (II.ii.18–25). On the Greek side, Diomedes pours contempt on Menelaus, Paris and Helen, reserving a special contempt for Helen's body:

> For every false drop in her bawdy veins
> A Grecian life hath sunk; for every scruple
> Of her contaminated carrion weight
> A Trojan hath been slain. (IV.i.71–74)

Driven by something like Hamlet's disgust with the female body, he sees the cause of the war as a piece of contaminated meat. Thersites, while agreeing that "All the argument is a whore and a cuckold" (II.iii.69–70), reduces the issue still further, cursing "those that war for a placket" (II. iii.19), a patch of contested ground even smaller than the one Fortinbras fights for. The theme returns on a smaller scale when Diomedes and Troilus fight over Cressida, and after winning one round Diomedes uses the language of chivalry: "I have chastised the amorous Trojan / And am her knight by proof" (V.v.4–5). If we take Thersites' view (and I want to hold on to that "if") the two men are simply doing what the two armies do, fighting for a whore. The one case of fighting for love in which the motive is powerful and the passion unequivocal is the rage at Patroclus' death that finally sends Achilles into action. He fights for his male lover with none of the hesitation and self-division the other men show when fighting for Helen. There is no woman in question here, and for a moment the division between war and love seals up.

It seals up in other ways. As the love of Romeo and Juliet comes to be infused with the hot blood and violence of the feud, throughout this play war and love are not just opposed to each other but seem at times disconcertingly like each other. Politics is to war what love (in this play) is to sex: a lot of talk, and then the bodies come together. War is the continuation of politics by other means, and sex is the continuation of love by other means. The result is a characteristic double action, as in the politicized rapes of Lucrece and Lavinia, and in Romeo's double loss of virginity. Here as in Verona there are two kinds of hot blood, except that what was energy in Verona seems more like sickness here. Hector attributes his brothers' enthusiasm for the war to "the hot passion of distempered blood" (II.ii.169). The other side of the equation is Paris' "hot blood begets hot thoughts, and hot thoughts beget hot deeds, and hot deeds is love" (III.i.124–25).

Two appetites are linked, and male combat is eroticized, when Achilles confesses,

> I have a woman's longing,
> An appetite that I am sick withal,
> To see great Hector in his weeds of peace. . . . (III.iii.239–41)

Aeneas greets Diomedes:

> By Venus' hand I swear,
> No man alive can love in such a sort
> The thing he means to kill more excellently. (IV.i.24–26)

Each man kills the thing he loves – or in this case, loves the thing he kills – and Aeneas' swearing by Venus, like Achilles' "woman's longing" to see Hector unarmed, marks the love in question as erotic. Cressida, a besieged woman in a besieged city, sees herself fighting a defensive war, lying "Upon my back to defend my belly, upon my wit to defend my wiles, upon my secrecy to defend mine honesty, my mask to defend my beauty, and you [Pandarus] to defend all these" (I.ii.251–54). As lying on her back hardly seems the most logical position for sexual defense,[1] Pandarus is an unlikely choice of defender. In the early scenes the Greeks are frustrated by their inability to take Troy, and Troilus by his inability to take Cressida. Cressida falls half way through the play; Troy will follow.

Hot blood cools in death: Achilles says of Hector, "I'll heat his blood with Greekish wine tonight, / Which with my scimitar I'll cool tomorrow" (V.i.1–2). Appetite turns away from a plate of cold leftovers: Troilus calls the remains of Cressida's love "The fragments, scraps, the bits and greasy relics" (V.ii.166). Love and war alike are haunted by frustration, bathos and failure. The opening of the Greek council scene is a prolonged meditation on the frustration of all human activity. According to Agamemnon, "Checks and disasters / Grow in the veins of actions highest reared" (I.iii.5–6). His image is of a tree twisted from its natural growth (7–9). It is not so much that the current turns awry, as in *Hamlet*; the force that twists it was there from the beginning, in its veins.

Troilus and Cressida, on their way to bed, contemplate the inherent frustrations of sex. Troilus declares, "This is the monstruosity in love, lady, that the will is infinite and the execution confined; that the desire is boundless and the act a slave to limit" (III.ii.77–80). There is nothing here of Juliet's "when I shall die, / Take him and cut him out in little stars" (III.ii.21–22), where orgasm puts the lovers in touch with eternity. Cressida has her own idea of monstrosity: "They say all lovers swear more performance than they are able, and yet reserve an ability that they never perform, vowing more than the perfection of ten and discharging less than the tenth part of one. They that have the voice of lions and the act of hares, are they not monsters?" (III.ii.81–86). Troilus complains that sex is over too soon; Cressida, that even while it lasts it is inadequate, either because the lover is holding back or because his ability does not match his boasts. In place of Juliet's shared orgasm, which wipes out individual identities and ignores the technicalities of the act, Cressida's reference to "discharging" shows a clinical, slightly amused awareness of what the man is doing. Pandarus has already warned where this kind of talk can lead: "she'll bereave you o'the deeds too, if she call your activity in question" (III.ii.54–56). Checks and disasters grow in the vein of actions highest reared, and two lovers heading for bed talk about frustration and disappointment while their go-between warns them that too much talk leads to impotence.

One reason why Troilus approaches sex with a certain anxiety is that in its very ecstasy there is something he fears:

> I do fear besides
> That I shall lose distinction in my joys,
> As doth a battle, when they charge on heaps
> The enemy flying. (III.ii.24–27)

Loss of distinction, a total blending with Romeo, was just what Juliet wanted; but Troilus needs to keep control (we shall see the consequences of this need in later scenes), and the loss of distinction makes him think of chaos on the battlefield. It is something like the loss of distinction Ulysses fears in the chaos of a disordered universe:

> Force should be right; or rather, right and wrong
> Between whose endless jars justice resides,
> Should lose their names, and so should justice too. (I.iii.116–18)

The fear of unnaming recalls "To be or not to be," where great enterprises lose the name of action. With justice, right and wrong losing their names there is a downward spiral from power to will to the universal, self-consuming wolf appetite (I.iii.119–24). (All this because Achilles is sulking in his tent; in this play, however daring the imaginative reach of its language, we are never far from bathos.) While Ulysses imagines "right" losing its meaning, Troilus greets Cressida's vow of fidelity, "O virtuous fight, / When right with right wars who shall be most right" (III.ii.166–67). He is positive where Ulysses sounds fearful, but the self-canceling language, the war of right with right, picks up some of the earlier speech's vision of absurdity and anticipates Troilus' later attempt to set Cressida's name against itself.

That attempt reduces Cressida, in Troilus' mind, to a shattered image of her former self: this is, and is not, Cressid. She is not, like Hector, literally killed; but the way his death is set up is close enough to the way the remaking of Cressida begins to suggest a parallel between the death of the man in war and the fragmentation of the woman. Cressida and Hector come to the Greek camp one after another. The Greek herald blows a trumpet to summon Hector, and Cressida enters. After she has been kissed in general by the Greeks, another trumpet sounds, and the group cry "The Trojan's trumpet" (IV.v.65) can easily be heard as "The Trojan strumpet." The pun connects her exit with Hector's entrance. Then the warrior, like the woman, is passed around and introduced to the Greeks, and the similarity in the stage action makes us wonder if Hector too is the Trojan strumpet. Achilles fixes him with a gaze that leads Hector to ask, "Why dost thou so oppress me with thine eye?" (IV.v.241). At first Achilles sounds like a butcher inspecting meat: "I will the second time, / As I would buy thee, view thee limb by limb" (IV.v.237–38). Then he starts carving:

> Tell me, you heavens, in which part of his body
> Shall I destroy him? Whether there, or there, or there?
> That I may give the local wound a name. . . . (IV.v.242–44)

The butcher becomes the lover constructing a blazon, surveying each part of the body in turn, and the act of naming is a way of getting power. The oppression Hector feels is like the oppression Lavinia must feel under the gaze of Chiron and Demetrius.

Refusing to stare back in the same way, Hector tries to keep the edge by finding Achilles' body less interesting than Achilles finds his. Achilles invites him, "Behold thy fill," but after a quick survey Hector shrugs, "Nay, I have done already" (IV.v.236). The insulting inference that Achilles is nothing special might indeed give Hector the edge if this were a pickup he was free to refuse. But this is a relationship to which he is committed, and within that relationship he is the target. In his death, set upon by a gang, he is outnumbered as Lavinia is in both rape sequences, and as Cressida is in the kissing scene. It is not, as an eroticized single combat might be, an encounter of two lovers each of whom values the other's body; it is more like a gang rape, and it ends with Hector's body being degraded, "at the murderer's horse's tail, / In beastly sort, dragged through the shameful field" (V.xi.4–5).[2] Achilles sees in Hector's death the fall of Troy: "So, Ilium, fall thou! Now, Troy, sink down!" (V.ix.11); Troilus' flat summary seems to add to the death of Troy the death of language: "Hector is dead. There is no more to say" (V.xi.22). In his reaction to Cressida's betrayal of him, Troilus sees language breaking apart; here, for a moment at least, it dies. The love story and the war story have much in common: they both deal in hot blood, they eroticize the body, and they end in ruin. In each case the ruin begins when a Trojan is passed from Greek to Greek, inspected, literally kissed in one case, imaginatively carved like meat in another, with (as in *Titus* and *Romeo*) the erotic turned menacing and violence eroticized. If the breakup of Cressida's identity plays at one level as cynical comedy, it acquires a more tragic coloring from the way it is shadowed by the war story. That darker color allows us to see it, like the killing and degradation of Hector, as an act of violation.

HOLDING OFF

In *Titus Andronicus* Chiron and Demetrius' professions of love lead with startling abruptness to the rape and transformation of Lavinia in the woods. The love story that leads to the breakup of Cressida's identity in the Greek camp takes a slower, subtler course. It works its way as the war does, through a world of divided selves, divided loyalties, with a constant undercurrent of doubt and frustration. As the Trojans are divided about the cause for which they fight, Troilus and Cressida approach love, and each other, with profound misgivings. From the start, love registers as damage and loss. Troilus feels it as an assault on his body, claiming that in speaking of Cressida Pandarus pours "in the open ulcer of my heart / Her eyes, her hair, her cheek, her gait, her voice" and lays "in every gash that love hath given me / The knife that made it" (I.i.50–51, 59–60). Waiting for Cressida, he imagines he is waiting to cross the Styx (III.ii.7–9), succumbs to vertigo – "I am giddy; expectation whirls me round" (III.ii.16) – and seems afraid of consummation: "Death, I fear me" (III.ii.20). The excitement of love has an edge of panic. Just as Romeo, pining for Rosaline, declares, "This is not Romeo, he's some other where" (I.i.196),

Pandarus claims that in love Troilus is not himself (I.ii.70). What Troilus says about Cressida at the end of the affair, Pandarus says about him at the beginning.

As Troilus is torn between loving and fighting, Cressida is torn between holding off and giving in. At first she is determined to hold off:

> more in Troilus thousandfold I see
> Than in the glass of Pandar's praise may be.
> Yet hold I off. Women are angels, wooing;
> Things won are done; joy's soul lies in the doing.
> That she beloved knows naught that knows not this:
> Men prize the thing ungained more than it is.
> That she was never yet that ever knew
> Love got so sweet as when desire did sue.
> Therefore this maxim out of love I teach:
> 'Achievement is command; ungained, beseech'.
> Then, though my heart's contents firm love doth bear,
> Nothing of that shall from mine eyes appear. (I.ii.275–86)

This early in the play she makes one of its crucial statements, and it may appear that while the men debate, learnedly and ponderously, Cressida has the sharpest mind on the stage. The squalid bathos of the killing of Hector, which ended Achilles' long period of holding off, illustrates her point that expectation, not consummation, is where the real pleasure lies – that in fact consummation is ruin. Hence her own conflict between desire and caution. Self-divided, her eye and heart at war, she is at least honest and articulate about her self-division, and understands it better than Hector and Achilles do theirs. Stephen J. Lynch calls her the only truly introspective character in the play, its only "trustworthy commentator."[3] Yet there is a glibness in her speech. Claire M. Tylee declares Cressida has no sense of self, and her account of her strategy is simply "bits of acquired 'wisdom.'"[4] Is there in fact an essential Cressida, a calculating and intelligent player in the game of love, or is she (as Strindberg describes his characters in the preface to *Miss Julie*) a collage of bits and pieces picked up from the surrounding culture?[5] The latter view seems borne out by the Cressida of the later scenes, more unstable and less in command than her first soliloquy would indicate.

At least her conventional wisdom puts her in tune with her world. Her fear that consummation will end the affair is justified by events. A striking difference between this play and *Romeo and Juliet* is that there is no hint of marriage, nothing to guarantee that this will be more than a one-night stand. Arguing for commitment to Helen as the cause of the war, Troilus

uses marriage as an analogy – "I take today a wife" (II.ii.61) – and the way
he develops the argument hints at his real view of the institution:

> How may I avoid,
> Although my will distaste what it elected,
> The wife I chose? (II.ii.65–67)

To be married is to be stuck. The Trojans are stuck with Helen, and
Troilus, not yet committed, may feel at some level that much as he wants
Cressida he would rather not be stuck with her. This is one reason why his
sexual excitement is tinged with the fear of loss of control.

Cressida holds back with overt calculation, afraid of loss. Troilus hesitates, afraid of commitment. It is Cressida's fear that comes true; loss is
built into the momentum of the story. As the lovers consummate their
affair, the external event that will end it, the exchange with Antenor, is
being negotiated. Checks and disasters grow in the veins of actions highest
reared. Heading for bed, the lovers themselves take vows that seem to
parody the vows of marriage,[6] capped by Pandarus' "If ever you prove false
to one another, . . . let all pitiful goers-between be called to the world's end
after my name: call them all panders" (III.ii.193–97). Game over. The
characters are trapped in their own predetermined story, a story the
audience already knows.[7] As we watch the defense of a city that for us
has already fallen, we watch lovers vow fidelity who for us are already a
byword for betrayal. The next morning Cressida declares, "Night hath
been too brief" (IV.ii.12); things won are done. They wake not to the sound
of a lark or a nightingale but to the cawing of "ribald crows" (IV.ii.9).

Yet Cressida has decided, against her own fears, to consummate the
affair. As it is Juliet who proposes marriage, it is Cressida who in III.ii
issues the sexual invitations. Her first words in the scene are "Will you
walk in, my lord?," to which Troilus replies, "O Cressida, how often have
I wished me thus!" (III.ii.59–60). He goes on to vow fidelity, and she has
to ask again, "Will you walk in, my lord?" (III.ii.95). While Troilus wants
to talk – he is now the one holding off – Cressida wants to get on with it.
This is one half of her self-division: she wants the act that she fears will be
the end of love, and she takes the initiative to get it.

She enters this scene as Lavinia enters her final scene, veiled (III.ii.45);
and in the first part of the scene, so long as Pandarus is on stage, she is
silent. But the difficulty this time lies not so much in how others read her
as in how she reads herself. She confesses love, rebukes herself for
confessing, and asks Troilus to stop her, finding herself helpless in speech
as Lavinia is in silence:

> Sweet, bid me hold my tongue,
> For in this rapture I shall surely speak
> The thing I shall repent. See, see, your silence,
> Cunning in dumbness, in my weakness draws
> My soul of counsel from me! Stop my mouth. (III.ii.125–29)

He takes what he thinks is the hint and kisses her; she tells him he has misread the signal – "'Twas not my purpose thus to beg a kiss" (III.ii.133) – and tries to leave. Silence has usurped the kiss's traditional function of drawing forth the soul; the kiss itself, which brings Romeo and Juliet together, seems for a moment to drive Troilus and Cressida apart.

She is torn even about leaving:

> I have a kind of self resides with you,
> But an unkind self that itself will leave
> To be another's fool. Where is my wit?
> I would be gone. I speak I know not what. (III.ii.143–46)

On the brink of consummating her love against her own advice, holding off and giving in, she feels her self split, her will divided, her language meaningless. Claiming she is torn between two selves, she plants an idea Troilus will develop: this is and is not Cressid.

REREADING CRESSIDA

The next morning, Pandarus asks, in effect, who's there? – "How now, how now, how go maidenheads? Here, you maid! Where's my cousin Cressid?" (IV.ii.24–25). There is, as with Lavinia, some blurring of her sexual identity. A line like "you men will never tarry" (IV.ii.17) makes her sound experienced; but Pandarus works from the assumption that she lost her virginity with Troilus.[8] In later Shakespearean tragedy his joke will be replayed, with a much more bitter edge. Othello greets Desdemona's insistence that she is not a whore,

> I cry you mercy then,
> I took you for that cunning whore of Venice
> That married with Othello. (IV.ii.90–92)

Finding Cleopatra with Thidias, Antony asks, "what's her name / Since she was Cleopatra?" (III.xiii.103–4). Both Antony and Othello see a woman who has betrayed them as having violated her own identity, become another person. All Pandarus is saying is that if this woman is a virgin she cannot be Cressida; but the way he says it suggests that Cressida has surrendered not just her body but her name. Troilus will take this further when he sees her with Diomedes.

Cressida becomes, like Helen, contested ground. The Trojans debate not only Helen's value but whether value dwells in the object itself or in the opinion of the person who values it. As Troilus turns Cressida over to Diomedes, the two men have a similar debate over her. To Troilus' "I charge thee use her well, even for my charge" (IV.iv.125) Diomedes replies,

> To her own worth
> She shall be prized; but that you say 'Be't so',
> I speak it in my spirit and honour: 'No'. (IV.iv.132–34)

Troilus says, in effect, she's worthy because I say so; Diomedes, she's worthy in herself. But his tribute to her beauty (IV.iv.116–19) has already made it clear that he is staking his claim as a rival lover – which means in this case a rival interpreter. They compete, like Hamlet and Laertes over Ophelia's grave, like the three sets of brothers who argue over Lavinia; and as they do so Cressida herself stands silent.

Having gone from self-contradiction to collapse to having her very name questioned (jokingly, but the joke bites deep) Cressida now appears to be a blank space, a tabula rasa on which men compete to write their own interpretations. In this state she is ready for anyone who will tell her what she is and what she will do. As he hands her over to Diomedes, Troilus has already begun the process of remaking her. The new Cressida he creates, with growing insistence, is the false Cressida whose defining act will be to betray him. Even as they vow fidelity on their way to bed, his statement of trust in her faithfulness comes with a deadly reservation: "O, that I thought it could be in a woman – / As, if it can, I will presume in you" (III.ii.153–54). When they learn they must part, his reiterated "Be true, be true" (IV.iii.57–73) betrays by its sheer insistence the expectation that she will be false. She sees what is happening, and protests: "what wicked deem is this?" (IV.iii.58). His attempts to placate her include a worry that "The Grecian youths are full of quality" (IV.iv.75), better than he is at singing, dancing and sweet talk (IV.iv.83–90). Claiming to mistrust his ability, he is actually claiming she has no capacity to hold out against seduction more expert than his.

Finally he puts it in the passive voice, a construction that denies her any will or agency:

> something may be done that we will not;
> And sometimes we are devils to ourselves,
> When we will tempt the frailty of our powers,
> Presuming on their changeful potency. (IV.iv.93–96)

He goes on to imagine an active self-betrayal – "devils to ourselves" – like that of Hamlet's enemy within. But by initially using the passive, and not using Cressida's name, he erases her as Hamlet never quite erases himself. Cressida will not do it; it will be done. This is a clue to the way Cressida is dramatized at certain points. We never see her decision to stop holding off and admit Troilus to her bed; or the moment when, having declared, "I will not go from Troy!" (IV.ii.110) she resigns herself to going; or the moment when she accepts Diomedes as her next lover. It is as though Cressida does not do these things; they are done.[9] And for Troilus (as for Hamlet when he generalizes about women) they are inevitable. Even before he sees Cressida in Diomedes' tent he makes it clear that he expects betrayal: "still sweet love is food for Fortune's tooth" (IV.v.293).

Though Cressida protests, she also co-operates. When he says "But be not tempted" she replies with a question, "Do you think I will?" (IV.iv.90–91), that could be indignant resistance, or a real question, asked out of genuine curiosity about her future.[10] One could even say that as she invited Troilus to bed, so in creating the false Cressida she has made the first move. Her vow of fidelity has already conveyed a hypnotic fascination with ruin: "When waterdrops have worn the stones of Troy, / And blind oblivion swallowed cities up" (III.ii.181–82). While Troilus asks to be remembered for truth she asks to be remembered for falsehood if she betrays him. Accordingly, her speech is not about her truth but about her falsehood:[11]

> As false
> As air, as water, wind, or sandy earth,
> As fox to lamb, or wolf to heifer's calf. . . . (III.ii.186–88)

These are the images that fill her mind as she goes off with Troilus, and they make falsehood seem (literally) natural. The next morning Troilus will tell her, in effect, that she will betray him; she is already telling herself. The scene that follows their departure for bed, and therefore coincides with the consummation, includes the dialogue of Achilles and Ulysses on the way people see themselves reflected in the eyes of others. Cressida will see her falsehood reflected, even created, in Troilus' warnings to her. The reflection works because of her own uncertainty about herself, and because like Achilles she sees what she is already prepared to see.

REREADING TROILUS

If she is prepared for a false Cressida, and even collaborates in its creation, she is also prepared for a false Troilus. There is some point in her morning-after question, when he urges her to go back to bed and keep warm, "Are you aweary of me?" (IV.ii.8). This is the end she feared. He starts to co-operate with her reading of him, as she does with his reading of her. His behavior when Aeneas comes with the news that Cressida is to be sent from Troy suggests he is ready to be rid of her. His reception of the bad news is pained, but resigned:

> TROILUS   Is it concluded so?
> AENEAS By Priam and the general state of Troy.
>   They are at hand and ready to effect it.
> TROILUS How my achievements mock me! (IV.ii.68–71)

He laments a *fait accompli*. The family, the state, the male group to which he belongs, have made the decision, and like Hector he submits to the group.

Breaking the news to Cressida, he laments with her over their fate; but he also makes it clear there is no choice. She asks, "I must, then, to the Grecians?" and he replies, "No remedy" (IV.iv.54). His gesture in giving her to Diomedes himself (Pandarus could have done it) is complex. He romanticizes it, seeing himself as a priest offering his own heart as sacrifice (IV.iii.6–9). But the gesture also asserts his rights in her as owner of the goods to be traded, and makes him symbolically complicit in her coming change of loyalty. Having anticipated the change in his warnings to her, he then hands her over to her next lover.

It is as though he needs Cressida to betray him,[12] and we should ask why. The answer lies, I think, in his determination to construct an image of himself as the epitome of truth. In the vows they exchange, that is how he sees himself remembered by posterity. When she counters his suspicions by asking if he will be true he replies, "Who, I? Alas, it is my vice, my fault" (IV.iv.101). He wishes she could match his truth, but makes it clear she cannot:

> that persuasion could but once convince me
> That my integrity and truth to you
> Might be affronted with the match and weight
> Of such a winnowed purity in love;
> How were I then uplifted! But alas,
> I am as true as truth's simplicity,
> And simpler than the infancy of truth. (III.ii.159–65)

He gives himself a satisfying pathos, as the pure young man too good for this wicked world, matched with a woman who will never meet his standard.

Troilus needs a false Cressida to set off and define his self-image as the true Troilus, and he needs that self-image because of his actual instability. Though in the Trojan council scene he argues eloquently for the value of keeping Helen, in the first scene he has spoken very differently: "I cannot fight upon this argument; / It is too starved a subject for my sword" (I. i.88–89). At the end of the scene he goes off to fight after all. In his own feelings for Cressida, as we have seen, he is torn between romanticized desire and the fear of unmanning and loss of control. There is, from the beginning, a part of him that does not want this love affair, at war with a part of him that does. In the end, Cressida's betrayal is (to put it coldly) useful to him: it frees him to return to the simple, socially approved role of warrior, his own reputation for truth intact.

This is not to deny that there is real grief in the lovers' parting. We sense it most strongly when they cling together for a few lines in silence, ignoring the chatter of Pandarus and feeling the closeness of each others' bodies for the last time (IV.iv.12–22). Speech tends to pull them apart; silence for a moment holds them together. Just as there is genuine concern in Titus' attempts to take Lavinia's pain on himself even as he brings her under his control, these lovers endure a loss that really feels painful to them, even as, at another level that we keep glimpsing, they are using each other – using their mutual suspicions to stabilize their sense of themselves, the false Cressida whose fears were justified, the true Troilus who has been betrayed. As Lucrece and Tarquin are terribly linked in the aftermath of the rape, Troilus and Cressida, as amid tears they fire stinging accusations at each other, are working together so closely that they establish the strongest bond, the most effective working relationship in the play. They need each other's betrayal as they needed each other's bodies, and together they satisfy that need. Hamlet uses words and pictures to fix reality in an unstable world; Troilus and Cressida use each other. It is one of Shakespeare's most searching, ironic depictions of relationship.

CRESSIDA AMONG THE GREEKS

Cressida goes to the Greeks to enact the role Troilus has set for her, the role she expects to play – though as we shall see questions remain as to just how she enters that role, and in what spirit she plays it. In the process we see the force of another relationship of which we previously had no inkling. She is returned to her father, at his request, in another case of a life-transition reversed.[13] Like Juliet trying to free herself from the feud, she protests, "I have forgot my father" (IV.ii.97). Yet she is symbolically bound to him. Calchas, like Helen, has a major effect on the story but only one onstage appearance. That appearance is telling. Just after the lovers have declared their vision of the future – Troilus will be remembered for truth, Cressida for falsehood, Pandarus as a pandar – Calchas declares his: "through the sight I bear in things to come, / I have abandoned Troy" (III.iii.4–5). He has the sense of impending ruin that Cressida has about her love affair, and in going over to the winning side she is, in more than a literal sense, following him. He has "Incurred a traitor's name" (III.iii.6), as she will. There may be more than an automatic social identification when Agamemnon calls her "Calchas' daughter" (IV.v.14), though we are so little used to thinking of her that way that it catches us by surprise. Calchas' last intervention in the play is as an offstage voice telling Diomedes, "She comes to you" (V.ii.5). In a small way, he has taken over from Pandarus. Compared with Titus or Capulet, Calchas does not loom large in his daughter's life or in the play; but she is still involved with him. He is associated not with stable patriarchal authority but with uprooting, disloyalty and fear of the future, and in that sense she is her father's daughter. This gives us yet another way of defining her: she is Calchas' Cressida.

For a while we are not sure who she is. When Diomedes comes to collect her, her vehement grief, and her protests against Troilus' mistrust, are replaced by silence. That silence persists in the first few moments of her entry into the Greek camp, recalling her initial silence in her meeting with Troilus. It is as though Cressida, before beginning a new relationship, has to go down into a silence from which she emerges changed and ready, leaving us to wonder what happened in the interval. The kissing scene, I have suggested, is the play's equivalent of the rape of Lavinia: a character is set upon, broken and changed. This time it happens before our eyes. Agamemnon, Achilles and Nestor kiss her; Patroclus kisses her twice, once for Menelaus and once for himself. Through all this she remains silent.[14] Kissing her after Nestor, Achilles offers, "I'll take that winter from your lips, fair lady" (IV.v.25), making her seem like a passive medium that can be printed with an image or wiped clean at will. This draws on the game Romeo and Juliet play with the notion of bestowing and removing sin on each other's lips by kissing. But they play that game together; Cressida just stands there. We may also remember Titus, accusing Chiron and Demetrius, calling Lavinia "This goodly summer with your winter mixed" (V.ii.171); Cressida by comparison is a smooth, non-stick surface from which impressions like Nestor's wintery kiss can easily be removed.

Cutting off Menelaus, Patroclus claims to be imitating Paris' rape of Helen: "thus popped Paris in his hardiment, / And parted thus you and your argument" (IV.v.29–30). Cressida now is a blank space on which the image of Helen can be printed. The next line, from Ulysses, is the inevitable horn-joke, and we are reminded that while the Trojans have a real debate over Helen, the Greeks, who are in theory fighting for Menelaus, treat him simply as a laughing stock. It is at this point that Cressida starts coming back to life. Behind her initial silence may be calculation, sexual interest, fear – we cannot tell. But when the jokes against Menelaus begin she senses a break in the Greek ranks, moves in at the point of weakness, and speaks for the first time:

> MENELAUS I'll have my kiss, sir. – Lady, by your leave.
> CRESSIDA In kissing, do you render or receive?
> MENELAUS Both take and give.
> CRESSIDA   I'll make my match to live,
>   The kiss you take is better than you give;
>   Therefore no kiss. (IV.v.36–40)

Having passively submitted to five kisses from four different men, she now sees kissing as reciprocal, a matter of giving and receiving, and reserves her right to accept or refuse. She refuses Menelaus. In fact after she first speaks no one else kisses her, as though her recovery of language is a way of defending her lips. This plays in reverse the ending of the courtship scene in *Henry V*, where Henry kisses Katherine and she is silent for the rest of the play: Cressida speaks, and the kissing stops. Both scenes differ markedly from the interplay of talking and kissing we see in *Romeo and Juliet*.

To Menelaus' "Every man is odd" Cressida replies, "No, Paris is not, for you know 'tis true / That you are odd, and he is even with you" (IV. v.43–45). She is not only gaining confidence; by joining in the general mockery of Menelaus she is becoming one of the boys. With Ulysses she becomes positively impudent, and he decides to put her in her place:

> ULYSSES . . .
>   May I, sweet lady, beg a kiss of you?
> CRESSIDA You may.
> ULYSSES   I do desire it.

CRESSIDA   Why, beg too.
ULYSSES Why then, for Venus' sake, give me a kiss,
      When Helen is a maid again, and his – (IV.v.48–51)

– meaning never. It is hard to say who wins this exchange. The
Cressida who makes Ulysses beg has come a long way, very fast, from
the silent, passive Cressida who began the scene;[15] but he may get the
edge back by refusing to beg, showing his contempt for her; either
because he wanted a kiss but balks at the price (in which case he loses)
or because he had set the dialogue up with this ending in mind (in which
case he wins).

At this point Diomedes pulls her out of the arena: "Lady, a word. I'll
bring you to your father" (IV.v.54). He is asserting his control over her,
but how we read that moment depends on how we read Cressida in this
scene. At a technical level she is caught up in the rhyming couplets as one
is caught in a dance or a game. She could be succumbing passively to the
pressure of the group, making herself promiscuously available, trying only
(and not quite successfully) to do it on her own terms. She could be
calculating that her survival depends on accommodating these men, and
she has to play along; she may be quite interested, and this could be a
wine-tasting session; or she could be using the sexual interest she arouses
to get control of the situation while keeping her own integrity intact.
These meanings can shade into each other; the main impression is that
Cressida goes down into silence and emerges with what looks like a new
strength, until she meets her match (or does she?) in Ulysses. In offering
to take her to her father, Diomedes could be protecting his own interest,
sparing her any further humiliation, or reasserting male authority over a
woman who is getting uppity. He could be stopping the match before she
loses any more points, or before she wins any more. Silent, she poses
problems of interpretation, as we have seen other silent characters do;
re-emerging into speech, she poses more problems.

Ulysses claims he can read her, because (anticipating the way Achilles
carves Hector) he can read her body:

> Fie, fie upon her!
> There's language in her eye, her cheek, her lip,
> Nay, her foot speaks; her wanton spirits look out
> At every joint and motive of her body.
> O, these encounterers, so glib of tongue,
> That give accosting welcome ere it comes,
> And wide unclasp the tables of their thoughts

> To every tickling reader! Set them down
> For sluttish spoils of opportunity
> And daughters of the game. (IV.v.55–64)

Perhaps. But we notice that he has Hamlet's trick of sliding into generalizations, together with his habit of jotting down striking phrases ("Set them down"). He claims he can read the thoughts of a character we have found opaque.[16] We may even remember Titus' overconfidence in reading the silent language of Lavinia. We certainly remember that Cressida made Ulysses beg for a kiss; this could be sour grapes. The Arden edition follows the Folio in placing the exit for Diomedes and Cressida at the end of this speech, and in the staging that results we do not just have to listen to Ulysses; we can watch Cressida as he speaks, testing his sense of her against ours. In this play of unstable, self-warring identities, confidence like that of Ulysses is bound to leave us suspicious.

Even if we agree that being kissed by several men makes Cressida *look* like a whore, we have to notice whose idea this was:

> AGAMEMNON Most dearly welcome to the Greeks, sweet lady.
> [*He kisses her.*]
> NESTOR Our general doth salute you with a kiss.
> ULYSSES Yet is the kindness but particular;
>   'Twere better she were kissed in general. (IV.v.19–22)

In Shakespeare's England the kiss of greeting was a common gesture of politeness; that is what Agamemnon offers. It is Ulysses who poisons the gesture by turning it into an image of female promiscuity, setting up a situation in which many men kiss Cressida, and then, as though his point has been made, calling her a slut. The Cressida he attacks is in that sense a Cressida he has invented. He sets against her an idealized tribute to Troilus, second-hand (he gets it from Aeneas) and with one major inaccuracy – "deedless in his tongue" (IV.v.99) does not sound like the Troilus we know – but offered with the same confidence as his attack on Cressida. Following the heroic code that denigrates the female, he plays Troilus' game of setting a true Troilus against a false Cressida; we may not find it so easy.

DIOMED'S CRESSIDA

If Cressida now seems more unstable and harder to read,[17] it may be because she is on her own in a strange world, having to make up a new character as she goes along. Calchas' description of his own entry into the Greek camp "As new into the world, strange, unacquainted" (III.iii.12), could describe his daughter. In the kissing scene she has a number of relationships, each of which lasts long enough for a kiss and a line or two of banter. In her last appearance she has, once again, one relationship, with Diomedes. It is, so far as we can judge, even more volatile and unstable than her relationship with Troilus. The reservation is important. We feel distanced from Cressida by the number of layers of commentary that come between us and her: Troilus, Ulysses, Thersites. It is like trying to see her through a crowd, and the number and length of the commentators' asides make them a constant distraction. Her scene with Diomedes comes to us in fragments, and includes a couple of moments when she whispers to him, leaving us further excluded (V.ii.8,36).

The whispering licenses the commentators to fill in the blanks, though in doing so they may be, like Ulysses in the kissing scene, not just interpreting but imposing:

> DIOMEDES [*to Cressida*] How now, my charge?
> CRESSIDA Now, my sweet guardian. Hark, a word with you.
>   [*She whispers to him.*]
> TROILUS [*aside*] Yea, so familiar?
> ULYSSES [*to Troilus, aside*] She will sing any man at first sight.
> THERSITES [*aside*] And any man may sing her, if he
>   can take her clef. She's noted. (V.ii.7–13)

"Charge" and "guardian" reveal an important dimension in the Cressida–Diomedes relationship: in the Greek camp she needs protection.[18] In the ensuing commentary that dimension is ignored. Troilus sees the whispering as familiar, as indeed it is; but Ulysses and Thersites go beyond this into their own view of Cressida as a woman who will offer herself to any man, not just this one, an assumption based on the kissing episode Ulysses himself created.

As the scene develops, Cressida seems to be playing her old game of hard-to-get, refusing the pledge she had offered, and trying to snatch it back once she has given it. She seems at once more open and more plaintive than she was with Troilus: "I prithee, do not hold me to mine oath. / Bid me do anything but that, sweet Greek" (V.ii.28–29). If she is less in control, one reason is that Diomedes plays the same game with her, quite successfully, threatening to leave and forcing her to call him back. The token in dispute is Troilus' sleeve (as a sign that Cressida is now alone she has to fetch it herself; there is no Pandarus to run errands) and even as she gives it away she is sentimental about it: "O pretty, pretty pledge!" (V.ii.83). Her attempt to take it back could be a genuine clinging to her old love, but Thersites sees it otherwise: "Now she sharpens. Well said, whetstone!" (V.ii.78–79). When Cressida tells Diomedes, "'Twas one's that loved me better than you will" (V.ii.96) she may be (as Thersites would have it) teasing and provoking him; or there may be a real sense of loss. The latter reading gives a sharper transition to the next line, "But now you have it, take it" (V.ii.97), where she seems to give in with a shrug. Her attitude to her old love shifts rapidly back and forth; so does her attitude to her new one, going from "I prithee, Diomed, visit me no more" (V.ii.77) to "You shall not go" (V.ii.107) and finally, as he leaves, "Ay, come. – O Jove! – Do, come. – I shall be plagued" (V.ii.111) in which she seems at her most helpless, needing him and chagrined at that need.[19] She may also love him: at one point she strokes his cheek (V.ii.53). One thing she clings to: she will not reveal her old lover's name. She is keeping something to herself, something Diomedes cannot have, and the way she keeps it is through silence. If the silence of Lavinia meant helplessness, this touch may help us read Cressida's silences, throughout the play, as self-protection. It is when she speaks that she loses control.

Even her one secret is taken from her, since Diomedes can easily identify the old lover by wearing the sleeve in battle and seeing who challenges it. In general Diomedes seems more assured, and more openly cynical, than Troilus was. His attack on Helen (IV.i.63–76) shows a misogyny as sharp as that of Ulysses. When Ulysses tells Troilus that Diomedes "gives all gaze and bent of amorous view / On the fair Cressid" (IV.v.282–3) we may be hearing of a romanticism that is the flip side of misogyny; or it may simply be the butcher's gaze Achilles bestows on Hector. None of this bodes well for Cressida; nor does Thersites' account of Diomed as a promise-breaker (V.i.88–92) or his hint that Patroclus is interested in her (V.ii.199–201). In Thersites' view she is not Diomed's Cressida but anybody's.

The scene is full of other characters watching and commenting on Cressida; she is as much on display in private as she was in public. Her own view of herself is given in her last soliloquy:

> Troilus, farewell! One eye yet looks on thee,
> But with my heart the other eye doth see.
> Ah, poor our sex! This fault in us I find:
> The error of our eye directs our mind.
> What error leads must err. O, then conclude:
> Minds swayed by eyes are full of turpitude. (V.ii.113–18)

The image of eyes looking in different directions has the grotesquerie of Claudius' "an auspicious and a dropping eye" (I.ii.11); but it also conveys a genuine, if brief, division of loyalties. Having bid farewell to Troilus she goes on talking about him, suggesting that her clinging to the sleeve was not just a flirtatious trick. Then her new loyalty becomes firm; the other eye and the heart work together, as opposed to the initial division of eye and heart when she was concealing her feelings for Troilus (I.ii.285–86). She still has to reconcile herself to what has happened. Now on her own, with no one else to tell her who she is, she could proclaim a self that is not Diomed's Cressida, or any man's, but Cressida's Cressida. Instead she finds refuge in a flatly conventional misogyny. "Ah, poor our sex" – I can't help it, I'm a woman – internalizes the cynical assumptions men make about women throughout the play, but with none of the anger and disgust. What follows, the light, glib lecture on the error of the eye, sounds like a passage from *A Midsummer Night's Dream.* Cressida is no longer taking responsibility for herself, and no longer taking herself seriously. With a shrug, she disappears from the stage.

Thersites' response to the soliloquy is utterly predictable, and has its own glibness: "A proof of strength she should not publish more, / Unless she said, 'My mind is now turned whore'" (V.ii.119–20). What we have seen is in some ways worse. A character of considerable wit and intelligence, capable of realistic appraisals of herself and the world, but dependent on relationship to give a sense of herself, has been through a series of relationships – with Troilus, with the Greek generals, with Diomedes – that break and fragment her, making her unclear to herself and to the audience, scrambling her motives in a way that makes any commentary on her seem reductive. She still shows moments of strength and self-command, and she can retreat into self-protective silence. But speech betrays her – even in the brighter, sharper manner of her first soliloquy we see the conventional cynicism to which she will return – and she ends in speech as Lavinia ends in silence. It is part of her tragedy that she makes herself sound like a character in a comedy. She accommodates herself to her fate by reducing what she could have expected of herself and her life, sinking into the conventional notion of fickle womanhood as Ophelia sinks into the water.[20] In so far as this is a male view, what happens here is the equivalent of the final entombments of Lavinia and Juliet.

Troilus' impassioned response, with its denunciation of the figure he has seen who "is and is not Cressid" and who calls into question beauty, loyalty, and "unity itself" (V.ii.144–53), is in its own way fraught with problems. The breadth of his generalization activates the quiet skepticism of Ulysses: when Troilus, resisting what he has seen, declares, "Let it not be believed, for womanhood! / Think, we had mothers," Ulysses, whose misogyny evidently has limits, replies, "What hath she done, Prince, that can soil our mothers?" (V.ii.135–36, 140). Troilus calls this new Cressida "Diomed's Cressida" (V.ii.144); but we have seen him working with her to create the image of a false Cressida to set against the true Troilus, and in that sense she is his Cressida after all. Like Cressida when she agreed to go to bed with him, he has got what he wanted and has to face the consequences. Finally, the wounded idealism of this speech, which suggests that he takes her betrayal far more seriously than she does – with the height of seriousness, in fact – evaporates more quickly and completely even than Cressida's love. Brecht's *Mother Courage*, in the scene in which Mother Courage sings the song of the Great Capitulation, distinguishes between the long rage needed to fight injustice and the short rage that blows over too quickly and changes nothing. Troilus' rage is a short rage.

UNSETTLING THE ENDING

The overinflation of Troilus' response and the comic banality of Cressida's add to the generic instability of the play and leave our own responses unstable. If a comic response is too little, a tragic response seems to be too much. In that as in other ways it is Cressida who brings the problems of the play most sharply into focus, gathering the general instability and self-division into one place. Or is saying that doing what Troilus does, making the character and her infidelity bear an excessive weight of meaning? That question is provoked by the way the play goes on without Cressida: like Lavinia and Ophelia, she fades from memory. For a while she is a cause for Troilus and Diomedes to fight over, Helen writ small. But when Troilus declares "as much as I do Cressid love, / So much by weight I hate her Diomed" (V.ii.174–75), in the equality of his motives we can see his focus shifting as Cressida's does. By the time of the rivals' last encounter Troilus has a new cause: "Pay the life thou owest me for my horse" (V. vi.8). As we can hear "The Trojan's trumpet" more than one way, behind "horse'" we can hear "whore." But the real point, I suspect, is that Troilus has lost interest in fighting for Cressida; he is a warrior, not a lover, and the horse (with an echo of Richard III?) is more important. As the battle goes on, he has other things to think about: Ajax' capture of Aeneas (V.vi.23), the death of Hector.

It is Pandarus, reappearing after we had almost forgotten his existence, who tries to keep the memory of Cressida going. He delivers a letter from "Yond poor girl" (V.iii.99) – his Cressida is the one he saw last, grief-stricken at leaving Troy – a letter Troilus tears and scatters:

> Words, words, mere words, no matter from the heart;
> Th'effect doth operate another way.
> [*He tears the letter and tosses it away.*]
> Go, wind, to wind! There turn and change together.
> (V.iii.107–9)

The existence of the letter implies that Cressida's turning to her new lover was less final than her soliloquy made it sound. Her self-division persists. But whatever feeling she now claims for Troilus is beyond interpretation, in a letter we never hear, in words (Hamlet's "words, words, words") that for Troilus are meaningless. In a touch that recalls Titus' image of a woman's words blown in the wind, the final glimpse of the love affair is torn, scattered paper, the fragmentation of Cressida literalized, and (it may be) left on stage to be kicked about by the feet of warriors through the next few scenes.

It looks like a decisive ending for the love plot. But we may sense behind the torn letter the damaged body of Lavinia, which marked not an ending but the beginning of a new effort of interpretation. As Lavinia's story ends without our feeling that we have a final reading of her, the cynicism of this ending, drawing as it does on the perspective of Thersites (who does not, we should notice, get the play's last word, however hard he tries to act as its chorus), should feel reductive. We cannot say "This was Cressida" and leave it at that. We should still be curious to read the letter, frustrated that we cannot. And as Troilus imagines a radical split in Cressida, there is sharp division in the way the war story ends. "Hector is dead. There is no more to say"; but there is. In the early scenes, alternating between an active phase of combat and a "dull and long-continued truce" (I.iii.262) we ask: is this war on or not?[21] At the end we ask, is this war over or not? V.x ends with Agamemnon's line, reacting to the death of Hector, "Great Troy is ours, and our sharp wars are ended" (10). V.xi begins with Aeneas – who stands for the future of Troy, beyond its destruction – ordering, "Stand ho! Yet are we masters of the field."

He does not yet know of the death of Hector. Troilus brings that news, and calls on the gods to make an end:

> Sit, gods, upon your thrones and smite at Troy!
> I say at once: let your brief plagues be mercy,
> And linger not our sure destructions on! (V.xi.7–9)

After Aeneas rebukes him, "My lord, you do discomfort all the host," he simply denies what he has said, and turns from despair to defiance:

> You understand me not that tell me so.
> I do not speak of flight, of fear, of death,
> But dare all imminence that gods and men
> Address their dangers in. (V.xi.10–14)

The jagged alternations of despair and defiance, as rapid as Hector's change of front, as volatile as Cressida's shifting tactics, continue through the scene. The play ends as it began, in the divided mind of Troilus. It ends by not ending, lacking the closure of his death.[22]

Except that this play seems to have as many endings as a Sibelius symphony.[23] Pandarus reappears to speak the epilogue.[23] In a final link between the love plot and the war plot, his diseased body recalls the putrefied corpse Hector found inside the glittering armour.[24] His diseases may be a displaced version of the tradition that Cressida (as in Henryson's *Testament of Cresseid*) contracted leprosy, and in that way he brings Cressida on to the stage yet again. Given that his sexual life seems to consist entirely of looking, commenting and imagining, was that how he was infected? And given that looking, commenting (and sometimes imagining) is what we have been doing through the play, are we at risk? We are in a crowded theatre, and Pandarus' final promise to bequeath us his diseases should make us nervous. As Troilus is implicated in the divided Cressida he watches in V.ii., we may be implicated too. We too watched, commented and interpreted. Registering the self-division of "this is and is not Cressid" – the self-division she shares with other characters – we may have been, like Troilus, betraying our own divided natures. Perhaps Thersites, whose curses, an elaborate extension of "A plague o' both your houses," call down disease on all parties, has had the last word after all and we ourselves are infected. We may protect ourselves by imagining that "Brethren and sisters of the hold-door trade" (V.xi.51) means Pandarus is addressing only a small section of the audience; but I think its real force is "hypocrite lecteur! – mon semblable, – mon frère!" The play, which breaks generic boundaries, ends by breaking the boundary that separates stage and audience.

If we are implicated in the tragedy – and is that finally too strong a word for a play in which people are destroyed before our eyes without the relief of dying? – it is because of our action as audience. The love-war conflict that tears the men apart may be confined, like Romeo's, within the play. But the action of reading and possibly misreading Cressida, performed by the men in the play, is our action too – as it was in the cases of Lavinia, Ophelia and Gertrude. As the feud pervades the love affair of *Romeo and Juliet*, interpretation pervades the love affair here, and in its own way it is just as damaging. We do not have to watch the rape of Lavinia, though we watch (and share) the men's struggles to read her afterwards. We have to watch violation of another kind, Cressida being kissed by the Greeks; then we see her flirting with Diomedes. From our own struggles to read those scenes and to decide whether to accept or resist the onstage readings (including, finally, Cressida's own) we come to share the play's sense of the instability of meaning, value and identity – and of how easily the latter in particular can be broken. Shakespeare's next experiment in tragedy will replace the general instability that centers on Cressida with the firm loyalty and chastity embodied in Desdemona; and the act of interpretation, about which we have doubts here and in *Hamlet*, will turn openly malignant.

CHAPTER 5

Othello: *I took you for that cunning whore of Venice*

INTERPRETING A MARRIAGE

Othello begins not just with the elopement of Othello and Desdemona but with the readings imposed on that elopement by Iago and Brabantio. We know what they think of it before we ourselves have a clear view of what has happened;[1] and what they see is an act of violation as shocking in its own way as what happens to Lavinia. Iago warns Brabantio that his house has been broken into: "Look to your house, your daughter and your bags! / Thieves, thieves!" (I.i.79). Brabantio's "How got she out?" (I.i.167) suggests that for Desdemona to have left the house at all is an outrage. Iago's order to Roderigo to raise the sort of clamor that is made "when by night and negligence the fire / Is spied in populous cities" (I. i.75–76) makes the elopement sound like a threat to the whole city. The stage picture confirms this sense of disruption, as Brabantio enters in his nightgown, accompanied by servants with torches, an old man dragged out of his bed at midnight. As the assault on Lavinia is also a Gothic assault on Rome, the attack on Brabantio's house seems linked with the political action: the Duke and Senators are also called up at night to deal with the impending Turkish attack on Cyprus. The Turks threaten a Venetian possession; Desdemona is a local girl carried off by an alien. She and Othello (like Tamora and Aaron) have crossed what a later age would call the color bar, and the racial insults begin when Roderigo calls Othello "the thicklips" (I.i.65) as though he cannot stand the thought of a black man kissing Desdemona.

Iago takes this farther, seeing a violation of kinds, a breaking of the barrier between one species and another. In the process he raises a fundamental question of identity. He bypasses the matter of names. The question is not, is this Othello? or is this Desdemona? The question is, are they human? "Even now, now, very now, an old black ram is tupping your white ewe" (I.i.87–88); "You'll have your daughter covered with a Barbary horse" (I.i.109–10). In the first image both partners are animals, and the outrage centers on the differences of age and color, differences that also operate in the human sphere. In that way both figures remain human, and the insult is metaphoric. In the second image the outrage deepens: Desdemona is a woman, "your daughter," copulating with a horse. Finally they become a single animal: "your daughter and the Moor are now making the beast with two backs" (I.i.114–15). Lavinia is reduced to a nameless thing, Cressida to a blank. Othello and Desdemona become not nameless or blank but all too clear: copulating animals whose relationship violates the normal, breaking the barriers of race, age and even species as Brabantio's house is violated.

Brabantio's view of Desdemona is unsettled in a more immediate and personal way. Titus' claim that he could read Lavinia left us, and at times Titus himself, uncertain. Brabantio thought he could read Desdemona; now he finds his daughter is a stranger, someone he never knew at all. She was "A maiden never bold" (I.iii.95) and now she has done this. She was "so opposite to marriage that she shunned / The wealthy, curled darlings of our nation" (I.ii.67–68). Now, instead of choosing a nice young Venetian, she has fallen in love "with what she feared to look on" (I.iii.99). What looked like proper restraint now seems a rejection of the normal. Of all the shocks Brabantio has to absorb, the one he finally fixes on is that Desdemona has deceived him. He once loved Othello and invited him into his house; in his last words to him (and his last words in the play) he warns him, man to man: "Look to her, Moor, if thou hast eyes to see: / She has deceived her father, and may thee" (I.iii.293–94). He does not question her identity in so many words, as Troilus does with Cressida. But in his sense that she is not the woman he thought she was the question of identity is latent; and it will come to the surface in Othello's ironic apology to the woman who is standing in front of him insisting on her chastity:

> I cry you mercy then,
> I took you for that cunning whore of Venice
> That married with Othello. (V.ii.90–92)

It is an inverted way of saying, as Brabantio does, you are not the woman I thought you were.

The gross imaginings of Iago in the first scene, when Desdemona and Othello have not yet appeared, introduce an obsession with visualizing hidden acts that will return with deadly effect later in the play. So will Brabantio's warning to Othello. But as we move through the opening scenes we realize that the Othello–Brabantio view of the marriage as an act of violation that calls Desdemona's identity into question is simply their interpretation, and open to challenge. Lavinia never clearly speaks for herself; Cressida never constructs a Cressida of her own to challenge the men's view of her. What gives this play a different dynamic is that Desdemona from the beginning has her own firm reading of what she has done. She begins with a straight denial that it is unnatural or abnormal. On the contrary, she has followed a life transition usual in her society: she has left her father and given herself to her husband. After acknowledging briefly "a divided duty" (I.iii.181) she insists she is doing no more than her mother did before her (I.iii.186–89). This may seem disingenuous, given that there is no hint of anything unconventional in her parents' marriage, or of its having been an elopement after a secret courtship;[2] but Desdemona's love of Othello is enough to make what she has done seem normal to her. She has, however, the honesty not to stop there. In referring to "My downright violence and scorn of fortunes" (I.iii.250)[3] she admits that from a conventional viewpoint what she has done is violently disruptive, of her own life if not of Venetian society. She has left her father forever. When the Duke, thinking conventionally, proposes that Desdemona return to her father's house during her husband's stay in Cyprus, Brabantio, Othello and Desdemona all protest and Desdemona acknowledges that her presence would "put my father in impatient thoughts / By being in his eye" (I.iii.243–44). The Duke's proposal reveals another aspect of the risk Desdemona has taken: she has left her father's home to marry a man who has no home. As a natural rite of passage that confirms the social order, marriage is a transition from one house to another; that pattern cannot work here. Desdemona's rejection of her origins is followed by a flight into the unknown.

In a sense Desdemona agrees with Brabantio; she is a new person. But she is the person she wants to be. She both admits and embraces the danger of her marriage. Official Venetian society, in the form of the Duke and the Senate, accepts it. They admire Othello (and need him) and Brabantio is politely but firmly overruled. The Turkish invasion is not, it seems, a simple parallel to Othello's violation of Brabantio's house: Othello is on the side of Venice, and his assignment is to defeat the Turkish enemy. The race hatred directed against him comes not from official society but from voices shouting in the streets in the dark, a kind of spoken graffiti. The view of the marriage as an act of violation begins to look like a misreading, a false start. Yet it is never completely dispelled. The official acceptance of the marriage is not quite decisive; it is hard to separate good will from political expediency, and from the fact that the state has other things on its mind than Brabantio's problem. And we may wonder if society at street level is ever appeased: late in the play, Emilia calls Desdemona's marriage "her most filthy bargain" (V.ii.153).

Another reading of the marriage, as extreme in its idealism as Iago's is in its cynicism, is offered by Cassio when Othello and Desdemona arrive in Cyprus. They have come triumphantly through the storm that has scattered the Turkish fleet, with the suggestion that Othello has beaten the enemy just by showing up. In Cassio's excited, romantic imagination the arrival of Othello and Desdemona on Cyprus is a supernatural event. Desdemona is "divine," circled and protected by the grace of heaven, which is not bestowed on her from above but something at her own level, an aura in which she moves (II.i.73–87). Othello is a life-giving god, coming to

> bless this bay with his tall ship,
> Make love's quick pants in Desdemona's arms,
> Give renewed fire to our extincted spirits
> And bring all Cyprus comfort! (II.i.79–82)

"Love's quick pants" links the speech with the voyeuristic imaginings of the sexual act that run through the play; but this time the emphasis is on breath, the sign of life, and Othello and Desdemona seem like fertility gods whose coupling will renew the community. Their marriage is not a side-issue in the victory over the Turks; it symbolizes and confirms that victory. This of course is Cassio's interpretation, as the beast with two backs was Iago's interpretation. What for Iago was beneath the normal order is for Cassio above it. In the move from the opening scene to the arrival on Cyprus the marriage that disrupted society now renews it, and what was unnatural is now supernatural. The common factor is that Othello and Desdemona are watched, commented on, subject to interpretation; and there lies the danger that will destroy them.

LOVE AND WAR

Brabantio and Iago see in the marriage of Othello and Desdemona a collision of opposites: black and white, Venetian and alien, age and youth. What Othello sees is a complementary partnership of opposites. They have sought each other out not despite their difference but because of it, each partner needing the other to supply a lack: "She loved me for the dangers I had passed / And I loved her that she did pity them"

(I.iii.168–69). In both views the marriage is founded on difference, and as the play goes on Othello's sense of the rightness of that foundation will be eroded, and the Iago–Brabantio view will re-emerge. From the beginning, we see the potential for trouble. Complementary opposites are still opposites, their linking requires negotiation, and for each partner there is not just something gained but something lost. Desdemona has lost security, and accepts the loss. Othello, in whose life story as he recounts it there are no cities or buildings, is giving up his open-air freedom, and is aware of making a sacrifice:

> But that I love the gentle Desdemona
> I would not my unhoused free condition
> Put into circumscription and confine
> For the sea's worth. (I.ii.25–28)

Desdemona is housebound, constantly drawn away from Othello's story by "the house affairs" (I.iii.148). To her, Othello's world is fascinating in its sheer otherness; to Othello the otherness of Desdemona's world is a source of unease. Apologizing to the Senate for his inability as an orator, he claims he has the language of war but is "little blest with the soft phrase of peace" (I.iii.83). It is an early hint of danger: he is moving into a world in which he feels inadequate.

The opposition of war and love we saw in *Troilus and Cressida* returns here. Cassio's dismissal of Bianca shows a conventional separation of the two spheres:

> I do attend here on the general
> And think it no addition, nor my wish,
> To have him see me womaned. (III.iv.193–95)

We think back to the Senate scene, and the Duke's assumption that Desdemona will stay home while Othello goes to war. Yet Desdemona insists on going, and this becomes the first source of tension within the marriage. It immediately puts Othello on the defensive. He has to assure the Senate that he can put his marriage on hold while he attends to war, and that if he failed to do so he would be not just unmanned but ridiculous: "Let housewives make a skillet of my helm" (I.iii.273). Like Romeo and Troilus he is open to the question: what is he, a lover or a fighter? (What is Pyramus, a lover or a tyrant?) Othello seems at first to have not just a secure sense of himself as a warrior but a confidence that he can play both roles because he knows how to rank them. Though newly married, he puts business first, telling Desdemona

> I have but an hour
> Of love, of worldly matter and direction
> To spend with thee. We must obey the time. (I.iii.299–301)

The time they must obey, as he sees it, is a time not of marriage but of war. She seems taken aback, as he is not, by the news that they must leave that night (I.iii.278–79). It is significant that they do not journey to Cyprus together. Othello goes first, while Iago stays behind to deal with the paperwork, and Desdemona (ominously) travels with Iago.

Love and war are separate, and Othello puts war first. He assures the Senate that though he would like his wife to be with him, it is not for any reason so low as sexual desire:

> I therefore beg it not
> To please the palate of my appetite,
> Nor to comply with heat, the young affects
> In me defunct, and proper satisfaction,
> But to be free and bounteous to her mind. (I.iii.262–66)

The heat and appetite associated with sex in *Troilus and Cressida* are not for him; he is too old. Desdemona may have other ideas. Her language is decorous, but her complaint that if she stays behind "The rites for which I love him are bereft me" (I.iii.258) sounds like a claim to the rites of the marriage bed. As Catherine Bates points out, Othello is going to Aphrodite's island, a dangerously female space in which his carefully constructed self will break apart.[4] Sex will become an obsession, and Desdemona's sexuality not a matter of indifference but a nightmare. The impossibility of Othello's maintaining an orderly division in his life is suggested when what appears to be his wedding night is interrupted by a brawl in the streets, and like Brabantio he is dragged out of bed, the bridegroom forced to be the general, the rites of love disrupted.[5] It is suggested again in IV.i when the disruption goes the other way: trying to do state business with Lodovico, he keeps turning aside to attack Desdemona; the tension runs so high that for the first time in the play he hits her (IV.i.239).

Desdemona compounds the problem by wanting a share in his military life. There is a telling ambiguity in her response to Othello's tales of adventure: "She wished / That heaven had made her such a man" (I.iii.163–64): she wants not just to have a man like this but to be a man like this. In her new life, with the landmarks of family and household removed, she aspires to a different, masculine identity. It is her own idea that she should accompany her husband to war. Othello allows her a share in his triumphant arrival on Cyprus, greeting her as "my fair warrior" (II.i.180); she will later see herself as betraying that role by thinking ill of him: "unhandsome warrior as I am" (III.iv.152).

It may seem that while Othello (with some difficulty) can literally be a lover as well as a warrior, Desdemona can be a warrior only in the realm of metaphor. In the stock thinking of the time, it was a grave impropriety for wives to follow their husbands to war; their role was to look after the home.[6] But Desdemona has no home, except with Othello; she must share his life. Her unconventional role as a military wife on the scene of action, like her unconventional marriage, gives her a chance for initiative most women would not have and seems admirable or improper according the speaker's interpretation. Cassio's complimentary reference to her as "our great captain's captain" (II.i.74) picks up her desire for a male identity; it shades into Iago's less complimentary "our general's wife is now the general" (II.iii.309–10). Ultimately, Iago sees her not as an honorary man but as all too much a woman, as her stronger sexuality destroys Othello's manhood:

> His soul is so enfettered to her love
> That she may make, unmake, do what she list,
> Even as her appetite shall play the god
> With his weak function. (II.iii.340–43)

Everything Othello promised the Senate would not happen has, according to Iago, come to pass, and this speech is an important move in his plot. It leads Cassio to play on Desdemona's interest in having a role in her husband's public life, with the result that she advises him to reappoint the lieutenant he had sacked for good military reasons. She does not just advise him but in a teasing, affectionate way, bullies him, as though she were indeed the captain's captain. She not only interferes with his public role but crowds him to the point where he has to beg, "leave me but a little to myself" (III.iii.85).

Seen in the most positive light, the marriage of Othello and Desdemona is a celebration of difference: their difference from the conventional world, their difference from each other. They are exceptional people in an exceptional relationship. Yet in taking them away from the norm, that relationship gives them new identities that are more troubling than liberating. Othello the lover keeps interfering with Othello the soldier. So does Desdemona the warrior. It is not so easy to be different in a society founded on conventional expectations of gender, and in their difference from convention lies the fear that the exceptional cannot be sustained. This fear, that "not another comfort like to this / Succeeds in unknown fate" (II.i.190–91), touches Othello in his triumphant arrival on Cyprus. It may explain why he declares, "When I love thee not / Chaos is come again" (III.iii.91–92); when, not if. He has a soldier's eye for trouble, knowing that to be on the heights is to be dangerously exposed.

IAGO AS READER

That the exceptional cannot be sustained is one of Iago's key ideas. In its service he casts people in stock roles, and he turns the delicate balance of opposites in Othello and Desdemona's marriage into mere incompatibility, bound to end in disaster. He speaks for the conventional world, he insists on the predictable, and he deals in generalizations.[7] Like Hamlet, Ulysses and Thersites, he generalizes particularly about women:

> Come on, come on, you are pictures out of doors,
> Bells in your parlours, wild-cats in your kitchens,
> Saints in your injuries, devils being offended,
> Players in your houswifery, and houswifes in . . .
> Your beds! (II.i.109–13; ellipsis in original)

On this subject he is a scrapbook of old jokes, and when he shows off by improvising verses on subjects thrown to him by his audience he is performing one of the stock routines of an Elizabethan clown. He is equally predictable on the subject of marriage. All that sex gets boring after a while, and when "the blood is made dull with the act of sport" (II.i.224–25) Desdemona "must change for youth"; "she must have change, she must" (I.iii.350, 352). That "must," insisted on defensively, is (like Cressida's view of erosion through time) the inevitability of nature, the way of the world. As for Othello, "These Moors are changeable in their wills" (I.iii.347). The plural says it all.

While the generalizations of Hamlet are a way of coping with a world that seems unreadable, the generalizations of Iago are a compensation for the mess inside. He reads the world confidently, but when in soliloquy he reports the workings of his own mind he descends into a fog of uncertainty and innuendo:

> I hate the Moor
> And it is thought abroad that 'twixt my sheets
> He's done my office. I know not if't be true,
> But I for mere suspicion in that kind
> Will do as if for surety. (I.iii.385–89)

A clear, public motive with its basis in known fact (he was passed over for promotion) is replaced by a private motive in a hidden world of sexual relations where gossip replaces knowledge and certainty is impossible. As Troilus' "This is and is not Cressid" reflects a split in himself, when Iago makes Othello feel the corrosive power of uncertainty he is making Othello mirror his own mind. Later he will throw in Cassio as an afterthought – "I fear Cassio with my night-cap too" (II.i.305) – as though once his mind has started he cannot shut it off until he has imagined all the ways he could be injured.[8]

The generalizations about women that give him such confidence when speaking to others, turned inward, work against him and make his mind a whirlpool of suspicion. Faced with Desdemona, the exceptional woman, he literally does not know what he feels:

> Now I do love her too,
> Not out of absolute lust, though peradventure
> I stand accountant for as great a sin –
> But partly led to diet my revenge. . . . (II.i.289–92)

Peradventure, partly; he cannot lock a single feeling into place. He emerges from the muddle with the notion that he will cuckold Othello as Othello has cuckolded him (293–97), but even that degree of control over his feelings for Desdemona vanishes as this plot is swallowed up by other possible plots. She provokes a jumble of feelings – lust, revenge, and whatever he might mean by love – leaving him unable to read himself. He will turn Desdemona into a problem of interpretation for Othello; he reacts to her first as a problem in interpreting himself.[9]

He seems to steady himself by turning to action. There is a note of relief when he manages to hatch a plot: "I have't!" (I.iii.402); "ay, that's the way!" (II.iii.382). But while he is clear about his tactics he is curiously vague about what he actually hopes to accomplish. Unable to cope even with the thought of Desdemona, he backs away from the idea of sleeping with her, a purpose that erodes as soon as he talks about it:

> nothing can or shall content my soul
> Till I am evened with him, wife for wife . . .
> Or, failing so, yet that I put the Moor
> At least into a jealousy so strong
> That judgment cannot cure. . . .
> (II.i.296–300; first ellipsis in original)

Make Othello jealous – is that all? "At least" implies something more, but what? When he says of Desdemona that he will "out of her own goodness make the net / That shall enmesh them all" (II.iii.356–57) the method is clear but the end is a generalized image of entrapment. When he declares "'Tis here, but yet confused: / Knavery's plain face is never seen, till used" (II.i.309–10) it amounts to saying, I'll know what I'm doing when I've done it.

As Othello needs Iago to teach him the ways of the world and the "truth" about his marriage, Iago needs Othello to give specific form to his generalized need to destroy. They are, like Othello and Desdemona, opposites who complete each other. Othello can think of the decisive end that seems to elude Iago's imagination: he tells him to kill Cassio. Iago responds by using reverse psychology to get Othello to kill Desdemona: "But let her live" (III.iii.477). It is as though for the first time he has seen the end of the story, but it takes Othello to get him there. Iago's resentments, feeding on themselves, issuing in no clear action, could go on forever like the gloating voice of Aaron. Once embodied in Othello's acts, Iago's plotting ends in two senses: it is fulfilled, and it is finished. Iago himself is weak at endings. Desdemona taunts him for the banal finish of his clown routine: "O, most lame and impotent conclusion!" (II.i.161). Othello is to kill Desdemona and Iago is to kill Cassio. Othello succeeds; Iago fails. He does not even manage to kill Roderigo. It is as though he hesitates to end because he wants to nurse his resentment forever. It is clear that he wants to torture Othello, not so clear that he wants to kill him. The sexual connotations of "I follow him to serve my turn upon him" (I.i.41) make his abuse of the Moor a parody of the sexual act, something that can be done over and over. (Othello will say of Desdemona, "she can turn, and turn, and yet go on / And turn again" [IV.i.253–54].) The relations of Iago and Othello are not just those of tempter and victim: like Troilus and Cressida they are bound by mutual need, constructing their story together. They come together, like Othello and Desdemona, from opposite poles of thought and experience; but their bond becomes closer than Othello's marriage, and that may be another reason why Iago uses sexual language for it.

Othello is as dangerous to Iago as Iago is to him. Here we turn from the question of Iago's motives – what he wants and why he wants it – to the deeper question of his identity. Iago's "Were I the Moor, I would not be Iago" (I.i.56) sounds cryptic just because its literal meaning is so flatly obvious we sense it has some other meaning we must tease out. What it suggests is a mutual cancellation of identity: Iago invades Othello, changing his nature, only to find he has left himself empty. Something like this happens in the writing of the play, as from III.iii. on Othello gains a terrible energy and Iago seems to diminish. His character is not expressed in action but cancelled in action.

Or does action reveal the self-cancellation that was always there? He tells Roderigo, clearly and simply, that he is not what he appears to be; then he goes one step further: "I am not what I am" (I.i.64). He is trying to get control of the cancellation of his identity, which he attributed to Othello a few lines earlier, by proclaiming it himself. Like "this is and is not Cressid," the statement is an impossibility in which language and meaning, not just identity, are self-cancelled. This time there is a note of blasphemy: Iago is master of the uncreating word, and the "I am" he cancels is the name of God. This is as close as we get to the heart of Iago, pure destruction as God is pure creation, issuing from non-identity, as God is pure identity.

This touches on a crucial point in the interplay of violation and identity. We have seen that acts of violation threaten the identities of Lavinia and Cressida; but it is not just the victims whose identities are called in question. Chiron and Demetrius become not Chiron and Demetrius but Rape and Murder. Perhaps this is what they always were: they tried to take Lavinia's humanity because they themselves were not human. Troilus tries to break Cressida's identity because his own is so deeply split. Othello and Desdemona begin with strongly defined, and opposite, identities, the warrior and the housebound woman; they are drawn together by difference and unsettled by difference. Iago will exploit that uncertainty to give Desdemona a new, fatal identity in Othello's eyes, and to destroy Othello's own identity in the process. The power he has to do this is the destructive power that issues from his own self-cancelled identity. Iago can make Othello take Desdemona for "that cunning whore of Venice" and reduce himself to "he that was Othello" because, as he proclaims of himself, "I am not what I am."

INTERPRETATION AS DAMAGE

Iago began the play by seeing the marriage of Othello and Desdemona as an act of violation. The real act of violation, however, was not the marriage but Iago's interpretation of it. Iago, we have noted, is not a decisive killer in the literal sense. What he does is turn interpretation into a destructive force. Plotting is not his strong point; he is not a playwright but a treacherously powerful critic. When Desdemona arrives on Cyprus, Iago and Roderigo watch Cassio kiss her and take her hand. Roderigo calls it courtesy; Iago calls it lechery (II.i.251–56). Desdemona, like Cressida on her arrival in the Greek camp and in the later eavesdropping scene, is watched and interpreted. This time the commentators disagree, and it is easy enough to take Roderigo's view. Yet Cassio does kiss Desdemona, they do hold hands, and like Cressida and Diomedes they say things we cannot hear. We can see what Iago's interpretation draws on. Commenting on what he claims is Desdemona's wedding night, Iago draws on Desdemona's actual boldness and frankness to replay Ulysses' reading of Cressida, using one of Ulysses' words, "game":

> CASSIO She's a most exquisite lady.
> IAGO And I'll warrant her full of game.
> CASSIO Indeed she's a most fresh and delicate creature.
> IAGO What an eye she has! Methinks it sounds a parley
>   to provocation.
> CASSIO An inviting eye; and yet methinks right modest.
> IAGO And when she speaks is it not an alarum to love?
> (II.iii.18–24)

Again there are competing interpretations, but we can feel Cassio drawn into Iago's reading ("an inviting eye") even as he tries to resist. They are looking at the same attractive woman, disagreeing only about how, and whether, she uses her attraction.

Iago uses Cassio and Roderigo for practice. His real task is to get Othello to reinterpret Desdemona. Though he will eventually dwell on things unseen, he starts with things seen:

> OTHELLO Was not that Cassio parted from my wife?
> IAGO Cassio, my lord? no, sure, I cannot think it
>   That he would steal away so guilty-like
>   Seeing you coming. (III.iii.38–40)

It was Cassio, and they both know it; and he would have been looking embarrassed, though not for the reason Iago will suggest. We see both the dishonesty of Iago's reading and its credibility.

He turns from things seen to things remembered, and from what we have seen to what for us is hearsay. Drawing closely on Brabantio's "She has deceived her father, and may thee" (I.iii.294), Iago declares:

> She did deceive her father, marrying you,
> And when she seemed to shake, and fear your looks,
> She loved them most. (IIII.iii.209–11)

By this account she deceived not only her father, but Othello himself. The last point raises a question. Did she really seem afraid of him? Othello replies, "And so she did" (211); is this a genuine memory or a false one, created by Iago's suggestion? Again Brabantio is at work; Iago is using his claim that Desdemona fell in love with what she feared to look on. Desdemona may have left her father behind, but he is returning to haunt Othello, through Iago in his role as the voice of society. Iago goes on to a more deadly suggestion, still drawing on Brabantio:

> Not to affect many proposed matches
> Of her own clime, complexion and degree,
> Whereto we see, in all things, nature tends –
> Foh! one may smell in such a will most rank,
> Foul disproportion, thoughts unnatural. (III.iii.233–37)

Iago declares, in effect: she must be depraved, she married you. Desdemona's marriage by its very nature carries the guarantee of adultery.[10] The obscene shouting in the streets, the racist insults that set the first crude interpretation of Othello's marriage, are now creeping back, masked as friendly warnings, couched in a new manner of polite regret.

Armed with our own knowledge of Desdemona, we resist. But on the news, which again Iago interprets in his own way, that Cassio acted as a go-between for the lovers (III.iii.70–74), we may be taken aback. There was at first no inkling of this. What else is there that we did not know? Iago begins, in his dealings with Roderigo and Cassio, with glib certainties. He goes on, in his dealings with Othello, to doubt and indecision, to provoking questions he refuses to answer, to hinting at the unseen. His initial strategy is not to tell Othello anything but to refuse to tell him, letting words like "honest," "think," and "indeed" bounce back as though they had hit a wall, leaving Othello to imagine what might be on the other side of that wall:

> thou echo'st me
> As if there were some monster in thy thought
> Too hideous to be shown. (III.iii.109–11)

To see the unseen will become his obsession, and Iago begins by refusing to let him see the monster. Then he relents. What he has been concealing is the green-eyed monster jealousy, and he lets Othello see it by warning him against it, giving him an image of what it is like to be jealous: "But O, what damned minutes tells he o'er / Who dotes yet doubts, suspects, yet strongly loves!" (III.iii.171–72). The result for Othello is an intolerable double reality, the equivalent of "This is and is not Cressid":[11]

> I think my wife be honest, and think she is not,
> I think that thou art just, and think thou art not.
> I'll have some proof. (III.iii.387–89)

As Troilus, playing on her insecurity, warned Cressida against falsehood and thereby gave Cressida a clear image of herself which she proceeded to act out, so Iago, warning Othello against jealousy, tells him what it will be like, giving him an image of himself as a jealous man which he proceeds to act out to the letter. In doing so he has created the position from which Othello will see Desdemona, and in turn himself.

LOOKING

Iago's first direct move echoes Brabantio: "Look to your wife, observe her well with Cassio" (III.iii.200). This picks up Othello's own resolution: "I'll see before I doubt" (III.iii.193), as though to see is to settle the matter. But as Othello's nightmare progresses he becomes anxious to see things he cannot see, anxious about what others have seen that was hidden from him. He asks Emilia, "You have seen nothing, then?" (IV.ii.1), clearly disbelieving her. An obsession with seeing runs through this play: things seen, like the handkerchief, things unseen but imagined, like Othello and Desdemona, then Desdemona and Cassio, making the beast with two backs. Seeing is believing, but more important for this play, believing is seeing.[12] This goes beyond the gaze directed at an onstage figure we have seen in *Titus*, *Hamlet* and *Troilus*. Now the gaze creates the figure.

As he wants to see, and finally does see, the monster in Iago's thought, Othello wants to see Cassio and Desdemona in the act: "give me the ocular proof"; "Make me to see't" (III.iii.363, 367). Iago obliges. Even as he tells Othello it is impossible to see what he wants, he makes him see not only the act but himself looking on: "Would you, the supervisor, grossly gape on? / Behold her topped?" (III.iii.398–99). The desire to look is itself corrupt; to the guilt of the act is added the guilt of the onlooker. Just because it is shameful, voyeurism has a guilty fascination, and a few simple words are all it takes to get a pornographic movie running in Othello's mind. Iago adds to the word "lie," "With her, on her, what you will" (IV.i.34). "With her" is simply an idea; "on her" creates the picture. "What you will" reminds Othello that this sight, which he cannot stand, is precisely the thing he wants. He is falling in love, like Desdemona, with what he fears to look on.

Iago is never far from blasphemy, and at one point he makes even God a voyeur: "In Venice they do let God see the pranks / They dare not show their husbands" (III.iii.205–6). The omniscient deity is a peeping Tom. Nor is the audience immune. We are not omniscient, and this turns us, as it turns Othello, to imagining the hidden. The play is full of unseen events about which we have to speculate,[13] and a question that recurs obsessively in criticism is, was the marriage of Othello and Desdemona ever consummated, and if so, when? The strongest evidence seems to put the consummation on the first night in Cyprus. Othello tells Desdemona, "The purchase made, the fruits are to ensue: / That profit's yet to come 'tween me and you" (II.iii.9–10). Iago puts it in his own way: "he hath not yet made wanton the night with her, and she is sport for Jove" (II.iii.16–17). (Given Jove's tendency to consummate his affairs in animal form, does the compliment conceal a reference back to the bestial images of the opening scene?) The couple are dragged out of bed by the street brawl, and the crude question arises: did they manage to do anything? They enter not just separately, but with attendants (II.iii.159.1, 244.1). Were they interrupted at an intimate moment or not? Looking back, did they really not manage consummation in Venice? Iago characteristically provides evidence that works against his own later statement in Cyprus, telling Cassio, "he tonight hath boarded a land carrack" (I.ii.50). How literally do we take the bawdy suggestion? Critics divide. The marriage is consummated in Venice;[14] it is consummated in Cyprus;[15] it is never consummated.[16] According to Michael Neill such arguments mirror "with disturbing fidelity the habit of obsessive speculation about concealed offstage action, into which the play entraps the viewer as it entraps its characters."[17] We find ourselves thinking about what Othello and Desdemona have done or not done, as Othello himself thinks about Desdemona and Cassio. At the end of *Troilus and Cressida* we were threatened with Pandarus' diseases. Now we seem to have caught Othello's. If we thought that whatever harm Iago does in the play we at least were safe from him, we have to think again.

Iago plays on Othello's need to see by his graphic account of sleeping with Cassio, who, dreaming he is with Desdemona, grips Iago's hand, kisses him and lays his leg over his thigh (III.iii.416–28). This is the scene Othello wants and fears, displaced several times: a report, a dream, and ultimately (we assume) a lie. But as a heterosexual love scene played by two male actors it evokes the performance conventions of Shakespeare's theatre, and prepares us for an encounter that actually takes place on stage, before our eyes and Othello's. In a scene Othello watches but cannot hear, leaving him free to interpret the language of gesture, Cassio not only describes how Bianca embraced him and tugged at him, but demonstrates it, impersonating Bianca and casting Iago as himself:

CASSIO . . .thither comes the bauble and, by this hand, falls me
   thus about my neck –
OTHELLO Crying 'O dear Cassio!' as it were: his gesture
   imports it.
CASSIO So hangs and lolls and weeps upon me, so shakes and
   pulls me! Ha, ha, ha!
OTHELLO Now he tells how she plucked him to my chamber.
                                                (IV.i.134–41)

What was narrative and speculation now becomes drama acted out in front of him. He becomes disconcertingly like a theatre audience, interpreting what he sees, filling in the dialogue of the dumb-show. Like an audience reading the actor as the character, he reads Cassio as Desdemona, not knowing he is really playing Bianca. In his own mind, his interpretation is powerful enough that he has now seen what at first he could only imagine.

In a later scene he turns to the real Desdemona and looks intently at her, interpreting what he sees, making her like Lavinia and Cressida a blank sheet on which he makes his own markings: "Was this fair paper, this most goodly book / Made to write 'whore' upon?" (IV.ii.72–73). The obscene scribble is his own, and he is not filling in a blank page but spoiling an image of purity. As the gaze gets more intimate he invites her to return it: "Let me see your eyes. / Look in my face" (IV.ii.25–26). As he contemplates her body, which he claims he has made the center of his life, he projects on to it his own blackness, reading that blackness as Brabantio and Iago have done, as a symbol of foulness:

> there where I have garnered up my heart,
> Where either I must live or bear no life,
> The fountain from the which my current runs
> Or else dries up – to be discarded thence!
> Or keep it as a cistern for foul toads
> To knot and gender in! Turn thy complexion there,
> Patience, thou young and rose-lipped cherubin,
> Ay, here look, grim as hell! (IV.ii.58–65)

The Quarto and Folio texts both print the last line as "I here looke grim as Hell," and we can hear that reading through the modernized version, as Othello's gaze turns to himself. To look grim as hell is to look black, like a devil. Othello cannot stop at the idea that he has been cut off from the source of his life, and simply discarded. He returns to the source and transforms it to a cistern full of copulating toads. Toads are black, and have devilish associations. (Aaron's child was described as a toad.) It is not enough that he can no longer drink from the fountain; he poisons it, and the poison is himself.

Othello has never shown Aaron's pride in his blackness. There is no one in this play to insist as Aaron does that black is beautiful. When Othello proclaims his faith in Desdemona by declaring "she had eyes and chose me" (III.iii.192) he implies that his appearance is a disability her love was able to overcome. She herself has said as much: "I saw Othello's visage in his mind" (I.iii.253). Black, it seems, is not beautiful. Both characters have accepted a color-coding we recognize as conventional to their society, expressed – naturally – by Iago: "So will I turn her virtue into pitch" (II.iii.355). What Othello sees in Desdemona now that he has rewritten her is his own visage:

> Her name, that was as fresh
> As Dian's visage, is now begrimed and black
> As my own face. (III.iii.389–91)[18]

Since she is the source of his life, what he sees in her corruption is his own.[19] The mutually attractive otherness that drew them together has collapsed into shared blackness, shared guilt. Troilus projected his own split reality on to Cressida; and we do not have to buy into the color-prejudice embodied in the imagery to take the point that what Othello sees when he gazes at Desdemona is the contamination of his own thought. Desdemona herself disappears.

THE TRAGEDY OF THE HANDKERCHIEF

Reading has become solipsism. What Othello sees when he stares at Desdemona is what he himself has put there; it was, in turn, put into his own mind by Iago; and Iago in turn was making Othello imitate his own obsessive jealousy. It is all in the mind, and Othello's demand for ocular proof leads to the creation of a series of vivid but imaginary pictures. Iago needs evidence more material than this. Desdemona, as we shall see, has a voice of her own and can fight off others' interpretations of her. She can even dispel Othello's fantasy, though not for long. But the handkerchief is a physical object. It is also voiceless and lifeless, with no way of resisting whatever interpretations the characters may offer. And over it, interpretation runs wild.

As Lavinia's rape is a hidden injury that remains unseen until she finds words for it herself, Desdemona's chastity is a hidden virtue that no amount of assertion can prove. Iago admits that knowledge of a woman's chastity is impossible, and that since honor can mean reputation or a physical state a woman can be honorable and dishonorable at once; but an external symbol can make all clear:

> Her honour is an essence that's unseen,
> They have it very oft that have it not.
> But for the handkerchief – (IV.i.16–18)

As Yorick's skull can solidify the idea of death for Hamlet, the handkerchief can solidify Desdemona's honor, or dishonor, for Othello. If she has it she is chaste; if she has given it away she is not.

Its actual role in the drama is not so simple. It begins with a horn-joke. Othello complains, "I have a pain upon my forehead, here" (III.iii.288). It is the old joke, from Iago's world, from the stock comic plotting this play daringly transmutes into tragedy. Desdemona offers to cure the headache by binding his brow with her handkerchief; what will be a cause of jealousy begins as a possible cure for it. But nothing can restrain the growth of Othello's horns. He replies, "Your napkin is too little" (III. iii.291). He does not seem to recognize the object as anything special; it is just "your napkin." Then he says, "Let it alone" (III.iii.292). It is on the ground and he tells her not to pick it up. What happened? Did he push it away? Did he drop it himself? Did she? Who, in fact, is responsible for losing it?[20] The ideal staging would be one in which the audience, distracted at the key moment, did not notice, and afterwards could not remember any more than Desdemona can (III.iv.23). Emilia, in conversation with Iago, blames Desdemona: "she let it drop by negligence" (III. iii.315). But blaming Desdemona is a practice the play as a whole discredits, and as we shall see Emilia is accumulating a sense of her own guilt here; it must be a relief to pass some of the blame.

Once lost, the little napkin starts to acquire value. As she picks it up, Emilia declares its meaning for Desdemona:

> she so loves the token
> – For he conjured her she should ever keep it –
> That she reserves it evermore about her
> To kiss and talk to. (III.iii.297–300)

Trying to get it back from Iago, she heightens its importance: "Poor lady, she'll run mad / When she shall lack it" (III.iii.321–22). Othello raises its value beyond the love-token it is for Desdemona, and radically extends its meaning:

> That handkerchief
> Did an Egyptian to my mother give,
> She was a charmer and could almost read
> The thoughts of people. She told her, while she kept it
> 'Twould make her amiable and subdue my father
> Entirely to her love; but if she lost it
> Or made a gift of it, my father's eye
> Should hold her loathed and his spirits should hunt
> After new fancies. (III.iv.57–65)

Its meanings work against each other. Sewed by a sibyl in "prophetic fury" (74), given by a woman to a woman, it is a token of the magic power women hold over men, a love-charm that will hold a man in place. The charmer could do – almost – what Othello wishes he could do, read the thoughts of people.[21] There is no indication that Othello's father even knew his mother had the handkerchief; it is one of those secrets women keep from men.[22]

On the other hand it shows how vulnerable women are: as Brabantio believes Othello could not have won Desdemona except by magic, in the story Othello constructs here a woman cannot hold a man's fidelity except by magic. The exotic myth is touched for a moment by the cynicism about men we shall see in Emilia: the handkerchief guarantees not female chastity but male chastity, and it takes magic to do that. Female chastity comes into play later: "it was dyed in mummy, which the skilful / Conserved of maidens' hearts" (III.iv.76–77). A maiden has preserved her body, but a preserved body is a dead one. In the last scene Othello will see the dead Desdemona as "Cold, cold, my girl, / Even like thy chastity" (V.ii.273–74). Far from playing into the story of the adulterous wife and the deceived husband, the handkerchief as Othello interprets it seems to be pulling away from that story. It is men who stray, and women who try to hold them. Women are still and unmoving, in chastity and in death. Yet we can also read Othello's anxieties here. Women have great power, and can subdue men. They keep secrets from them. Just to keep the handkerchief is a token of loyalty, and women can be loved only if they are loyal ("'Twould make her amiable"). Finally, and most terribly, it is in death that a woman's chastity is preserved; Othello will see Desdemona as chaste only after he has killed her.

We have come a long way from "your napkin is too little." Othello's imagination is running free, both pulling away from his intolerable situation and exploring it. In the last scene he turns the story completely around; the handkerchief was "An antique token / My father gave my mother" (V.ii.214–15). The power and authority are now male; the sibyl and the Egyptian charmer have disappeared. And Othello has killed Desdemona, because she lost the handkerchief he gave her. It has picked up a new, narrower meaning – male power – from the plot in which it has been involved, and lost much of its mystery and complexity. We have already seen its meaning shrink into bawdy innuendo when one cynic gives it to another. Emilia tells Iago "I have a thing for you" and he replies "it is a common thing" (III.iii.305–6). When Cassio gives it to Bianca to take the work out, it triggers her jealousy as it triggers Othello's, but more simply and naturally: "This is some token of a newer friend" (III.iv.181). She throws it back to him, as a sign of her own self-respect. Passed from hand to hand, it suggests how people traffic with each other in the way of the world.

Desdemona's insistence that it is not lost is a lie and a truth: the literal handkerchief is lost, but the loyalty Othello makes it symbolize is not. Her line "It is not lost, but what an if it were?" (III.iv.85) virtually summarizes the play. The fantasy Iago constructs for Othello to turn into action explores the consequences of "what if"; the main statement, "It is not lost," is the reality of Desdemona's chastity that grounds the play. Taking it, as Othello seems to be doing, as a sign of her honesty, she can say "It is not lost." Literally it is lost; but this time the fact is meaningless and the interpretation is the reality. The play's usual procedure, in which interpretation is a terrible error, is thrown into reverse.

The handkerchief works for and against Iago, creating a false picture of Desdemona's guilt and finally a true picture of his own. It is Emilia, who steals it at the beginning, making it a vehicle for falsehood, who turns it to truth at the end. She has her own tragedy. Stealing the handkerchief and giving it to Iago, knowing what it means to Desdemona, is a serious betrayal, and she knows it. When Desdemona asks about it she tells a flat lie: "I know not, madam" (III.iv.24). She is onstage when Othello challenges Desdemona about the handkerchief, she must see the consequences of what she has done, and she says nothing. As she steals it, we hear a voice that has been heard throughout human history:

> what he will do with it
> Heaven knows, not I,
> I nothing, but to please his fantasy. (III.iii.301–3)

I don't want to know, I'm only following orders. She may even anticipate the story Othello constructs in which the handkerchief is the way a woman can hold a man. She steals it because her "wayward husband" (III.iii.296) has asked her to; now he may be less wayward.

We may be tempted to cover for Emilia, whose brusque common sense makes her the play's most engaging character, by saying that in the rush of the story we do not think about her responsibility. But at the end, as Desdemona lies dead, Emilia reveals that she has thought about it herself, and should have acted on her thought: "O villainy! / I thought so then: I'll kill myself for grief!" (V.ii.188–89). She has an inkling of how Iago used the handkerchief, even before the truth comes out. When Othello reveals that the handkerchief was his evidence, she blurts out the whole story. Iago, drawing on a stock view of women's responsibilities, tells her to be quiet and go home (V.ii.179, 193). But Emilia has a deeper sense of her responsibility than that. When she says, "Perchance, Iago, I will ne'er go home" (V.ii.194), she is both declaring an end to her marriage and implying that after what she is about to say she does not expect to get out of the room alive. She says it, for Desdemona's sake, and Iago kills her. Because of the handkerchief, which in one version of its meaning was supposed to guarantee a woman's hold over a man, two marriages have ended in the husband killing the wife.

The handkerchief is a false sign of Desdemona's betrayal of Othello, but a true sign of Iago's betrayal of him, of Emilia's betrayal of Desdemona, her betrayal of Iago, and her final loyalty to her mistress. For Bianca it is a false sign and a true one; Cassio does not have a new love, as she thinks, but his cavalier attitude to her is betrayal enough, and she is right to suspect him. If as many critics have suggested the strawberry decoration is a sign of virginal blood on the wedding sheets, it should have been symbolic proof of Desdemona's chastity.[23] But Karen Newman tells us that "In cinquecento Venice, possession of a lady's handkerchief was considered proof of adultery and led to stringent punishments." She adds that the strawberry decoration "figures" Desdemona's "sexual parts": nipples, lips, clitoris.[24] By such a reading, to watch the handkerchief passed around is to watch Desdemona passed around like Cressida in the kissing scene, to see Othello's jealous fantasies acted out.

The handkerchief signifies Desdemona's loyalty, and her disloyalty; it is a vehicle for betrayal and for commitment; it figures female power, and male power. And behind the plethora of meanings we can still hear, "Your napkin is too little." Is it, like Fortinbras' patch of Poland, too trivial to carry the weight and complexity of meaning imposed on it? Notoriously, Thomas Rymer thought so. His proposal that this should be called "the *Tragedy of the Handkerchief*" and that the moral of the tragedy was "a warning to all good Wives that they look well to their Linnen" was his way of saying that the token was made to mean too much. For him the Tragedy of the Handkerchief was like the (yet unwritten) Rape of the Lock.[25] He added, with ironic helpfulness, "Had it been *Desdemona's* Garter, the Sagacious *Moor* might have smelt a Rat."[26] As a token of betrayal, a garter would certainly have been clearer and simpler. The tragedy of the handkerchief as Shakespeare wrote it is indeed that it means too much, but not in Rymer's sense. It is a token not of mighty contests rising from trivial things but of a struggle to establish meaning in a world in which reality is broken by conflicting interpretations.

DESDEMONA REPLIES

Desdemona is at the center of that struggle. In that she resembles Lavinia, Cressida, Ophelia and Gertrude. At one point Othello's gaze seems to break her apart. When she insists on her honesty he apologizes for mistaking her: "I took you for that cunning whore of Venice / That married with Othello" (IV.ii.91–92). He has so thoroughly rewritten her that if she is chaste, as she knows she is, then she cannot be herself; and for her to assert her truth is to deny herself, leaving her with no identity at all. But Desdemona is not simply a text to be misread. If the handkerchief embodies the power of interpretation to remake reality, Desdemona embodies the human integrity that resists that power. She has her own voice, and initially at least a firmly grounded sense of herself, as Juliet does. Lavinia is literally denied a voice, and Cressida is too unsure of herself, too inclined to retreat to the conventional wisdom about women that is Iago's stock in trade, to set up a powerful counterinterpretation to the way the men read her. Desdemona on the other hand is clear, resists Iago's interpretation just by being what she is, and throughout the play establishes a powerful counterforce. We have seen her insist on her own reading of her marriage. When she arrives on Cyprus she is coming, like Cressida, into a military encampment, and the entertainment Iago provides in his misogynist clown routine is a version of the welcome Ulysses contrives for Cressida. She has no trouble resisting, and in her mockery she is quite acute about the origins of Iago's thinking: "These are old fond paradoxes to make fools laugh i'th' alehouse" (II.i.139–39).

Faced with Othello's attacks on her, Desdemona fights back. Her response to his obsession with the handkerchief is, "I'faith, you are to blame" (III.iv.98). When he strikes her, she retorts, "I have not deserved this" (IV.i.240). Left briefly alone, she releases anger with a flash of sarcasm:

'Tis meet I should be used so, very meet.
How have I been behaved that he might stick
The small'st opinion on my greatest misuse? (IV.ii.109–11)

Sure of herself, she is bewildered about Othello: "I understand a fury in
your words, / But not the words" (IV.ii.32–33). The question, why is he
talking this way? becomes the question, who is he? This is and is not
Othello: "My lord is not my lord, nor should I know him / Were he in
favour as in humour altered" (III.iv.125–26). His appearance, from being
something to apologize for, has become the only guarantee of his reality.
When Emilia later refers to "my lord," Desdemona does not seem to
know who she means (IV.ii.100–4). Each sees the other's identity breaking
apart, and of the two Desdemona has the greater reason.

Emilia sees what has happened as the way of the world, generalizing
about men as Iago generalizes about women:

> They are all but stomachs, and we all but food:
> They eat us hungerly, and when they are full
> They belch us. (III.iv.105–7)

Desdemona produces a softened and tactful version of Emilia's view,
attributing Othello's strange new mood to a natural dying of kindness
through time, making it seem ordinary:

> Nay, we must think men are not gods
> Nor of them look for such observancy
> As fits the bridal. (III.iv.149–51)

Her later cry, "O these men, these men!" (IV.iii.59) has the same effect of
retreating to a generalization, and a touch of Emilia's voice. This is
one way of coping with Othello. But Desdemona cannot buy completely
into the Iago–Emilia view of men and women. Emilia argues that
men cheat on women, women cheat on men, and turnabout is fair play
(IV.iii.85–102). Something of this drifts into Desdemona's misremem-
bered version of the willow song: "If I court moe women, you'll couch
with moe men" (IV.iii.56). But this view denies Desdemona's sense of
herself. When she is more in control she refuses to believe there are
women who would betray their husbands (IV.iii.60–68). Her refusal
seems naive and overdone; but she is clinging her sense of her own
chastity and trying to buttress it with a generalization of her own. She is
not exceptional, not alone; half the human race is like her.

Troilus insisted on his own truth, to make it stand out against the
falsehood of Cressida. Desdemona not only insists that she has all women

on her side, but, torn between resistance and acceptance, starts to rewrite
Othello as he has rewritten her:

> My love doth so approve him
> That even his stubbornness, his checks, his frowns
> – Prithee unpin me – have grace and favour. (IV.iii.17–19)

She reinterprets him through her love as he reinterprets her through his
jealousy, seeing beauty in his ugly conduct as he sees the foulness in her
beauty. As she says this she is undressing for bed, the bed in which he will
kill her. The word "approve" returns in her revision of the willow song:
"Let nobody blame him, his scorn I approve," which she herself recognizes as a slip: "Nay, that's not next" (IV.iii.51–52). (The actual line is "Let
nobody blame me, her scorns I do prove": just the opposite.) The more
unguarded she becomes, letting Emilia unpin her, letting words drift
through her mind, the more she seems to be moving, Cressida-like,
towards an acceptance of Othello's view of her – or at least towards the
conventional role of the Griselda figure, patiently putting up with abuse, a
role that up to now she has refused to play. Her sense of her own integrity
seems in danger of fading.

In the murder scene Desdemona fights back, verbally and physically.
But after her apparent death, she revives long enough to speak of her
own murder, and proclaims a double reality. Speaking from the border
of life and death, she at once resists and accepts what Othello has done.
"O falsely, falsely murdered" and "A guiltless death I die" (V.ii.115, 121) are
the words of the Desdemona who could say "I have not deserved this."
But when Emilia asks her to name her killer and she replies, "Nobody. I
myself. Farewell. / Commend me to my kind lord" (V.ii.122–23) we hear
the Desdemona of the willow song. Iago's "I am not what I am" is self-
cancellation. Othello's "I think my wife be honest, and think she is
not," like Troilus' "This is and is not Cressid," is unbearable bewilderment. Desdemona declares two contradictory realities, each one set out
separately, each asserted at full strength. One is her knowledge of her
innocence: there Othello stands condemned. The other is her love for
him: there, as in Cordelia's "No cause, no cause," the offense never
occurred, and he is innocent. What guilt there is she takes on herself.
For a moment this seems to involve the cancellation of Othello's identity:
Desdemona was killed by "Nobody." Then "Nobody" is succeeded by
"my kind lord." In two lines she has obliterated him, then re-made him.

If we are tempted to take her second view as a lie or a fantasy, the
savagery of Othello's "She's like a liar gone to burning hell: / 'Twas I that

killed her" (V.ii.127–28) makes us think again. A truth so stated is a truth we feel bound to reject. Othello, as we have seen, cannot live with contradictory realities, and has to come down on one side. But Desdemona, with her last breath and with none of Troilus' sense of effort, asserts a contradiction and holds it. Throughout the play she has been interpreted, and interpretation has been a deadly assault, a violation of her being. Her responses have been complex and contradictory, and have challenged the audience's own capacity to interpret. By dying on a contradiction Desdemona does not just resist interpretation; she controls and extends it, opposing to its reductiveness a double vision of Othello and of herself.

INTERPRETING A MURDER

As Desdemona produces contradictory readings of her own death, Othello's own view of what he is doing is torn – beginning with shifting plans about the means of killing. At first he wants to use poison. It will allow him to kill Desdemona at a distance, by remote control, and avoid a confrontation. He seems if anything afraid of her: "I'll not expostulate with her, lest her body and beauty unprovide my mind again" (IV.i.201–2). "Again" leads us to think back to moments when that actually happened: when Desdemona walked on stage, and just the sight of her led Othello to declare, "If she be false, O then heaven mocks itself, / I'll not believe it" (III.iii.281–82); when just thinking of her beauty made Othello feel "the pity of it" (IV.i.192–93) and got Iago seriously worried: "Nay, that's not your way" (IV.i.183). But poison satisfies neither Iago's malice nor his sense of drama: he wants Desdemona strangled in her bed, "even the bed she hath contaminated" (IV.i.205). Behind the moral glibness are even more malign thoughts: Iago wants Othello personally committed to the deed, and he wants Desdemona to know who is killing her. As a result the confrontation takes place, and it is as unsettling as Othello feared it would be. Not for the first time, Iago has unleashed a force of whose full power he has no inkling. It is the sheer force of Desdemona's presence.

Othello goes from violent fantasies of dismemberment – "I'll tear her all to pieces!" (III.iii.434); "I will chop her into messes!" (IV.i.197) – to a promise of bloodshed as he sets out to do the deed: "Thy bed, lust-stained, shall with lust's blood be spotted" (V.i.36). The blood on the bed will be a grotesque parody of the blood that proves the bride's virginity on her wedding night. When he enters the chamber, however, her presence

transforms him. He approaches with a new caution and respect the body
he planned to tear to pieces:

> Yet I'll not shed her blood
> Nor scar that whiter skin of hers than snow
> And smooth as monumental alabaster. (V.ii.3–5)

This is no longer the sexual body of his jealous fantasies, glimpsed in the
act of copulation. But it is not Desdemona's natural, living body either.
With a touch of Marcus trying to turn the wounded Lavinia into language, he transforms her into the statue on her own tomb. With the same
words, he celebrates her purity – the white skin, so different from his own
– and freezes her in death. Like his linking of chastity and death in the
myth he constructed around the handkerchief, this shows him trying to
control the disturbance Desdemona's body creates in him, the hot, moist
hand in which he read her sexuality, by fixing her forever as a cold
monument.[27]

But he cannot resist kissing her, and the touch of her lips breaks his
control. Her body resists his attempt to turn it into alabaster. The statue
breathes, and the breath starts the very counterargument he was afraid of:
"O balmy breath, that dost almost persuade / Justice to break her sword!"
(V.ii.16–17). We think back to the quick breathing of love Cassio imagined, and beyond this play to Lear's desperate need for Cordelia's
breath, and the breath that comes from the sculptured Hermione, the
first clue that she is not (or no longer) a statue. Desdemona resists
Othello's reading of her just by breathing, just by being alive. Then she
wakes up, speaks, defends herself, pleads, struggles, and goes on speaking
after her apparent death.[28] Even in death her look continues the confrontation Othello had wanted to avoid:

> When we shall meet at compt
> That look of thine will hurl my soul from heaven
> And fiends will snatch at it. (V.ii.271–73)[29]

She continues to send out contradictory messages: her last words were of
forgiveness, yet now her look judges and condemns him. He tried to fix
her in his imagination as a statue, but the vitality and complexity of
Desdemona in life, her shifting responses to his cruelty, continue beyond
death.

Her resistance opens a division in himself, and his own sense of what he
is doing begins to shift. Though apparently convinced of her guilt, he still
asks her to confess in order to cleanse her soul before death (V.ii.26–32). Is

there a part of him that is unconvinced, that needs to hear her proclaim her own guilt? Her resistance denies him this certainty, and he complains she makes him "call what I intend to do, / A murder, which I thought a sacrifice!' (V.ii.64–65). "Call" is significant: it is important for him not just to do the deed but to find the right name for it, the right interpretation. As a sacrifice, it would cleanse the world by removing an evil from it: "Yet she must die, else she'll betray more men" (V.ii.6). But if she is innocent, the killing is itself an evil. And that is how it looks: the poise and dignity of Othello's opening speech, the priest approaching the altar for a sacrifice, give way to a shouting, violent struggle on the bed that tells us we are watching a murder.

As we have seen before, the question, who is this person? leads to the question, what is this act? A murder, a sacrifice – or, as in the last scene of *Romeo and Juliet*, a grim enactment of a wedding night, the consummation of the marriage Iago and Brabantio presented as itself a violation? Desdemona has asked for her wedding sheets. Othello's threat to stain the bed with blood, and his admission, "when I have plucked the rose / I cannot give it vital growth again" (V.ii.13–14) suggest taking her virginity. Her painfully innocent question, "Will you come to bed, my lord?" (V.ii.24) not only implies she is expecting him, after so much bewildering anger, to make love; it acquires an extra dimension if we assume the marriage has not been consummated. To consummate it now will prove her innocence.[30] Instead we watch them struggling on the bed, a parody of love-making more grotesque and violent than the controlled, symbolic love-deaths of Romeo and Juliet. We have been brought at last into the bedroom of the play's voyeuristic imaginings. The bed is on stage in front of us. And what we see enacted on it is more terrible than anything we, or Othello, have been goaded into imagining.

A murder, a sacrifice, a wedding night; Desdemona as the deflowered bride, the sacrifice dying for the common good, the innocent victim struggling helplessly against a murderer – this is the questioning of the act even as it happens, that Othello wanted to avoid. When the truth about Iago comes out there are more questions. The revelation of his duplicity has less impact than the desperate, futile questioning of the man himself. What is Iago? Othello asks the question interpreters have been asking ever since, the question to which Iago himself had so many answers that he seemed to have no answer at all: "Will you, I pray, demand that demi-devil/Why he hath thus ensnared my soul and body?" (V.ii.298–99). If Iago were a devil there would be no need to ask; he simply did what devils do. If he is at least partly human, there is a need. Having tried to justify his own act by giving it a meaning, calling it a sacrifice, Othello looks for a meaning in Iago as though it will somehow control the horror, making it bearable by making it understandable. Iago denies him that consolation: "Demand me nothing. What you know, you know. / From this time forth I never will speak word" (V.i.300–1). There is talk of torturing him but not of killing him; he will be suspended in endless silence as Aaron is suspended in endless speech. Even knowledge is self-cancelled, a tautology that loops back on itself in a way that denies significance: "What you know, you know" has the shape of "I am not what I am." Iago clearly means his refusal to sound impressive, even heroic. It is a way of keeping power in his defeat by keeping to himself the meaning of his act, denying it to anyone else.[31] But all there is to be known of him is that negative, self-canceling identity.

HE THAT WAS OTHELLO

Gratiano responds to Iago's silence with a conventional threat, "Torments will ope your lips." Othello's response is more cryptic: "Well, thou dost best" (V.ii.303). He agrees with Iago's decision to keep silent. Is this a contemptuous dismissal, implying that Iago would have nothing to say? Or does Othello want Iago's sense of mystery preserved, since it creates a mystery in himself, putting him beyond conventional judgment? Like Lucrece and Tarquin these two have established a terrible bond. They have been together where no one else in the play has been, and affected each other more deeply than any other pair of characters. There is an understanding between them that goes beyond speech, beyond any interpretation we can devise. When Othello made Iago his lieutenant, and Iago replied, "I am your own for ever" (III.iii.482), we saw that bond formed; now we are sensing, without fully seeing, how deep it runs. Othello seems to understand better than we do why Iago is silent.

But Othello does not himself retreat to silence; that would indeed be to join Iago forever. He returns to speech to free himself from Iago and to establish his own meaning. In parallel with his examination of Iago, the questioning of his deed is bound up with the questioning of his identity. He makes that identity sound fragmented, like Cressida's. To Lodovico's "Where is this rash and most unfortunate man?" he replies, "That's he that was Othello[;] here I am" (V.ii.280–81).[32] (My name was Don Andrea.) Having complained of the loss of manhood – "I am not valiant neither, / But every puny whipster gets my sword" (V.ii.241–42) – he seems to have become a blank where Othello once was. In that way he is like the Ghost in *Hamlet*, a thing that looks like the late king. And like the Ghost he seems enervated in the domestic, female space of the bedroom. It is as though the killing was a love-making that sapped his strength. As the warrior is finished so is the lover: having said that the current of his life runs from Desdemona he has stopped that current, and it may seem there is nothing of him left.

Yet there is still someone who unlike Iago can say "I am," and the "he that was Othello" is still he, not it. He offers a self-definition that combines murder and sacrifice but he offers it with a shrug, as though it hardly mattered: "Why, anything; / An honourable murderer, if you will" (V.ii.290–91). "If you will" turns the responsibility for meaning over to the survivors; he is what they will make of him. But as he preserves something of himself in "here I am" he comes back from his initial indifference to show Hamlet's concern for the way his story will be told: "When you shall these unlucky deeds relate,/Speak of me as I am" (V. ii.339–40). "I am" again; he seems about to reconstruct his broken identity.

The story he relates sounds for a while like an exercise in self-justifica-tion. He denies responsibility with the word "unlucky" (after killing Tybalt, Romeo called himself "fortune's fool" [III.i.138]), then calls for a nicely balanced judgment:

> Nothing extenuate,
> Nor set down aught in malice. Then must you speak
> Of one that loved not wisely, but too well;
> Of one not easily jealous, but, being wrought,
> Perplexed in the extreme. . . . (V.ii.340–44)

He goes on to dwell on his own sorrow and loss. It sounds like a plea in mitigation, an attempt to throw himself on the sympathy of the court. It also sounds like an attempt to detach himself from what he has been, and what he has done: he speaks not of "I" but of "one." That part of his summary he wants written, fixed, like the words that enable revenge in *Titus*: "Set you down this" (V.ii.349). Then he returns to speech, the medium in which Aaron expressed not his suffering but his pride and sense of achievement. In the process "one" vanishes and "I" returns:

> And say besides that in Aleppo once
> Where a malignant and a turbanned Turk
> Beat a Venetian and traduced the state,
> I took by the throat the circumcised dog
> And smote him – thus! (V.ii.350–54)

The split identity of "he that was Othello" acquires a new meaning. There are two Othellos, as there were two Hamlets and two Cressidas. One is the enemy within, the hated foreigner, the Turk – drowned and forgotten in act II, returning within the hero himself. The Turkish invasion has happened after all. In act I the Turk made a feint towards Rhodes and then headed for Cyprus. Now he has surprised us again. The other Othello is the representative of the state, the judge and executioner, who kills the Turk, and who speaks like the hero of a white supremacist adventure fantasy dispatching an undesirable alien.

The hero then turns to the woman he has avenged and dies on a kiss. The conflicting roles of lover and warrior are resolved in the chivalric manner; he has defended his lady's honor against the man who wronged her. But he is that man. He speaks of the "I" who killed the Turk. But as the blade enters his body "I" and the Turk become one. The last kiss comes from Desdemona's avenger, and from her murderer. He has matched her doubleness with a doubleness of his own. Their love is cemented and violated at once. That love began in storytelling, and it ends with his last story, a story that issues in action. So far as justice is done, the action is satisfying; but the onlookers' exclamations, "O bloody period! . . . All that's spoke is marred" (V.ii.355) suggest that the action has spoiled the story by its violence. In place of the control and finally the detachment conferred by a constructed meaning, the onlookers are forced to confront the deed itself. In a play full of looking, and of visual imagining, we would expect a significant stage picture at the end, and we get one. But Lodovico, having demanded that Iago "Look on the tragic loading of this bed," like rubbing a dog's nose in the mess it has made, adds, "The object poisons sight, / Let it be hid" (V.ii.361–63). Husband and wife lying together might suggest a resolution, but as Michael Neill has argued, the fact that there are three bodies on the bed figures the adultery that never happened.[33] As darkness comes with dawn for Romeo and Juliet and then for Verona, it is as though the fantasy that haunted Othello's mind has never been dispelled, but still hovers in the room, as though his final attempt at the control of meaning has failed.

It matters, however, that what shares the bed with Othello and Desdemona is not just any third body, to create an image of a love triangle. It is Emilia. As Paris, dragged by Romeo into Juliet's final resting place, seems to bring with him the ordinary, violent society from which the lovers tried to isolate themselves, Emilia has spoken through much of the play for a commonsense cynicism like Iago's. The handkerchief became dangerous when she stole it. At the cost of her own life, she has rescued Desdemona's reputation; but she has never reconciled herself to the marriage, and throughout the last scene she fires at Othello racist insults like the shouting in the streets that greeted his elopement: he is a black devil, Desdemona's "most filthy bargain"; she is probably thinking of his skin color when she calls him "ignorant as dirt" (V.ii.153, 160). Othello has tried to interpret his deed as a love-death, ending with a kiss; the stage picture, without Emilia, would make it seem a consummation like that of Romeo and Juliet. With Emilia, that interpretation breaks open, and we see it as the wedding night of a marriage that street-level Venice saw from the first as an act of violation; naturally, another act of violation is its consummation.

Brabantio too is brought into the last scene by the announcement of his death (V.ii.202–4). His voice, like the voices shouting in the streets in the opening scene, has never quite been silenced. The Brabantio–Iago view of the marriage as an act of violation seemed for a while to be a damaging interpretation we could dismiss and put behind us. But as Iago and even Emilia keep it alive, the play slowly and insidiously confirms it. The differences that drew Othello and Desdemona together, shocking to the conventional mind, unsettle their identities and lead to mutual estrangement. Othello re-creates Desdemona's identity: she becomes (as Cressida becomes Diomed's Cressida), "that cunning whore of Venice" – Brabantio's Desdemona, a woman not to be trusted. But his destruction of her identity really reflects the destruction of his own. The driving force behind all this is Iago, who sets out to destroy other identities, having none of his own. That is all a non-being can do: destroy. His weapon is interpretation, and the openness of the handkerchief to different readings shows how powerful interpretation can be, how infinitely malleable reality can seem. Desdemona, not just by her integrity but by the sheer power of her physical presence, fights back against the interpretations imposed on her. Realizing the truth too late, Othello can deal with what he has done only by splitting himself in two: Othello and he that was Othello, "I" and the Turk. He can only reintegrate himself as (figuratively at least) he consummated his marriage – by another act of violation, a stroke of the blade that reintegrates his identity only by ending his life. What Romeo talks about, when he offers by killing himself to kill the name that has offended Juliet (III.iii.101–7), Othello actually does. He can be who he is only by killing what he has become; and he cannot separate the one from the other. It is a grim variation on Titus' insistence that Lavinia is still Lavinia, the insistence that was meant to keep Lavinia alive.

CHAPTER 6

King Lear: *We have no such daughter*

UNMAKING CORDELIA

When Chiron and Demetrius rape and mutilate Lavinia, they try to destroy her as a human being, leaving her with a life that is no life at all. It is her father who takes the lead in trying to restore whatever life she can have, trying to bring her back into the relationship. In the first scene of *King Lear*, Cordelia endures a cruel twist on Lavinia's fate: it is her father who tries to annihilate her. He does this most obviously in the curse he utters when he banishes her, an attack that leaves no mark on her body but aims at destroying her humanity, her relationships and her identity, even more completely than Chiron and Demetrius destroy Lavinia's. Lear has defined Cordelia as his daughter, and if she is not his daughter she is nothing. The long ordeals of Lavinia, Cressida and Desdemona take up much of their respective plays. Cordelia's is compressed into the first scene, after which she disappears for a long time as though Lear has truly annihilated her. But as Othello in trying to destroy Desdemona's identity actually destroys his own, so Lear's attack on Cordelia means that he is the one who breaks apart. From the self-violation of Lear's identity, chaos spreads through his family and his kingdom, as identities and the structures of relationship that depend on them break down.

The annihilation of Cordelia and ultimately of Lear is implicit in the love-test. Chaos starts, as it so often does, with an attempt to impose order. Lear has at the beginning a clear image of Cordelia. She is the daughter who loves him best, who will make the best speech, who will get the biggest share of the kingdom and the privilege of his company for the rest of his life. But this fantasy, no less than the curse, annihilates Cordelia herself. It allows her no space for her own decisions, her own needs, her own life. From the start, she is not real to Lear; he has constructed a version of her in his mind, as Othello does with Desdemona. Othello's fantasy is that Desdemona has betrayed him. Lear's fantasy is that

Cordelia loves him totally. In the service of that fantasy Lear constructs a rigged, artificial love-test in which Cordelia's victory is foreordained. Simple arithmetic tells us he has it planned that way: since Goneril and Regan go first, once their shares have been determined, hers is also. Lear virtually admits the test is rigged: his first pronouncement is "we have divided / In three our kingdom" (I.i.36–37).[1] The phrasing of his question, "Which of you shall we say doth love us most" (I.i.51) makes the issue depend on his own judgment. He has already made that judgment, and expects them to confirm it. He has imagined how they will speak, putting words in their mouths – Cordelia's in particular – as Titus does to Lavinia. What looks like a free experiment has a determined end; an act of surrender is an act of control.

The unreality of the occasion is reflected in the vagueness of its language. Goneril offers a love expressed in large generalities, "Beyond what can be valued, rich or rare" (I.i.57). Regan offers the same, only more so. Lear in turn divides a map that has no distinguishing features, each section of the country being equally lush, "With shadowy forests and with champaigns riched, / With plenteous rivers and wide-skirted meads" (I.i.64–65). We cannot relate this to any known geography, or tell where the divisions fall. The kingdom, like the love, is idealized to the point of unreality.[2]

Lear's fantasy, like Othello's, deals in absolutes, and breaks against the reality of the woman on whom it centers. Yet, just as the simple chastity Desdemona embodies is expressed in complex and contradictory ways, so the truth Cordelia proclaims is full of paradoxes. Her refusal to speak registers as a silence, anticipating her final, terrible silence at the end of the play. Behind Lear and Cordelia we glimpse Titus and Lavinia, a father desperately trying to get speech from a silent daughter – except that Lear has silenced Cordelia himself by demanding a speech she cannot give. Yet while Lavinia says nothing Cordelia says "Nothing," and that makes a difference. She is not just tongue-tied; she *says*, quite articulately, that she is tongue-tied. She actually speaks far more than her sisters. She has a number of asides, the only character in the first scene to do so. While Goneril's declaration is seven lines and Regan's (making just enough effort to go one better) is eight, Cordelia has two speeches explaining her lack of speech, totaling thirteen lines.[3]

While the language of her father and sisters has been vague, Cordelia's is concrete. She makes her difficulty sound physical: "my love's / More ponderous than my tongue"; "I cannot heave / My heart into my mouth" (I.i.77–78, 91–92). When Goneril claimed "A love that makes breath poor and speech unable" (I.i.60) the easy flow of the lines belied her claim.

Cordelia conveys the sheer weight of her love, pressing down on her tongue and keeping her heart from rising. When she speaks of heaving her heart into her mouth, she makes speech seem a violent internal disruption, as though her love could be spoken only at terrible cost. And so we get a limited version of it, duty responding to nurture. What is held back is the love that appears later in the play, breaking the pattern of exchange by meeting genuine injuries with a grace that refuses to acknowledge them ("No cause, no cause") and costing Cordelia nothing less than her life. The language of bargaining Lear has established in the opening scene is so inadequate to this fuller love that to speak it now would be a betrayal; it has to wait until language can contain it. Meanwhile Cordelia falls in line with what language is doing now, speaking of love as a matter of exchange and insisting on keeping it realistic:

> You have begot me, bred me, loved me. I
> Return those duties back as are right fit,
> Obey you, love you, and most honour you. (I.i.96–98)

This at least touches on actions rather than vague feelings, and unlike her sisters, who talk airily about their love, Cordelia draws on a history of shared life.

Particularly in the Folio version, Cordelia's clear yet inadequate speech may also be in play with literal silence. The Folio adds to Lear's invitation a final word, "Speak" (I.i.86), suggesting that Cordelia's first response has been to say nothing, and he has to prod her. The Quarto goes straight from Cordelia's "Nothing my lord" to Lear's "How, nothing can come of nothing." The Folio slows and expands the exchange, with Lear repeating "Nothing" and Cordelia confirming it: "Nothing" (I.i.87–90). The effect is to hold the word suspended in silence by inviting the actors to pause between each repetition, so that we hear both "Nothing" and nothing. Lavinia's silence is unbroken; in Cordelia there is a play of speech that explores the meaning of silence and silence that isolates speech, setting words apart for examination.

There is another sense in which the speech of Cordelia reads as silence. It registers as such on Lear, because she is not saying what he wants to hear. And so he takes her sensible, measured profession of love as a flat refusal of it. If she is not giving him what he wants, she is giving him nothing. She joins a line of women in Shakespearean tragedy – Lavinia, Cressida, Desdemona – whose men one way or another misread them. What he wants is everything. Goneril and Regan claim to offer total, unqualified love, and Lear expects no less from Cordelia. Instead she asks,

> Why have my sisters husbands, if they say
> They love you all? Haply when I shall wed,
> That lord whose hand must take my plight shall carry
> Half my love with him, half my care and duty. (I.i.99–102)

She falls again into the language of measurement and exchange Lear himself has set up: if the kingdom is divisible, so is her love. If love is quantifiable, then there is only so much to go around. Again Cordelia draws on reality: while her own marriage is still in the offing, Cornwall and Albany, just by being there, make her point that women sometimes have husbands.

What Lear had in mind is revealed when he complains, "I loved her most, and thought to set my rest / On her kind nursery" (I.i.124–25). While Cordelia is ready to move forward to marriage as the next stage of her life, Lear wants a regression and an inversion: he will be the child and she will be his nurse, even his mother. There seems no place for a husband in this picture. Arguably, what he really wants is a marriage with Cordelia, with the love-test functioning as the bride's promise to her husband.[4] Later there will be a hint of sexual rivalry in Lear's bitter reference to 'the hot-blooded France' (II.ii.401). In the unguarded speech of madness he tells the attendants who have come to take him to his daughter, "I will die bravely, like a smug bridegroom" (IV.vi.194). If Cordelia senses this as an undercurrent in the opening scene, no wonder her response is silence followed by a carefully measured account of what a daughter owes a father. Incest blurs identities (as in *Hamlet* – "My uncle-father and aunt-mother") and suggestions of incest hover over the love-test, blurring Lear's relationship with Cordelia. These suggestions, according to James B. Driscoll, create not so much a subtext of literal incest as "a metaphor for an evil that pervades all [Lear's] relationships," his insistence on making absolute demands.[5] In particular, as Lynda E. Boose points out, Lear is asking for "pledges that would nullify those required by the wedding ceremony,"[6] and that is just Cordelia's point. On what is supposed to be the day of her betrothal Lear seems bent on making her marriage impossible.

The opening dialogue of *Antony and Cleopatra* playfully rewrites the opening of *King Lear*, with Cleopatra asking "If it be love indeed, tell me how much" and countering Antony's claim that his love is beyond reckoning, "I'll set a bourn how far to be beloved" (I.i.14–16). Lear cannot set a bourn; for him it is all or nothing, and when Cordelia will not give him everything he tries to annihilate her. Unable to accept a love divided between himself and her husband, he declares, "Thou hast her, France; let her be thine, for we / Have no such daughter" (I.i.264–65). When Marcus introduced the raped and mutilated Lavinia with the words "This was thy daughter" Titus replied "Why Marcus, so she is." Lear reverses that, not for a daughter who has been raped but for a daughter who is about to be married. Cordelia professed to love him "According to my bond" (I.i.93). Lear tears up that bond: "Here I disclaim all my paternal care, / Propinquity and property of blood" (I.i.114–15). She has claimed, "You have begot me, bred me" (I.i.96); he denies it. Having created her, he uncreates her, swearing "By all the operation of the orbs / From whom we do exist and cease to be" (I.i.112–13). Chiron and Demetrius tried to dehumanize Lavinia; Lear goes further, trying to uncreate Cordelia.

He tries not just to annihilate her but to put her into a parody relationship with himself, conveyed in negative language: "Unfriended, new adopted to our hate, / Dowered with our curse and strangered with our oath" (I.i.204–5). He violates his relationship with her by violating the language of relationship. In a similar way he tries to blight her marriage: "Thy truth then be thy dower" (for France, it will be); "Let pride, which she calls plainness, marry her" (I.i.109, 130). As what Othello saw in Desdemona was the corruption of his own imagination, the unnaturalness Lear sees in Cordelia reflects his own unnaturalness:

> The barbarous Scythian,
> Or he that makes his generation messes
> To gorge his appetite, shall to my bosom
> Be as well neighboured, pitied and relieved,
> As thou my sometime daughter. (I.i.117–21)

In his total, life-denying demands, he himself is the cannibal father who eats his own child. We may catch an echo of Chiron's protest against Titus, killer of sons and host at a cannibal feast: "Was never Scythia half so barbarous!" (I.i.134). Lear's attempt to unmake Cordelia seems a complete reversal of his view of her at the beginning of the scene; but it is also an expression of it. At the beginning he saw her as a source of total love and protection, all directed at him; in her own person she was nothing. When she asserts her own reality, and he counterattacks by reducing her to nothing, this simply brings to the surface what he was doing to her all along. Nothing has come of nothing.

UNMAKING THE KINGDOM

In the words, "we / Have no such daughter" Lear tries to unmake his relationship with Cordelia. Yet that was the relationship on which he had

centered his life, and the future of his kingdom. Lear's original plan might
have produced a tense but viable political settlement, and it would have
kept him out of the hands of Goneril and Regan.[7] With Cordelia gone,
the center is knocked out of that plan, and the consequences do not stop
there. Lavinia's rape shadows the world of *Titus Andronicus* through
metaphor and analogy. In a far more practical and literal way, the
decisions Lear makes because of his banishment of Cordelia lead to the
unraveling of his kingdom, and of his own identity.

Even his initial plan for a political division was full of contradictions. In
the play's opening line, "I thought the King had more affected the Duke
of Albany than Cornwall" (I.i.1–2), Kent makes it clear the division is
already made, sees it as a division between the men, and links it not to the
daughters' professions of love but to Lear's opinion of their husbands. He
is surprised at the even division between Albany and Cornwall; Lear is not
just contradictory but capricious. For a man giving away power he shows
a cunning mastery of one of its tricks, riveting attention on himself by
making everyone wonder what on earth he is doing. But the contradiction
also suggests in Lear's thinking a dangerous instability. Once Cordelia has
gone that instability comes to the surface. Through much of *Titus* we have
to watch Lavinia undergo the consequences of her initial violation. For
about the same length of time in *King Lear*, Cordelia vanishes. She is as
strikingly absent as Lavinia is strikingly present. In that absence, we watch
the consequences for Lear and for his society. "We / Have no such
daughter" means not just the destruction of one person but the destruction of a relationship. And in the scenes that follow, the whole idea of
relationship seems to crumble. Moreover, if Lear is Cordelia's father and
she is not his daughter, then what is he? In a trick Lear himself will later
turn on Goneril, the loss of her identity means the loss of his.

By the same token, Lear's two-part division of the kingdom, impro-
vised in the wake of Cordelia's banishment, recoils on himself: he becomes the one divided.[8] He divides his time between Goneril and Regan,
and divides his office in two:

> only we shall retain
> The name, and all th'addition to a king: the sway,
> Revenue, execution of the rest,
> Beloved sons, be yours. . . . (I.i.136–39)

His asking the Dukes to part a coronet between them (I.i.139) – and how
are they supposed to do that?[9] – symbolizes the way he has split his own
office. He is and is not the king; it is a perfect recipe for political

confusion. Without Cordelia to nurse him, he will need to protect himself not just with the trappings of authority but with some measure of its reality. The hundred knights on whom he insists, and who will be a basic source of tension, are part of the "addition" to a king, and a real power to call on in difficulty. The fact that they turn out to be no help at all except to his daughters, who use them as an excuse to turn on him, suggests that in dividing his office he has actually emptied it out, reducing himself as he tried to reduce Cordelia, to nothing. And from now on the crack that has begun in the center will run through the whole kingdom. Part of Lear's original design was to prevent future strife (I.i.43–44). We are not far into the new dispensation before we hear rumors of war between Albany and Cornwall, and before the end of the first scene Goneril and Regan are already squaring off; we hear it in Regan's quick insistence that Goneril gets Lear first (I.i.288–89).

Lear began with everything, in his own mind, settled. Meeting Cordelia's resistance he annihilates her, then reduces his own kingship to absurdity and his kingdom to civil war. The extent of the disruption he causes is suggested by the way the Gloucester plot echoes the Lear plot. The most significant parallel is not, as we might have expected, between the two fathers: it is between Lear and Edmund, the massive disruptive force at the center of the play's first scene, and the disruptive force on a domestic level at the center of its second. Edmund's being born at all was a social offense, and we shall see the play return to this in its last view of him. Though there is evidence that Gloucester loves his sons equally (I.i.17–18), there is still something anomalous – "Half-blooded" (V.iii.81) is Albany's phrase – about Edmund, and Gloucester's jocular evasiveness about acknowledging him – "His breeding, sir, hath been at my charge" (I.i.8) – leaves his identity for a moment uncertain (I.i.7–11). As Lear is and is not king, Edmund is and is not Gloucester's son. This is not their only similarity. While Lear gives land away and Edmund seeks to acquire it, they both use it as a measure of status. Lear, ignoring the integrity of his kingdom, rewards professions of love with land; Edmund, in defiance of "the plague of custom" and "The curiosity of nations" (I.ii.3–4), plans to use land to confirm his worth and resolve his identity. You can tell a loving daughter, and a true gentleman, by the land they own. The echoes multiply as "Edgar" (in Edmund's forged letter) proposes that "the father should be as ward to the son and the son manage his revenue" – Goneril and Regan take a similar view of Lear – and offers to share half Gloucester's revenue with his brother (I.ii.71–74, 53).

While the Gloucester plot begins as literally independent of the Lear plot, in that Edmund's scheme does not hinge on anything that happened in the first scene, the echoes back and forth suggest Lear has touched some hidden spring, releasing a force of disorder that ranges beyond the immediate consequences of his own actions. In the storm, Lear

> Bids the wind blow the earth into the sea,
> Or swell the curled waters 'bove the main,
> That things may change, or cease . . . (III.i.5–7)

Like the cosmic language of Titus, this annihilates boundaries. While in the Creation the voice of God separated the land and the sea, here the voice of Lear tries to annihilate distinction in an act of uncreation. It is the disruptive, uncreating Lear of act I, writ small in Edmund, writ large in his vision of a self-destroying cosmos.

CHAOS

The central scenes of the play are an extended dramatization of chaos, through the heavens, through society, and within the human body. We have seen how in other plays an act of violation puts language, meaning and identity into crisis. All that and more happens here, with the emphasis falling on problems of order and relationship. Titus called Rome a wilderness of tigers. In *Lear*, as the structures of society crumble, we have a much fuller sense of what such a world would look like. Ulysses saw universal chaos because Achilles was sulking in his tent; Troilus imagined the collapse of value and meaning because he saw Cressida with another man. In *Lear*, chaos of that sort is not just talked about but unleashed before our eyes, for reasons – Lear's unmaking of his relationship with Cordelia, and of his kingdom – that are free of the incongruity that haunts the earlier play. The vision of chaos is more compelling still because we see it not just in apocalyptic imaginings but in small, precise details.

We realize how political language has been inverted when Oswald reports, in some bewilderment, Albany's attempt to put it right:

> Of Gloucester's treachery
> And of the loyal service of his son,
> When I informed him, then he called me sot,
> And told me I had turned the wrong side out. (IV.ii.6–9)

The Fool's jokes are pervaded by the idea of inversion: he accuses Lear of making his daughters his mothers and putting down his own breeches for

a whipping (I.iv.163–65), getting not the nursing he expected from
Cordelia but the punishment due to a naughty child. The King himself
becomes a great baby, expecting demand feeding: "Let me not stay a
jot for dinner; go, get it ready" (I.iv.8). He is also a noisy rebel, an
outsider, demanding the attention of Regan and Cornwall by creating
the sort of disturbance Iago and Roderigo created in the streets of
Venice: "at their chamber door I'll beat the drum / Till it cry sleep to
death" (II.ii.307–8). In *Macbeth* it is a regicide who murders sleep; here it
is the King.

In an inverted world, true loyalty takes the form of rebellion: Kent's
rebellion against Lear is intended to serve him, as is the rebellion of
Cornwall's servant during the blinding of Gloucester. The world is upside
down, and they are trying to give it an extra turn to set it right.[10] Kent is
banished, and the servant is killed and thrown on a dunghill. If the world
were simply inverted the old pattern would still be visible, and the next
turn of the wheel would indeed restore it. But the world has blown apart
and the pattern is gone. There is a new world order, exemplified in
Cornwall. We see him improvising a power structure of his own, drawing
on anyone who might be useful. Edmund is his first catch: "Natures of
such deep trust we shall much need; / You we first seize on" (II.i.116–17).
Edmund's kind of trust will indeed be useful to him. Rewarding the
young man's betrayal of his father, Cornwall says of the information that
Gloucester is trafficking with the enemy, "True or false, it hath made thee
Earl of Gloucester" (III.v.17–18). We glimpse the working of a police state,
modern and early modern: accusation is the instrument of authority, and
the question of its truth or falsehood is irrelevant. In the service of this
authority, betraying a family member is a special virtue. In bestowing the
earldom Cornwall is taking a king's prerogative and ignoring the question
of Edmund's legitimacy. He is making up a society as he goes along. We
glimpse what that society will be like when the King's messenger is put in
the stocks, and Gloucester's apology makes it clear that the issue is not
right or authority but Cornwall's temperament and the kind of mood he
is in (II.ii.280–301). In a passage the Folio cuts (as though to deny us the
comfort of having the issue clarified), Albany sees behind this new world
order the solipsism of evil: "Wisdom and goodness to the vile seem vile; /
Filths savour but themselves" (IV.ii.39–40).

With inherent order gone, we are left with a structure of bargains and
deals, the structure Lear himself introduced in the first scene. Lear hopes
for better treatment from Regan than he had from Goneril, not just
because she remembers the bond Cordelia invoked, "The offices of

nature, bond of childhood," but because "Thy half o' the kingdom hast thou not forgot" (II.ii.367–69). He expects her love because he paid for it. He clings to the terms of the love-test, measuring his daughters' love by the number of knights they will allow him: "Thy fifty yet doth double five and twenty, / And thou art twice her love" (II.ii.448–49). As love comes with a price, authority comes with a reward. Edmund steels his Captain to the task of killing Lear and Cordelia by telling him there is promotion in it. Justice, mad and ineffectual in the Quarto-only trial in the farmhouse, is materialized in Lear's later vision of society (a Folio addition):

> Plate sin with gold,
> And the strong lance of justice hurtless breaks;
> Arm it in rags, a pigmy's straw does pierce it. (IV.vi.161–63)

Innocence is neither presumed nor proven; like love, it is bought. In this world, Kent's explanation of Oswald rings true: a tailor made him. He is an artificial creature belonging to a world in which value and identity have become material things, and we remember that tailors are in business.

BECOMING NOTHING

Kent's explanation of Oswald's origin is a comic spin-off from the central question of identity. Oswald has his own sense of who Lear is. When the King asks him "who am I, sir?" Oswald replies, "My lady's father" (I.iv.76–77). For the tailor-made man Lear has no traditional authority, no inherent identity; the marks that identify him are those that are relevant to Oswald as he does his own job. Lear has brought this on himself, unmaking his own identity: to his challenge, "Dost thou call me fool, boy?" the Fool replies, "All thy other titles thou hast given away; that thou wast born with" (I.iv.141–43). As Oswald sees the essence of Lear in the relationships of his own household, the Fool identifies him as a fool. We may see Oswald as blind and the Fool as insightful; but they share a solipsism, a tendency to define others in terms of themselves, that we shall see again in Lear.

Women in earlier plays have their identities unsettled by men in what for the latter is the crucial area of sexual conduct: this is and is not Cressid, I took you for that cunning whore of Venice. Now the process is reversed, as women unsettle a man in the male roles of king and father. Lear sees what is happening:

LEAR Does any here know me? why, this is not Lear.
Does Lear walk thus, speak thus? Where are his eyes?
Either his notion weakens, or his discernings are lethargied – Ha!
sleeping or waking? Sure 'tis not so. Who is it that can tell me
who I am?
FOOL Lear's shadow.
LEAR I would learn that, for by the marks of sovereignty, knowledge
and reason, I should be false persuaded I had daughters.
FOOL Which they will make an obedient father.
LEAR Your name, fair gentlewoman?   (I.iv.217–27)

He feels a second, alien identity inside him, like Hamlet's madness or
Othello's Turk: something that walks and talks differently and has somehow usurped his being. It is part of the disturbance that unlike Hamlet or
Othello he cannot at first name this alien thing. The Fool calls it Lear's
shadow. In the Quarto version of this passage it is Lear who says "Lear's
shadow," answering his own question, but by having the Fool give the
answer the Folio dramatizes the idea that Lear needs someone else to tell
him who he is.[11] If this woman is not his daughter, then he is not Lear.
This cuts both ways: at the end of this passage Lear pretends not to know
Goneril as he has pretended not to know himself. She has gone the way of
Cordelia, and is no longer his daughter. All of this is an ironic pretense on
Lear's part, as is his later kneeling to Regan to apologize for being old and
to beg raiment, bed and food. But in both cases Lear's irony is a way of
dramatizing what is really happening: here, he shows that as relationships
crumble, so do the identities that depend on relationship.

Is there any identity that does not? The Fool's answer would seem to be
no; his relationships gone, Lear has no identity left: "Thou hast pared thy
wit o'both sides and left nothing i'the middle"; "I am better than thou art
now. I am a fool, thou art nothing" (I.iv.177–79, 184–85). He no longer
has even the title he was born with, "fool." Because Cordelia said "Nothing" he reduced her to nothing; but in the process he has reduced himself
to nothing. Of course what storms across the stage of the Globe, or of any
theatre where *King Lear* is played, is not nothing but a solid actor –
preferably for this part, an actor with a strong presence. That is another
meaning of "Lear's shadow," since for Shakespeare (as at the end of *A
Midsummer Night's Dream*) "shadow" can mean "actor." The metatheatrical awareness the word triggers functions like the metatheatrical quality
of the Ghost in *Hamlet* ("You hear this fellow in the cellarage" [I.v.159]):
it is a further unsettling of identity. But while within the performance the

real presence of the actor suggests Lear is not a person but a part to be played, within the play the real presence of the character contradicts the idea that he is nothing. As Cordelia's "Nothing" turns out to be a careful and detailed statement about her inability to express her love, and Edmund's letter, which he calls "Nothing" (I.ii.32), will destroy an entire family, the "nothing" which is Lear is a formidable presence, raging and suffering. But the rage and the suffering are triggered in large measure by the fear of reduction to nothing, the fear that lies behind Lear's sense that some other, unnamed thing has taken over his being. If that thing is Lear, then perhaps Lear himself is nothing. What we see is neither identity nor nothingness, but a terrible struggle between the two.

Edgar undergoes a similar experience, but he is more in control of it. Creating the figure of Poor Tom, he names the being who will usurp his nature and gives a detailed account of him. Meanwhile, "Edgar I nothing am" (II.ii.192). He seems to enact literally the undoing of one's own identity that characters in earlier plays have expressed in language: Juliet's "I am not I if there be such an 'I'" (III.ii.48); Iago's "I am not what I am" (I.i.64). Juliet and Iago, like Lear, continue to be strong presences, and even Coriolanus' attempt to unmake his identity can produce only "a kind of nothing" (V.i.13) through which the original character shows all too clearly. We have seen the reality of Cordelia resist Lear's attempts to make her nothing. Tom is so vivid, and Edgar as an independent character has been so shadowy up to this point in the play, that Edgar may indeed appear to have reduced himself to nothing as Tom takes over. Yet through persistent asides, and the continuing presence of the actor we know as Edgar, this "nothing" continues to be something. And he continues to have relationships. As Lear claims to have lost his identity because of his daughters' treatment of him, Edgar is reduced to nothing by his father, who declares "I never got him" (II.i.78). If Gloucester never got him, he does not exist. To that he extent he suffers the uncreation Lear attempts with Cordelia. The name Edgar surrenders was given to him by Lear, who was his godfather (II.i.91–92). In the scenes that follow after Edgar's apparent reduction of himself to nothing, his strongest relationships will be first with Lear and then with Gloucester, as the original sequence, birth and then name-giving, runs backward and Edgar returns to his origin.

ATTACKING THE BODY

As the sheer physical presence of Desdemona sets up a powerful counter-force to the insinuations of Iago, so the "nothing" to which the characters seem to reduce each other, or themselves, is denied by a simple fact of performance, the bodies of the actors who play them. But as the self is constantly under attack in this play, so is the body. Lear's curse leaves Cordelia's body (unlike Lavinia's) untouched. But in language and action, physical suffering is dispersed through the rest of the play. Tom, "whipped from tithing to tithing and stocked" (III.iv.130), enacts the fate of the displaced poor in Elizabethan society, and his reference to the stocks recalls the fate of Kent in Cornwall's new order. (In a juxtaposition that used to be obscured by the scene-breaks of traditional editing, Kent is onstage in the stocks during the soliloquy in which Edgar creates Tom.) Pursued and threatened, Tom also enacts Edgar's own sense of displacement, and perhaps Edmund's as well. Edmund too has no place in society,[12] and behind the character who seems to have wiped out Edgar we see not only Edgar but his brother. They are also linked through what turns out to be one of the play's key images, the body turning against itself. Edmund wounds himself, onstage (the audience always winces) to build up his case against Edgar. Bedlam beggars, according to Edgar, "Strike in their numbed and mortified bare arms / Pins, wooden pricks, nails, sprigs of rosemary" (II.ii.186–87). Whether he literally does this to himself or not, Edgar, naked in the storm, has adopted a disguise that ensures physical suffering. He has turned against his own body.

In language and action the little world of man reproduces the rebellions that are taking place in the larger world as children turn against parents and subjects against a king. Lear says of ingratitude, "Is it not as this mouth should tear this hand / For lifting food to't?" (III.iv.15–16). He threatens, "Old fond eyes, / Beweep this cause again, I'll pluck ye out" (I.iv.293–94). We see him strike his own forehead: "Beat at this gate that let thy folly in / And thy dear judgment out" (I.iv.263–64). Lavinia's body was attacked by Chiron and Demetrius, men mutilating a woman. Lear speaks of attacking and mutilating his own body as though to destroy an enemy within, and that enemy is the woman's part of him: "O, how this mother swells up toward my heart! / *Hysterica passio*, down, thou climbing sorrow" (II.ii.246–47). The hysteria he fears is a female ailment, a wandering womb.[13] His refusal to cry shows the same resistance: "let not women's weapons, water-drops, / Stain my man's cheeks" (II.ii.466–67). As Romeo and Troilus fear being effeminized by love, Lear fears being effeminized by passion, and for him the threat is physical.

At one point he fears not passion but corruption, and the woman within has a name: Goneril. If Lear and his daughters are (like man and wife in *Hamlet*) one flesh, then that flesh is sullied:

> But yet thou art my flesh, my blood, my daughter,
> Or rather a disease that's in my flesh,
> Which I must needs call mine. Thou art a boil,
> A plague sore, or embossed carbuncle
> In my corrupted blood. (II.ii.410–14)

Goneril has not just taken his identity: she has invaded his body in a parody of sex, sullying it as Chiron and Demetrius sullied Lavinia, "This goodly summer with your winter mixed" (V.ii.171). If Lear seems to have a compulsion to control his daughters totally or to banish them totally – and this includes Cordelia – it may be because he fears and loathes their flesh-and-blood involvement with him, fears and loathes the woman in himself.

Lear's disgust at the corrupt female presence in his body links with a general recoil from female sexuality. Gloucester's reference to Edmund's birth, "Do you smell a fault?" (I.i.15) hints at his own corruption and Edmund's, but "fault" can mean vagina,[14] and Lear thinks he knows where the smell comes from:

Down from the waist they are centaurs, though women all above. But to the girdle do the gods inherit, beneath is all the fiend's: there's hell, there's darkness, there is the sulphurous pit, burning, scalding, stench, consumption! Fie, fie, fie! Pah, pah! Give me an ounce of civet, good apothecary, to sweeten my imagination. (IV.vi.121–27)

It is not just his imagination that needs sweetening. On "Pah! Pah!" he seems to be spitting a foul taste out of his mouth. This grim fantasy builds on his vision of "yon simp'ring dame, / Whose face between her forks presages snow" (IV.vi.116–17), where the inverted language suggests an inverted body, a face in the crotch (as in medieval drawings of devils), with a hint of oral sex. In a smaller, meaner way Regan is preoccupied with what lies between Goneril's legs, and what Edmund is doing there: "But have you never found my brother's way / To the forfended place?" (V.i.10–11). In the imaginations of the play's characters a vagina is a fault, the pit of hell, and a taboo.

But Tom, no less than the simpering dame, is a "forked animal" (III. iv.106). The Fool has a line of codpiece jokes and penis jokes (III.ii.26–40; I.v.49–50). The "fault" was not just that of Edmund's unnamed mother; Gloucester took part in the sport. When Lear, quelling yet another rebellion in his body, cries, "O me, my heart! My rising heart! But down!" the Fool's bawdy reply invokes another rebellious organ: "Cry to it, nuncle, as the cockney did to the eels when she put 'em i'the paste alive: she knapped 'em o' the coxcombs with a stick, and cried, 'Down, wantons, down!'" (II.ii.310–14). There are similar overtones in Edmund's view of generational conflict: "The younger rises when the old doth fall" (III.iii.24). Contemplating Tom, Lear sees male guilt in procreation:

> Is it the fashion that discarded fathers
> Should have thus little mercy on their flesh?
> Judicious punishment, 'twas this flesh begot
> Those pelican daughters. (III.iv.71–74)

Tom-Edgar responds with a penis-joke: "Pillicock sat on Pillicock hill" (III.iv.75). Even without a female component, the male body is the enemy within, to be punished for the sin of begetting. In the storm Lear calls for a breaking of male and female bodies alike and a cosmic onanism: "Crack nature's moulds, all germens spill at once / That make ingrateful man" (III.ii.8–9).

   The male body's sin, as Lear sees it, is in the getting of daughters. (They are "ingrateful man.") In his madness he is willing to "Let copulation thrive" so long as the result is male children: "To't, luxury, pell-mell, for I lack soldiers" (IV.vi.112, 115). But at one point his denial of procreation is comprehensive. His most terrifying counterattack is his curse on Goneril's body, which centers on the fact that it is a woman's body. Undoing his own view of the future when he divided the kingdom – "To thine and Albany's issues / Be this perpetual" (I.i.66–67) – Lear now demands that nature work against itself:

> Suspend thy purpose if thou didst intend
> To make this creature fruitful.
> Into her womb convey sterility,
> Dry up in her the organs of increase,
> And from her derogate body never spring
> A babe to honour her. (I.iv.268–73)

He imagines sterility not as an internal condition but as a force attacking Goneril's body from outside, a force he can summon himself. If she has a child, the curse continues, it will attack and mark her body: "Let it stamp wrinkles in her brow of youth, / With cadent tears fret channels in her cheeks" (I.iv.276–77). His disowning of Goneril is an extended version of his disowning of Cordelia. Having tried to block one daughter's marriage, he tries to block the other daughter's motherhood. Having divided his kingdom he tries to put an end to his family.

In the Quarto Albany claims Goneril has already sterilized herself:

> She that herself will sliver and disbranch
> From her material sap perforce must wither,
> And come to deadly use. (IV.ii.35–37)

Tom is not only beaten but tortures himself; Goneril is not only sterilized but sterilizes herself by denying the human bond, severing herself from the paternal body of Lear. (The fusion of bodies that Lear sees as corrupt Albany sees as nourishing.) While Albany thinks he understands the source of Goneril's cruelty, Lear imagines himself looking for the source of Regan's: "Then let them anatomize Regan; see what breeds about her heart. Is there any cause in nature that make these hard hearts?" (III.vi.73–75). In Lear's imagination Goneril is invaded and scarred and Regan is sliced open. In both cases it is the female body, its capacity to breed, that preoccupies him. As Goneril may breed a child to torment her, Regan is breeding something about her heart (an unnatural place for breeding) that has made her evil. Lear imagines his daughters invading and corrupting his body; in turn he wants to invade, examine and destroy theirs.

The blinding of Gloucester begins as a female counterattack on a man. It is Goneril, who has said she loves her father "Dearer than eyesight" (I. i.56), who first gets the idea: "Pluck out his eyes!" (III.vii.5). Regan pulls hair from the old man's beard; the blinding itself can be seen as a symbolic castration.[15] But the atrocity transcends the male–female conflict, so that we can no longer say (if we were tempted to) that cruelty is the fault of women, or of men. Gloucester is attacked by a man and a woman; and Cornwall's threat to put out his eyes with his foot recalls the moment in *Lucrece* when Tarquin puts out the light with his foot (673).[16] When she is raped Lavinia is attacked as a woman; when her hands are cut off and her tongue cut out she is attacked as a person. So is Gloucester when he is blinded, and the atrocity is equally basic in denying him a faculty we depend on and usually take for granted. (A friend who worked for a medical publisher told me the pictures no one wanted to deal with were of hand injuries and eye injuries.) This time there is no hiding. Gloucester is attacked on stage, we have to watch every moment of it, and there is no Marcus to decorate it in language. We confront the thing itself.

As rebellions in the human body correspond to rebellions in society, the attack on Gloucester's body is an attack on a whole range of social codes. When he pleads, "you are my guests" (III.vii.30) he invokes one of the sacred relationships in early societies. Cornwall is not only his guest but his "worthy arch and patron" (II.i.59). Gloucester is in his own house, which his guests and patrons have taken from him (III.iii.2–4); in Grigori Kozintsev's 1970 film he is at his own fireside. When he declares "I am tied to the stake and I must stand the course" (III.vii.53) he realizes he is not in society after all but in a bear-baiting arena, and he is the bear. Beneath the descent to the animal is a descent to the material. His tormentors seem excited by the frailty of his body: "Bind fast his corky arms" (III.vii.29). His eye, as Cornwall plucks it out, is no longer a precious organ but a mere object: "Out, vile jelly" (III.vii.82). We have seen the reduction of humanity to the material in social relations; now we confront the final implications of that descent.

As Gloucester loses his eyes he learns the truth about his sons. But to say that blindness brings insight and suffering brings wisdom, and to leave it at that, is to settle for an easier comfort than the play offers. We must first assimilate the play's clearest message about suffering: it hurts. What we then can say is that while in *Titus Andronicus* we become more sharply aware of language because Lavinia is mute, in *King Lear* we become more sharply aware of sight because Gloucester is blind. What begins as metaphor, as in the Lear–Kent exchange, "Out of my sight!" "See better, Lear" (I.i.158–59), becomes a persistent focusing of the audience's vision as the characters focus their own. We have to look at Lear: "O thou side-piercing sight" (IV.vi.85); "Was this a face / To be opposed against the warring winds?" (IV.vii.31–32). Lear in turn demands that his hearers, and the audience, look at things only he can see: "When I do stare, see how the subject quakes" (IV.vi.107); "Behold yon simp'ring dame" (IV.vi.116); "Look, look, a mouse" (IV.vi.88). Having nagged at the blind Gloucester to read the challenge he thinks he is holding, Lear finally takes the point that Gloucester cannot see, and turns sight back into a metaphor: "A man may see how this world goes with no eyes. Look with thine ears" (IV.vi.146–47). This is what we have been doing as we listen to Lear describe his hallucinations: told to look at something we cannot see, we feel an empathy with Gloucester. The solution is to listen and to see with an inward eye.

Gloucester claims his own way of seeing the world; "I see it feelingly" (IV.vi.145). Feeling – with the emphasis on the physical – is Gloucester's cure for the corruption of the world and for his own sin. He asks the gods,

> Let the superfluous and lust-dieted man
> That slaves your ordinance, that will not see
> Because he does not feel, feel your power quickly. . . .
>   (IV.i.70–72)

Lear has a similar cure for the indifference of authority, himself included, to the poor of the kingdom: "Expose thyself to feel what wretches feel" (III.iv.34). Having tormented his body as Poor Tom, Edgar introduces one of his later impersonations as

> A most poor man, made tame to fortune's blows,
> Who by the art of known and feeling sorrows,
> Am pregnant to good pity. (IV.vi.217–19)

Suffering hurts; but in making sufferers aware that others are suffering too, it may help them begin the work of binding a broken world together. That is one reason why the characters are always telling themselves, and each other, to look. And as the blinding of Gloucester makes us more sharply aware of eyesight, giving a new urgency to the persistent gazing we have seen in *Titus*, *Hamlet* and *Othello*, behind this is the fundamental reality of human beings, conveyed in the actor's body. No being who suffers and feels can be called "nothing." And so it is on the basis of suffering that the play's relationships are slowly and painfully reconstructed. But the process is not simple, as restoration is infused with memories of the damage it is trying to cure.

THE CRUELTY OF KINDNESS

In *Titus*, a group gathers around Lavinia, trying to offer care and comfort; but here, with a madman leading a blind man and a blind man trying to kiss the hand of a mad king, it becomes harder to tell sufferers and caregivers apart. This is a hospital in which the patients are looking after each other. And as in Titus' tending of Lavinia there is something invasive and self-preoccupied, so the images of relationship are shot through with a continuing solipsism, a focus on oneself even in moments of sympathy. This touches Lear's first truly outgoing moment, when he notices that the Fool is enduring the same storm as he is: "Come on, my boy. How dost my boy? Art cold? / I am cold myself" (III.ii.68–69). He is sorry for the Fool, and sorry for himself, and the two motives cannot be separated. The moment has the same double-edged quality as Titus' attempt to make Lavinia's pain his own. It may even be that the Fool's condition makes Lear for the first time fully aware of his own. Having had a grand shouting match with the storm, he notices with sudden humility that he is shivering.

His most extraordinary moment of fellow-feeling is with Poor Tom. The King confronts a naked madman and sees a mirror-image of himself:

"Didst thou give all to thy two daughters? And art thou come to this?" (III.iv.48–49). This is the moment when Lear suddenly loses hold on literal reality, and the madness he has dreaded engulfs him. As the externals fall away Lear can see across the social divide that separates king and beggar, and what he sees is that the madman is suffering like him, and he is suffering like the madman. Like Titus trying to imitate Lavinia's mutilation in his own body, Lear tries to make the resemblance complete by tearing his clothes off. Edgar, in a soliloquy the Folio cuts, finds comfort in the mirroring of his sufferings with Lear's: "How light and portable my pain seems now, / When that which makes me bend makes the King bow" (III.vi.105–6). Lear finds not a sharing of grief that lightens the burden but a confirmation of his obsessed view of the world, in which all suffering is caused by ungrateful daughters. His bonding with Tom at once puts into action his theoretical notion of caring for the poor of his kingdom now he knows what they are enduring, and drives him more deeply into himself.[17] Like Lavinia he can sometimes break out of his private world for a moment of recognition, a touch of reality; but these moments only emphasize his self-enclosure. It was solipsism that led Othello to misread Desdemona; and while the effect here is not so sinister it prevents us from reading Lear's development in the middle scenes as a straight line of spiritual progress. In so far as he is getting out of himself he is escaping from the Lear of the first scene; but in so far as he is trapped in himself, he is still that Lear.

There is something more sinister in Edgar's bonding with the blinded Gloucester. This apparent image of kindness is one of the most complex and difficult relationships in the play; it is not just a matter of (in France's words) taking up what's cast away (I.i.255). One reason for Edgar's fellow-feeling with Lear is "He childed as I fathered" (III.vi.107). This equates Gloucester with Goneril and Regan, and brings to the surface a resentment that shows implicitly elsewhere. When Gloucester enters with a torch Edgar calls him "the foul fiend Flibbertigibbet" (III.iv.112). He imagines Tom as one that "served the lust of my mistress' heart and did the act of darkness with her. . . . One that slept in the contriving of lust and waked to do it" (III.iv.84–88). He warns Lear, "Keep thy foot out of brothels, thy hand out of plackets" (III.iv.94–95). This is a moralizing madman, obsessed with sex, warning Lear against lust and punished for it himself. He has smelled his father's fault, and is lashing it in his own person. Taking his father's guilt on himself he is also taking the punishment; but is there a hint that Gloucester too should suffer this way?

When Gloucester says of his wronged son, "Might I but live to see thee in my touch, / I'd say I had eyes again" (IV.i.25–26), he seeks a comfort Edgar could easily give him. Edgar holds back. He touches his father, but the touch conveys no recognition, and he plays role after role in order to keep his identity hidden. Gloucester took away Edgar's identity by breaking their relationship ("I never got him"). Edgar in turn uses this loss of identity against his father, practically as a weapon. (Is there a touch of Iago here, the man whose non-identity led him to attack others?) No longer Edgar, he can use his freedom to be anybody as a chance to manipulate his father; and in that manipulation he exploits Gloucester's own loss. As Titus uses Lavinia's silence to take over her voice himself, Edgar uses Gloucester's blindness to get into his mind and re-invent the world for him, a process Gloucester, helpless though he is, tries to resist:

> GLOUCESTER When shall I come to the top of that same hill?
> EDGAR You do climb up it now. Look how we labour.
> GLOUCESTER Methinks the ground is even.
> EDGAR   Horrible steep.
>   Hark, do you hear the sea?
> GLOUCESTER   No, truly.
> EDGAR Why then, your other senses grow imperfect
>   By your eyes' anguish.
> GLOUCESTER   So may it be indeed.
>   Methinks thy voice is altered and thou speak'st
>   In better phrase and manner than thou didst.
> EDGAR You're much deceived; in nothing am I changed
>   But in my garments.
> GLOUCESTER   Methinks you're better spoken.
>   (IV.vi.1–10)

If we could hear a dialogue between Lavinia and those who are trying to speak for her it might sound something like this. Not just seeing for him, but denying the truth of Gloucester's remaining senses, Edgar seems to be trying to disconnect him completely from reality, putting him in an invented world of Edgar's own making. Gloucester offers the resistance Lavinia might offer if only she could speak. We can see and hear the truth of Gloucester's perception: the stage is flat and Edgar has dropped the Tom voice for standard English. We may see one man looking after another, but we hear a struggle between control and resistance.

As other characters are continually telling Lavinia to speak, Edgar tells Gloucester, "Look up a-height. . . . Do but look up" (IV.vi.58–59). The cruelty seems if anything more deliberate. Edgar in one sense is being cruel only to be kind, creating the invented scene at Dover to frustrate Gloucester's plan for suicide. Edgar sees suicide as a devilish temptation. The fiend kept offering Tom the means of death: knives, halters, ratsbane (III.iv.53–54). It was a fiend, Edgar in his next role claims, who led Gloucester to the brink of the cliff (IV.vi.67–72). Yet not to be able to die when life is unendurable is itself one of the torments of hell: versions of this torment are wished on Aaron and Iago. Edgar leads Gloucester to the threshold: "Give me your hand: you are now within a foot / Of th'extreme verge" (IV.vi.25–26). Gloucester prepares to cross that threshold alone, as we all have to: "Let go my hand" (IV.vi.28). After such careful preparation the anticlimax of continuing life is unbearable: "Is wretchedness deprived that benefit / To end itself by death?" (IV.vi.61–62). When we hear Edmund is seeking his father "In pity of his misery to dispatch / His nighted life" (IV.v.14–15) we may wonder for a moment which son is really the good one. We ask the same question when Edgar tells the blind man to look.

I have been following the undercurrent of cruelty in Edgar's dealings with his father, seeing their new bonding as riddled with old tensions; but of course this is only one component in a complex relationship. Edgar is also looking after Gloucester as Lear hoped Cordelia would look after him; he later says he has learned of his father's sufferings "By nursing them" (V.iii.180). Throughout their shared journey he is torn between a desire to end the charade and a compulsion to keep it going: "I cannot daub it further . . . And yet I must" (IV.i.55–57). Tom's physical self-torment is reflected in Edgar's self-rebukes for the role he is playing: "Bad is the trade that must play fool to sorrow, / Angering itself and others" (IV.i.40–41). Even when the story is over he cannot recount it without beating himself, with a word that links his guilt to his father's: "Never – o fault! – revealed myself unto him / Until some half-hour past" (V.iii.191–92).

Edgar resents his father, toys with him, and hates himself for doing it because he loves him. The love is seen in the simplest of gestures, vital for Romeo and Juliet and denied to Lavinia, the taking of hands. At first Edgar says "Give me thy arm" (IV.i.81), limiting the contact and suggesting an element of coercion as he pushes and steers the old man. By the end of their journey together the command has changed to "Give me your hand; / I'll lead you to some biding" (IV.vi.219–20) and finally, after the disaster of the lost battle, "Give me thy hand; come on" (V.ii.7). They are refugees, but they flee together.

UNMAKING LEAR

As Gloucester rewards the unknown man who is helping him – "Here, take this purse" (IV.i.67) – Lear rewards the man who, kneeling and kissing his hand, has acknowledged his kingship: "If thou wilt weep my fortunes, take my eyes." Lear's self-preoccupation is typical, but it is followed by a breakthrough of simple recognition: "I know thee well enough, thy name is Gloucester" (IV.vi.172–73). Gloucester has already recognized Lear as he cannot recognize Edgar: "I know that voice"; "Is't not the King?" (IV.vi.95, 106). He sets up the fuller restoration of identity that Cordelia offers. She seems free of the self-division and ambiguity that afflicts Edgar. She reverses the damage her sisters have done. They denied Lear his hundred knights; Cordelia's command, "A century send forth" (IV.iv.6) symbolically restores them. Like Albany turning political language right side up, she restores Lear's titles: "How does my royal lord? How fares your majesty?"[18] (IV.vii.44). As he sleeps she kisses him:

> O my dear father, restoration hang
> Thy medicine on my lips, and let this kiss
> Repair those violent harms that my two sisters
> Have in thy reverence made. (IV.vii.26–29)

After all the assaults on the body, verbal and literal, the relief of this moment is such that she seems to be healing not just her father but the whole play. Desdemona in her last moments creates a double reality, calling herself "falsely murdered" while exonerating her "kind lord." Cordelia simplifies this to a single new reality, wiping out the real offense Lear has done her. Prepared to drink poison from her hands, Lear compares her with her sisters, "You have some cause, they had not," and Cordelia replies, "No cause, no cause" (IV.vii.75).

Yet her return to England with a French army recalls the final situations of *Titus Andronicus* and *Hamlet*: the rescue mission is also an enemy invasion. It puts Albany in particular in an ambiguous position: "It touches us as France invades our land, / Not bolds the King" (V.i.25–26). Half his loyalty is with the other side, but he has to defend his country. In large measure Cordelia's return is responsible for the blinding of Gloucester. From Cornwall's opening declaration "the army of France is landed" (III.vii.2–3) he and Regan are obsessed with the danger of Gloucester's contact with the enemy and the fact that he has sent the King to Dover. They are made cruel by fear. Cordelia brings not just salvation but trouble.

When her attendants come for Lear, he runs away. As in the ambiguous political situation, so in Lear's deranged mind, Cordelia's mission seems like enemy action. He cannot face her, and she has some trouble facing him. When he wakes, Cordelia is at first reluctant to speak to him, asking the Gentleman to do it for her (IV.vii.43). It may be that, remembering what happened the last time she spoke to Lear, she is afraid of her own words. Lear's first response to his restoration is "You do me wrong to take me out o'the grave" (IV.vii.45). Though he is never, like Gloucester, overtly suicidal, he has earlier seen the grave as a place of shelter and protection, swearing as he banishes Cordelia, "So be my grave my peace" (I.i.126) and telling Tom "thou wert better in a grave than to answer with thy uncovered body this extremity of the skies" (III.iv.99-100). We remember the shock of Old Hamlet's bursting out of the grave, and we may also think of the warning over the author's grave in Holy Trinity Church in Stratford-upon-Avon. Lear's first waking thought is that his return to life is a violation; it is grave-robbing seen from the viewpoint of the dead.

In this new life he feels helpless and vulnerable: "Pray do not mock me. / I am a very foolish, fond old man" (IV.vii.59–60). He sees himself as Goneril and Regan did, and when told he is in his own kingdom replies "Do not abuse me" (IV.vii.77). Their view of him offered a comfort like that of the grave, the comfort of giving up and accepting that his life was over. Now he is forced to begin again, and he tries to retreat, as he ran from Cordelia's soldiers, as Lavinia ran from Marcus. In these moments of withdrawal, neither wants human ties restored; neither wants life to go on. Lear puts at first the greatest imaginable distance between himself and Cordelia, the distance between heaven and hell:

> Thou art a soul in bliss, but I am bound
> Upon a wheel of fire that mine own tears
> Do scald like molten lead. (IV.vii.46–48)

After what he has wanted from her, and done to her, just to look at her is a punishment. Even so the sight of Ophelia made Hamlet feel corrupt, and Othello imagined Desdemona's look on Judgment Day consigning him to hell. There may also be a memory of Lear's fear and loathing at having a daughter's flesh mingled with his; he now tries for the most radical separation he can imagine. He is saying, again, "We / Have no such daughter."

He turns from her to consider himself, and finds he cannot get himself in focus:

> I should ev'en die with pity
> To see another thus. I know not what to say.
> I will not swear these are my hands: let's see –
> I feel this pinprick. Would I were assured
> Of my condition. (IV.vii.53–57)

In earlier scenes his pity for other people was bound up with pity for himself. Now to understand what he feels about himself he has to begin by imagining another person. The person remains hypothetical and Lear retreats, baffled, language itself failing him. Turning to his body as a sign of his physical reality, he feels detached from it, not sure this is really him. The taking of hands established relationship for Romeo and Juliet, Edgar and Gloucester; looking at his own hands, Lear feels disconnected from them. As in kneeling to Cordelia he is doing with perfect seriousness what he did ironically when he knelt to Regan, he is now taking his early, sarcastic "this is not Lear" and wondering if it is the simple truth. Even what should in this play be the ultimate test of reality – he can feel pain – does not convince him.

From this point he never again speaks his own name. The recognition he gropes towards and achieves, undoing the curse he uttered in the first scene, is "I think this lady / To be my child Cordelia" (IV.vii.69–70). Though he feels disoriented by his own body, he tests reality by touching hers: "Be your tears wet? Yes, faith" (IV.vii.71). Earlier she has asked him "hold your hands in benediction o'er me!" with an implied assurance that those are indeed his hands; he kneels instead and she pleads with him not to (IV.vii.58–59). The gestures that imply hierarchy, his authority over her, and the inversion of that in her authority over him, are both refused. The gesture that brings them together is his touch on her face. At the opening of V.ii as they go into battle the Quarto stage direction "*Cordelia with her father in her hand*" has them repeat the gesture that binds Edgar and Gloucester. The wording hints that Cordelia is leading him and setting the pace. Lear tried to unmake Cordelia. Confronted with her again he tries not only to retreat but to unmake himself. All the things that defined him, and that others, over his protests, tried to take away – kingship, authority, his own name – he now tries to surrender.

It is as though violation and the loss of identity, so terrible to Lavinia, so pervasive in this play as Lear's attempt to annihilate Cordelia recoils on himself and leads to chaos in his kingdom, have returned now as instruments of grace. Lear being forced out of his grave, denied the peace of death, is given a new life; and losing his identity has freed him from the solipsism and egotism that blocked his full engagement with the world.

The very instruments that did such damage in the first scene have undone that damage. Yet, as the sense of marriage as violation that darkens the opening of *Othello* returns to haunt the rest of the play, so the opening of *King Lear* returns to disturb the Lear–Cordelia reunion, troubling its beauty as the relationship of Gloucester and Edgar is troubled by cruelty. This reunion is Lear's original fantasy come true.[19] Cordelia is looking after him, and her husband has vanished. In the Quarto the King of France lands briefly in Britain and then returns; in the Folio he is simply not there. Is this one reason why Lear comes to accept his happiness so slowly? Either it is too good to be true, or he realizes what was unnatural in that fantasy and no longer wants it, is even afraid of it. His question "Am I in France?" (IV.vii.76) acknowledges Cordelia's marriage as she herself does not. Either he is afraid the dream is incomplete, or he is showing that he is willing to accept Cordelia's new life. Perhaps he is trying to ground this new experience in reality, as Cordelia in the first scene tried to ground love in reality. The pain of "Do not abuse me" (IV. vii.77) on being told he is still in Britain suggests the question was asked in hope, not fear. He would find Cordelia's nursing easier to take if her husband were there, freeing him from the taint of total possession of his daughter.[20] With France not there, the best he can do is ask Cordelia to "forget and forgive" (IV.vii.83–84).

As there is lingering tension in the bonding of Edgar and Gloucester, the Lear–Cordelia reunion is shot through with memories of the old trouble it tries to resolve. This makes it difficult, for Lear especially; but it also makes it moving and convincing simply because it is difficult. When he responds to their defeat and capture by imagining a new life for them together, Lear seems to have forgotten the difficulty. There is a new confidence, a fierce possessiveness, in his cry,

> Have I caught thee? [*Embraces her.*]
> He that parts us shall bring a brand from heaven,
> And fire us hence like foxes. (V.iii.21–23)

That only some force from heaven can part them suggests he thinks of this as a marriage. His fantasy that in prison they will have a happy, playful life together, just the two of them, looking (like Chaucer's Troilus after his death) with amused detachment at the world, recalls Titus and Lavinia together forever in the tomb. The difficulty of their reunion, in which Lear acknowledged her separateness and was shy about claiming anything from her, was a saving difficulty. His confidence restored and his inhibitions gone, he is regressing to something like the unnatural demands of the first scene, though his manner has changed from overbearing authority to easy self-assurance. Once again he needs Cordelia to bring him back to reality. She tries in one line, the last words we hear her speak: "Shall we not see these daughters and these sisters?" (V.iii.8). As she did when she reminded him of her husband, she is trying to make him think of other people, other relationships. She knows the political reality of their situation, she is prepared to confront their enemies, and given the context there is intelligent irony in the words "daughters" and "sisters." He brushes all this aside in favor of his own view of a happy ending. But the play has shown that relationships are at their fullest – not their happiest, their fullest – when they acknowledge trouble; and we are on the brink of a series of endings – the doing of justice, the re-tying of severed bonds, the recovery of identity – in which the trouble will be overwhelming. We have seen that *Titus*, *Hamlet* and *Troilus* have unsettled endings. Here, the trouble Lear began when he severed his bond with Cordelia has never quite been dispelled; it returns in his attempt to construct a fantasy life with her, an attempt that takes us back to the first scene. As Lear's initial violation of Cordelia sent shock waves through the rest of the play, his reversion to his old way of thinking precedes what may be the most troubled ending in Shakespeare. Lear and Cordelia seem at first withdrawn from that ending; there is so much business to do that does not concern them. But they withdraw only to return with devastating force. The chaos of the play began with them, and returns to them.

TROUBLED RESOLUTIONS

In the second half of the play there is a general convergence on Dover. It is the place where salvation, and enemy invasion, will come to Britain, and the place where Gloucester wants to die. Literally no one ever seems to get there; in the later scenes there is no clear sense of where we are. But Dover's contradictory meanings prepare us for a series of endings as full of contradiction as the play's opening. In the Swift-like satire of Lear's madness, there seems no possibility of justice in this world. Edgar's act in challenging and killing Edmund looks like justice at last. The champion appears on the third sounding, as in the opening scene it was the third daughter who spoke the truth. For G. Wilson Knight the trumpets suggest nothing less than the Last Judgment.[21] But justice takes the form of fratricide, the first murder. The suggestions of brother killing brother in the match between Hamlet and Laertes become literal here. Change places and handy-dandy, which is the punishment, which is the crime?

As Hamlet sees the man who will kill him as a mirror image of himself, there has from the beginning been a rapport between Edmund and Edgar, suggested by the similarity of their names. It is Edmund who first introduces Tom o' Bedlam (I.ii.135–36); Edgar seems to share his brother's skepticism about astrology (I.ii.142). Edgar comes into the last scene as Edmund came into the first, with an obscure identity and a need to establish himself. He declares "my name is lost" (V.iii.119); to get it back he will have to kill his brother. He claims to be "noble as the adversary / I come to cope withal" and "no less in blood" (V.iii.121–22, 165). While Lear at first puts himself at a great distance from the daughter who is trying to save him, Edgar in a complementary play of opposites puts himself surprisingly close to the brother he is going to kill. Laertes asks Hamlet to exchange forgiveness with him; Edgar, having given him his death-wound, offers to "exchange charity" with Edmund (V.iii.164).

Yet "charity" does not seem quite the word for what follows. Reclaiming his name and announcing his relationship with Edmund, Edgar leaves one thing unsaid. "My name is Edgar and thy father's son" (V.iii.167): there is distance as well as bonding here. Though in their first dialogue they both used the word freely (I.ii.138–40, 169–70), now Edgar cannot say, "I am your brother." We may recall Chiron and Demetrius and their refusal to acknowledge the black baby, the brother they wanted to kill. It is their father who links Edmund and Edgar, and the brothers agree on a final, extraordinary judgment of him. Edgar sees Gloucester's blinding as the gods' "judicious punishment" (III.iv.73) for getting Edmund: "The dark and vicious place where thee he got / Cost him his eyes." Edmund replies, "Thou'st spoken right, 'tis true; / The wheel is come full circle, I am here" (V.iii.170–73). There is a grim order in the linking of images: the eye, the vagina, the wheel. In a play much concerned with a return to origins, with birth and begetting, Edmund's begetting was a crime for which he and his father have been condemned and punished, Gloucester with blindness and Edmund with death. We have traveled a long way from Gloucester's "yet was his mother fair, there was good sport at his making, and the whoreson must be acknowledged" (I.ii.21–23). Agreeing with Edgar's judgment, Edmund has condemned both his parents, and his own origin. Lear saw his return to life as an outrage. Here, it seems to both brothers an outrage that Edmund was born at all. In his initial attack on Cordelia, Lear made a similar attempt to unwish her birth: "Better thou / Hadst not been born than not to have pleased me better" (I.i.235–36). Agreeing with his brother's judgment, Edmund does what

Albany (in the Quarto) accuses Goneril of doing: he condemns his own origin (IV.ii.33-34). It would be better if he had not been born.

Yet Edmund cannot accept this total condemnation of his life, any more than Cordelia does. The immediate answer for Cordelia is a new, albeit shadowy, life with France, a new relationship in which she is valued. Edmund finds a twisted, parodic version of this in his relationship with Goneril and Regan. While they have squabbled over him in a mean and petty way and he has looked at their rivalry with amused detachment, Edmund's vow to Goneril "Yours in the ranks of death" (IV.ii.25) seems in the end more than just a romantic flourish. Though for Albany the corpses of Goneril and Regan are "this object" (V.iii.237) and Edmund's own death "but a trifle here" (V.iii.294), Edmund tries for something like the marriage-deaths of *Romeo and Juliet* and *Othello*: "I was contracted to them both; all three / Now marry in an instant" (V.iii.227-28). The attempt is desperate: there are no death-kisses, no final dialogue. The idea of a three-way marriage recalls the three bodies on the bed in *Othello*, ironically fusing marriage with adultery, including Gloucester's adultery that created Edmund in the first place. But Edmund's need to see his worth confirmed in this imagined marriage is captured in one line: "Yet Edmund was beloved" (V.iii.238). Again he is following Lear: having tried to establish his value by acquiring land, he tries in the end to establish it by claiming love.

Edmund's story ends with death in marriage, Gloucester's with death in a family reunion. Lear's recognition of Gloucester took him back to his birth, and to all human births:

> I know thee well enough, thy name is Gloucester.
> Thou must be patient. We came crying hither:
> Thou knowst the first time that we smell the air
> We wawl and cry. (IV.vi.173–76)

The smell in the air is the smell of mortality Lear finds on his own hand, the smell of sex in procreation. Lear recognizes Gloucester's name and the human condition together, as Edgar too will link name-giving with copulation and death. Edgar's naming of himself entails killing his brother; and having done so he recounts that by the same act he killed his father. The recognition he held off for so long brought Gloucester the death Edgar had at first denied him, as the old man's heart "'Twixt two extremes of passion, joy and grief, / Burst smilingly" (V.iii.197–98). Edgar re-establishes the identity he lost; but in restoring his relationships with his father and his brother he kills them both.

Reunion, that brought Lear out of the grave, puts Gloucester in it. But it also brings Edmund to a sense of relationship that goes beyond the savage moralizing about his birth he has shared with Edgar and his strained attempt to see his value in a three-person marriage. Edgar's story of their father's death triggers the first stirrings of Edmund's impulse to save Lear and Cordelia (V.iii.198–99). The thought that Goneril and Regan have died for him takes him the rest of the way. Is it the sight of their bodies that breaks the final barrier and makes him command a reprieve? He has only heard of the power of Gloucester's love for Edgar, a love that kills. Now he sees a demonstration of the sisters' love for him. But perhaps it is the mere sight of death, the body itself, that makes him see the value of life and makes him want to save the prisoners he himself has condemned. In any case a final irony touches the sisters: in life, they tried to destroy their father; in death, unwittingly, they might save him. The order comes too late; as an attendant carries Edmund off, Lear enters carrying Cordelia. At the Globe two different doors could be used, making Edmund's exit and Lear's entrance complement each other like figures on a weatherclock. Edmund has failed. But there may be one break in the relentless cruelty of the final scene: he dies offstage, not knowing he has failed.

In his reunion with Cordelia Lear's original fantasy of being nursed by her came true. That was succeeded in the first scene by another fantasy: he wanted her annihilated. That fantasy in turn comes true: "we / Have no such daughter" (I.i.264–65) is now a terrible reality. The end of Othello's marriage was haunted by the way it began; so is the end of Lear's relationship with Cordelia. But as Laertes says of Ophelia's madness, this nothing's more than matter; the annihilation of Cordelia produces her closest relationship with her father. Lear wanted to crawl unburdened towards death. Now he comes onstage carrying the burden of Cordelia's body. Physically, it is the closest relationship they have had. Her body, like Lavinia's, is the dominant presence in the scene, the thing we have to look at whether we can face it or not. In her first scene she alternated speech and silence; now her silence is more eloquent than speech. Lear wanted her to nurse him. Now he is nursing her, tending her, trying to bring her out of the grave. He caresses her name as Juliet did Romeo's: "Cordelia, Cordelia, stay a little" (V.iii.269). As in the blinding of Gloucester, there is no retreat into imaginative language, nothing like the lyrical rewriting of Lavinia's wounds or the turning of Desdemona into monumental alabaster. Instead, language is a stark confrontation with the thing itself: "Never, never, never, never, never" (V.iii.307). Such relief as Lear finds comes from an occasional wavering of his attention as other, shadowy figures temporarily distract him, and, just once, the dead Cordelia seems to become someone else: "And my poor fool is hanged" (V.iii.304).

In *Titus*, *Romeo* and *Othello* kisses were bestowed in death. Lear's intense concentration on Cordelia's lips may suggest the final claim of love, the claim he has never quite learned to withdraw. But more immediately what he wants is words, even breath. We hear one side of a dialogue with the dead: "Cordelia, Cordelia, stay a little. Ha? / What is't thou sayst?"; "I killed the slave that was a-hanging thee" (V.iii.269–70, 272). In his imagination she moves back and forth across the final threshold: "This feather stirs, she lives"; "now she's gone for ever" (V. iii.263, 268). As we found an empathy with Gloucester, being told to look at things we could not see, we may feel an empathy with Lear's desperate hope. The original stage directions for Lear's entrance specify that he is carrying Cordelia, not that she is dead; for all we can tell she could be still alive.[22] But we have seen links between mirroring and death, in the relations of Titus and Tamora, Hamlet and Laertes, Edmund and Edgar; and when Lear cries,

> Lend me a looking-glass;
> If that her breath will mist or stain the stone,
> Why then she lives. (V.iii.259–61)

– he is looking for signs of life in images of death: a mirror, a stone.

In the Quarto Lear virtually kills himself with a last attack on his own body: "Break, heart, I prithee break" (V.iii.311). Those are his last words; language kills. In the Folio that line is given to Kent and Lear dies with an intense concentration on Cordelia's body: "Look on her: look, her lips, / Look there, look there!" (V.iii.309–10). Here we (and Lear's imagined hearers, whoever they are) are told, as we have been told all through the play, to look. In the Quarto language kills; here, sight kills, drawing on the intensity of the relationship that is concentrated in Lear's final gaze. Throughout the last scene he has been unable to focus that gaze properly on anyone else: "Who are you? / Mine eyes are not o'the best, I'll tell you straight"; "This is a dull sight: are you not Kent?" (V.iii.276–77, 280). His fantasy of a private world to share with Cordelia alone, in which no one else matters, has in a terrible way come true. Edgar's command, "Look up, my lord" (V.iii.311) would draw his gaze away from Cordelia; it falls on dead ears, and draws Kent's rebuke: "Vex not his ghost; O, let him pass" (V.iii.312). Kent knows that Lear's concentration on Cordelia is killing him, as the final bonding with Edgar killed Gloucester; and he knows that Lear should die. In the Quarto, where language kills, Albany says of Lear, "He knows not what he sees"; sight has emptied out. In the Folio, where sight kills, the line is "He knows not what he says" (V.iii.291). Language has emptied out.

Lear, in his private world, is unable to concentrate on the others. Those whose role it is to sort out the public world find their concentration returning to Lear. Albany tries for an ordered ending, then gives up:

> All friends shall taste
> The wages of their virtue and all foes
> The cup of their deservings. O, see, see! (V.iii.301–3)

Language dies and sight takes over. So for Edgar does feeling. His last speech begins, "The weight of this sad time we must obey" (V.iii.322) as though he could feel the weight of the dead Cordelia in his own arms. We remember the weight of love that pressed down on Cordelia's tongue. When Edgar adds, "The oldest hath borne most" (V.iii.324) it is a tribute to the sheer value of the dead thing Lear has carried.

In "borne," the line also puns on birth.[23] The play has conflated the beginning and end of life, with Edmund reminded of his conception as he dies and a father cradling a dead child as he might cradle a newborn baby. Lear's love for Cordelia begins as an unregulated, self-centered demand and ends as an attempt to drag her back across the threshold of death. He began by trying to deny the reality of Cordelia's life; he ends by trying to deny the reality of her death. He has asked for more than life, and death, can offer. He is punished for demanding love and punished for loving, not by any regulating gods but by the conditions of life itself, the separateness of one person from another, the finality of death. When Kent says, "The wonder is he hath endured so long; / He but usurped his life" (V.iii.315-16) there is a suggestion in the word "usurped" that goes beyond the surface meaning that Lear has been living on borrowed time. Hamlet's father was accused of usurping the night, as though his return to life is illegitimate. Now we hear another king accused of usurpation, not for returning to life after death but simply for living, for having been born in the first place. "He but usurped his life": in a final link between Lear and Edmund we sense that to live at all is an illegitimate act for which life itself is the punishment.

The brutal power of *King Lear* has always seemed to center on the death of Cordelia – its shocking unexpectedness, its lack of justice. Yet this ending is latent in the play from the beginning. Lear's initial act of violation is his attempt to unmake Cordelia's identity, the result of which is the unmaking of his own. The pattern is by now familiar, and goes back to Chiron and Demetrius, whose attempt to reduce Lavinia to a nameless thing reduces them in turn to Rape and Murder. Lear tries to resist the loss of his identity when that loss stems from attacks on him by Goneril and Regan. Yet when Cordelia tries to give his identity back, he refuses to take it. Touched with healing – music, fresh garments, a restoring kiss – he reacts as though he is being tortured, bound upon a wheel of fire. To take identity away is violation; but to give it back is also violation. And when he eventually accepts the new life Cordelia has to offer, Lear sets up the conditions for his final agony, in which his initial curse comes true, and kills him by killing her. It was in relationship that he had hoped for happiness; it is relationship that kills him. The subplot plays its own variations on this: Edgar's tending of Gloucester has an element of torture; and in restoring his own identity and his relationships with his father and brother, Edgar kills them both. To say that life is our punishment for being born is not, for this play, just a large generalization. *King Lear* shows death latent in birth, as the wheel comes full circle when Edmund condemns his birth as he dies, and Lear enters carrying a dead body as though it were a newborn child. The play sees violation not just in Lear's attack on Cordelia, but in the restoration of identity and relationship that seems to counter that attack. In the aftermath of Lavinia's rape we saw something coercive, something not unlike the rape itself, in her family's attempts to comfort her. In *King Lear*, hurt and healing are so twisted together that they cannot be separated.

CHAPTER 7

Macbeth: *A deed without a name*

INTERPRETING A MURDER

We have seen that acts of violation unsettle the identities of both the victims and the perpetrators. Chiron and Demetrius are reduced to Rape and Murder. The loss of Cressida's identity is bound up with, and in part created by, the instability of Troilus. Othello, re-making Desdemona, undoes himself; and Lear, trying to turn Cordelia into nothing, becomes nothing himself. Sometimes the lost identity is in play with a new one that can be named: Hamlet's madness, taking over Hamlet; the cunning whore of Venice, taking over Desdemona; Diomed's Cressida. But the new identity is often nameless: a figure like your father, he that was Othello, the thing that looks like Lear. It all goes back to "This was thy daughter" and beyond that to "My name was Don Andrea." We have also seen that the identities of the acts themselves become unsettled. Romeo's killing Tybalt and his breaking into the Capulet tomb color, and are colored by, the consummation of his marriage with Juliet. Lavinia's rape and her marriage shadow each other; so do Desdemona's murder and her wedding night. In *Macbeth* there seems to be no question about Duncan's identity, or Macbeth's, and when Macbeth kills Duncan there seems to be no ambiguity about the act. There are many ways to describe it, all images of violation. However, beneath these descriptions – and this is the first note struck when the murder is discovered – is the idea that the act is unnameable. This time it is not the perpetrator or the victim but the act itself whose identity is unfixed.

The murder, like the rape of Lavinia, takes place offstage. We never see the body; but in the moments that follow its discovery, the characters, led by Macduff, try to do what Lavinia's family has to do: find words for what has happened. Macduff's first reaction is a generalized shock, in a single word that, like Lear's "never," can only repeat itself as though there is nothing more to say. He goes on to declare the failure of thought (like the "thoughts beyond the reaches of our souls" [I.iv.56] the Ghost triggers in *Hamlet*) and the failure of language: "O horror! horror! horror! / Tongue nor heart cannot conceive, nor name thee!" (II.iii.64–65). In *Titus, Hamlet* and *Othello* looking, like speaking, is a way to fix reality. Macduff warns Macbeth and Lennox that the murder does to sight what it does to thought and language: "Approach the chamber, and destroy your sight / With a new Gorgon!" (II.iii.72–73).

In between, he has found an image to embody his sense of violation. There is after all a way to name it and a way to describe it:

> Most sacrilegious Murther hath broke ope
> The Lord's anointed temple, and stole thence
> The life o'th'building! (II.iii.68–70)

As Lavinia's body is for Aaron a rifled treasury (I.i.631) and her rape is like an enemy breaking into a city, so the temple of Duncan's body, the body of an anointed king, has been broken into. Speaking to Malcolm and Donalbain, Macduff finds an image in family terms: "The spring, the head, the fountain of your blood / Is stopp'd; the very source of it is stopp'd" (II.iii.98-99). Othello saw Desdemona's body as the spring that gave him life; Duncan was that for his sons, and now, with the spring stopped, it as though their own lives will dry up. Blocked parenthood is, as we shall see, an obsessive theme in the play. Duncan's murder is the death of a king, the death of a father, the stopping of life itself.

But these images of violation alternate with moments when meaning seems to break down. Calling the sleepers to awake, Macduff talks as though what has happened is not the ultimate crime but the ultimate judgment:

> up, up, and see
> The great doom's image! – Malcolm! Banquo!
> As from your graves rise up, and walk like sprites,
> To countenance this horror! (II.iii.78–81)

Lady Macbeth calls the bell "a hideous trumpet" (II.iii.82), and Banquo's "when we have our naked frailties hid" (II.iii.126) recalls naked souls rising from their graves in a Doomsday painting.[1] Hamlet's father breaking out of his grave, the disturbance of domestic peace when Brabantio is roused from his bed – these images are now expanded, both in language and in action, as half-dressed people, alarmed and bewildered, fill the stage. As in *King Lear* the first murder and the Last Judgment seem conflated, so here the horror of this one crime and the horror of ultimate judgment – the judgment Macbeth told himself he was prepared to risk (I.vii.1–7) – become one. The meaning of Duncan's murder expands beyond the kingdom and the family to become the essence of all crime, and crime itself, in a breakdown of meaning, infiltrates the idea of judgment.

In the midst of his own struggle to say what has happened, Macduff tells Macbeth and Lennox, "Do not bid me speak: / See, and then speak yourselves" (II.iii.73–74). Macbeth echoes Macduff's sense of ultimate ruin – "renown, and grace, is dead; / The wine of life is drawn" (II.iii.94–95) – but goes on to strike a slightly false note: "Here lay Duncan, / His silver skin lac'd with his golden blood" (II.iii.111-12). There is a touch of Marcus here, covering the physical horror in ersatz beauty.[2] Lady Macbeth's "What! in our house?" (II.iii.88) seems false in the other direction, in its apparent banality; though in its own way it is telling. Her earlier line, "The doors are open" (II.ii.5) establishes the conditions for murder: as for Macduff a temple has been violated, for Lady Macbeth a threshold is crossed, a house no longer affords protection. The difference is that she opened those doors herself. It is the perpetrators who have the greatest difficulty finding words for the deed; Macbeth overdecorates, Lady Macbeth under-reacts while revealing more than she intends to.

There is also some difficulty about naming the doers of the deed. Malcolm's reaction to the news raises the question of agency, and seems designed to start a revenge action: "O! by whom?" Lennox's reply is guarded: "Those of his chamber, as it seem'd, had done't" (II.iii.100–1). "As it seem'd" keeps the question open, as does Macbeth's revelation that he killed the grooms, putting them beyond interrogation. Left alone, Malcolm and Donalbain suspect everybody – "Let's not consort with them" (II.iii.135) and decide to flee the country. For a while the deed seems to lack a doer. Then in the following scenes, suspicion spreads, as agentless as the murder itself. There is no detective work, no handkerchief to give a clue, no equivalent of Lavinia writing in the sand. Macduff is apprehensive about the new reign, Banquo suspects the truth, but keeps his thoughts to himself, and by III.vi the roundabout sarcasm of Lennox accuses Macbeth without quite using the words. It is as though agency has been suspended. The horror of the murder is clear, and has many dimensions; part of its horror is that it seems to float free of the actions and the knowledge of particular people.

Throughout *Macbeth*, the language dwells obsessively on unnameable deeds; and these deeds are done by done by unnameable agents. The question of identity shifts into the question of agency. "Who's there?" becomes "who did this?" In most cases we can give an answer, or think we can. But when we look for the answers given in the play, we find its language slides and dissolves. Language itself is now in the condition of Lavinia after the rape: something terrible has happened, but it cannot say what it was, or who did it. When Hamlet denies responsibility for the death of Polonius – "Hamlet does it not, Hamlet denies it" (V.ii.232) he names himself twice, and the denial is an implicit self-accusation. There is no such clarity in the language of *Macbeth*.

THINGS UNNAMEABLE

Long before the murder itself, a curious vagueness about who is doing what pervades the language of the play. It is clear that Duncan's generals are fighting an invasion and a rebellion, but the messengers' reports that give details are oddly murky. The Captain, describing Macbeth's confrontation with Macdonwald, declares that Macbeth

> carv'd out his passage,
> Till he fac'd the slave;
> Which ne'er shook hands, nor bade farewell to him,
> Till he unseam'd him from the nave to th' chops,
> And fix'd his head upon our battlements. (I.ii.19–23)

Who did the killing? The antecedent of "which" seems to be "the slave," Macdonwald; the antecedents of "he" and "him" in the next line are ambiguous. By the end of the passage it is evidently Macbeth who has killed Macdonwald, but the initial effect is of an action in which we cannot distinguish the actors. This concealment of agency becomes one of the key effects of the play. The narrative confusion continues when Macbeth confronts either the King of Norway or the traitor Cawdor in hand-to-hand combat, and at first it is not clear which one he is fighting. Again there is a problem of antecedents; Macbeth "Confronted him with self-comparisons" (I.ii.56), but who is "him"? "Rebellious" in the next line suggests Cawdor. But in the following scene confusion is worse confounded when Macbeth seems to know nothing of Cawdor's treachery.[3]

The riddling language of the witches participates in – and since they begin the play may be said to trigger – the general uncertainty. Their paradoxes can be decoded: "When the battle's lost and won" (I.i.4) and "Lesser than Macbeth, and greater" (I.iii.65) are riddles that do not require an Oedipus to solve them. "Fair is foul, and foul is fair" (I.i.11) is a simple moral inversion, and when Macbeth echoes it in his first line, "So foul and fair a day I have not seen" (I.iii.38) he turns it into another fairly easy riddle. But the cumulative effect is that, just as the body turns against itself in *Lear*, so words are set to fight each other, even cancel each other out. Macbeth's first line disturbs us not by the particular riddle it poses but by the way it shows him participating in this general self-canceling of language. It is an effect we have seen before: this is and is not Cressid, I think my wife be honest, and think she is not.[4] Words are "As two spent swimmers, that do cling together / And choke their art" (I.ii.8–9).

Choking suggests the swimmers will drown. The next stage after self-cancellation is that words disappear, as the witches do. In their charm "Thrice to thine, and thrice to mine" (I.iii.35) we cannot tell what they are talking about. There, a word seems missing; when they describe their action in the cauldron scene as "A deed without a name" (IV.i.49) a word is deliberately erased. At times, like the Ghost in *Hamlet*, they are silent under questioning, as they are with Banquo in their first encounter; they speak only to Macbeth. Then they reverse themselves, speaking only to Banquo; when Macbeth wants to hear more their response to his repeated questions is silence. On "Speak, I charge you" (I.iii.78) they vanish, as the Ghost did on a similar command.

Like Lavinia and the Ghost, the witches provoke the question, "what are you?" (I.iii.47). A puzzle about their identity is built into the text. In the Folio speech headings they are identified only by number; in its stage directions they are witches, and for convenience I have adopted the general practice of calling them that. But that word is used only once in the play's dialogue (I.iii.6). Elsewhere they are (with variations) weird sisters; that is what they call themselves (I.iii.32). (The adjective derives from the Old English word for fate or destiny.) In earlier versions of the story their identities are shifting and uncertain: they are variously wildly dressed women, goddesses of destiny, nymphs or fairies, women of striking beauty, demons in the form of women.[5] Banquo's questions are like the questioning of the Ghost in *Hamlet*, alternatives tried out against silence:

> What are these,
> So wither'd and so wild in their attire,
> That look not like th'inhabitants o' th' earth,
> And yet are on't? Live you? Or are you aught
> That man may question? You seem to understand me,
> By each at once her choppy finger laying
> Upon her skinny lips: you should be women,
> And yet your beards forbid me to interpret
> That you are so. (I.iii.39–47)

Of the earth or not, alive or not, questionable or not, women or not: they inhabit a series of border zones, with something nameable on one side of the border and something unnameable on the other. Bombarded with questions, they say nothing about themselves, replying only with riddling statements about their questioners. The mystery deepens in the cauldron scene, when they refer to "our masters" (IV.i.63) and these masters turn out to be apparitions who rise at the witches' bidding. Who in fact are the masters, the witches or the spirits? And what are those spirits?

This sense of an encounter with the unknowable touches even the Porter scene. The Porter brings solid reality into the murky world of the play: jokes about drink, sex and urine; stock comedy about tailors, farmers and equivocators. But the Porter, having invoked Beelzebub, cannot remember "th' other devil's name" (II.iii.8). His three imaginary visitants are followed by an unknown fourth. The Porter gets no further than "What are you?" (II.iii.18), then breaks off his routine. What, not who: in a play that follows with almost comic rigor the old storytelling rule of three, the introduction of a fourth is a brief glimpse beyond the border into something truly unknown, and unknowable – unless the fourth visitant is Macduff, who appears at this point as a totally new character and who has, we shall see, his own uncanniness.

The suppression of agency, the self-canceling of language, encounters with the unnameable – all these come to a head around the murder of Duncan. Macbeth and Lady Macbeth compulsively use the passive voice to talk about the murder, concealing their own agency in the act as Troilus suppresses agency in his warning to Cressida, "something may be done that we will not" (IV.iv.93). "He that's coming / Must be provided for" (I.v.65–66); "If it were done, when 'tis done, then 'twere well / It were done quickly" (I.vii.1–2); "I go, and it is done" (II.i.62). Not only does the deed have no doer, it has no name. "Provided for" conflates murder with hospitality in a remark that heard out of context would be perfectly innocent. Elsewhere the deed is "it": the word applied compulsively to a character, the Ghost, in *Hamlet* is here applied just as compulsively to an act. Lady Macbeth's strong impulse to drive her husband to murder meets an equally strong counterforce in her refusal to say what she actually means:

> what thou wouldst highly
> That wouldst thou holily; wouldst not play false,
> And yet wouldst wrongly win; thou'dst have, great Glamis,
> That which cries, 'Thus thou must do,' if thou have it;
> And that which rather thou dost fear to do,
> Than wishest should be undone. (I.v.20–25)

While she accuses her husband of fear, her own fear of the words that will name the deed drives her into a series of desperate evasions.

Macbeth's incomplete sentence "And falls on th' other –" (I.vii.28) anticipates his inability to say "Amen," the word that gives closure. The grooms have asked for blessing, and a murderer cannot complete that thought. As we shall see, part of Macbeth's horror is that the murder itself remains forever unfinished, and the failure of his language to give closure is a warning of that larger failure. It is practically a physical blockage: "'Amen' / Stuck in my throat" (II.ii.31–32). Cordelia feels love pressing her tongue down; eventually she is strangled. So is Desdemona. Lavinia loses her tongue. Macduff's tongue fails him (II.iii.64–65). But Macbeth's problem is with the word itself, which blocks the passage that would utter it. Elsewhere language is ambiguous. Lady Macbeth's "All our service, / In every point twice done, and then done double" (I.vi.14–15) conceals a wicked pun on "double" as treacherous, and leads to Macbeth's "He's here in double trust" (I.vii.12), where the pun seems no longer under the speaker's control but built into the language. "My thought, whose murther yet is but fantastical" (I.iii.139) is equivocation of another kind. Macbeth speaks the forbidden word for once, but while admitting he is thinking of murder he also suggests that thought itself is murdered, as if to suppress the word it is in the act of speaking. Words destroy each other: "This supernatural soliciting / Cannot be ill; cannot be good" (I.iii.130–31) leaves nothing but a blank; so does "nothing is, but what is not' (I.iii.142). The self-canceling of identity in Iago's "I am not what I am" is extended to action and finally to existence itself.

UNMAKING MACBETH

The disconnection and internal conflict that affect language also affect the body – or, more precisely, the language that imagines the body. Tarquin in *Lucrece* is in some ways an early study for Macbeth, but in one respect he is radically different. The components of his being work together: "His drumming heart cheers up his burning eye, / His eye commends the leading to his hand" (435–36). Macbeth commands,

> Stars, hide your fires!
> Let not light see my black and deep desires;
> The eye wink at the hand; yet let that be,
> Which the eye fears, when it is done, to see. (I.iv.50–53)

The disconnection of eye and hand recalls Cressida's disconnection of eye and heart (I.ii.285–86). While Tarquin is active, Macbeth characteristically retreats to "let that be" and "when it is done." He also calls for a disconnection between the act and the external world that might see it, as he will later ask the earth not to hear his footsteps (II.i.56–58). More startlingly, Lady Macbeth commands "That my keen knife see not the wound it makes" (I.v.52). Since it is the knife (not Lady Macbeth) that does the killing it must be a sentient being, and she wants it blocked from the sight of its own deed.

As language turns against itself, so does the body. Macbeth feels an internal disruption that recalls *King Lear*:

> why do I yield to that suggestion
> Whose horrid image doth unfix my hair,
> And make my seated heart knock at my ribs,
> Against the use of nature? (I.iii.134–37)

We have seen that those who do acts of violation undo themselves. Othello and Lear lose their names. Macbeth never loses his name; but he seems to lose contact with his own body. He looks at his own hands and, like Lear, fails to recognize them:

> What hands are here? Ha! they pluck out mine eyes.
> Will all great Neptune's ocean wash this blood
> Clean from my hand? No, this my hand will rather
> The multitudinous seas incarnadine
> Making the green one red. (II.ii.58–62)

In the first line the echoes of *Lear* work backwards, from the reunion with Cordelia to the blinding of Gloucester, as Macbeth's own hands, initially unfamiliar, seem to turn against him and Duncan's blood becomes his own. He called for darkness so that he could kill Duncan, and tried to conceal the deed in language so that he could not see it. Now, in killing Duncan he has blinded himself; except that he can still see the blood with terrible clarity, and it runs out of control as his hands did. Titus and Lear saw the sea flooding the land; Macbeth sees his own guilt flooding the sea. The world outside the private consciousness, which he and Lady Macbeth asked to hear nothing and see nothing of the murder, now registers nothing else. As Macbeth is internally disconnected, the border between himself and the life outside himself breaks; the thoughts he has tried to suppress now confront him everywhere he looks. And that border, dividing "me" from "not me," is the border that defines identity.

Far from being silent and unknowing, the outside world sends back disembodied voices, like the calls of "Graymalkin" and "Paddock" (I.i.8–9) the witches hear. Macbeth hears something as he leaves Duncan's chamber (II.ii.14–17); we never know what. In the chamber he hears a voice cry "Sleep no more!" but to Lady Macbeth's question "Who was it that thus cried?" (II.ii.34, 43) there is no answer. We seem to be in a kind of anti-drama without actors in which things are done, but no one does them, things are said but no one says them. Macbeth projects himself into an allegorical play where it is "wither'd Murther," not Macbeth himself, who walks the stage "thus with his stealthy pace" (II.i.52–54) towards the exit that stands for Duncan's chamber.[6] "Thus" implies Macbeth is walking as he speaks the line. His direction has been set by the unseen dagger: "Thou marshall'st me the way that I was going" (II.i.42). It is not the killer who guides the dagger but the dagger that guides the killer. Even Macbeth's evasions are out of his control, for they recoil on him as statements of truth. He is indeed withered murder: like Chiron and Demetrius in their roles as Rape and Murder, he is becoming his own crime; through the rest of the play we will see him wither and, like Goneril, come to deadly use.

That he lets a dagger lead him is a sign that his own will is suspended. Lady Macbeth complains that when circumstances were wrong for the deed he was willing to make them right: now they are right, "That their fitness now / Does unmake you" (I.vii.53–54). She sees his refusal to act as an unmaking of his being. But for Macbeth it is action itself that unmakes him: "To know my deed, 'twere best not know myself" (II.ii.72). It is not just that "to live with what he has done, he must erase his knowledge of himself";[7] in declaring that consciousness of the deed and consciousness of himself cannot exist together, he suggests that he and the deed cannot exist together. Instead of a character expressing himself in action, this action cancels a character. This was the fate of Tarquin: "So that in vent'ring ill we leave to be / The things we are" (148–49); it was the fate of Othello when he turned against Desdemona, of Lear when he turned against Cordelia.

HAUNTED BY MACBETH

The deed Macbeth tried to imagine as beyond his will or agency is now beyond his control. He has said, "I go, and it is done" (II.i.62). Lady Macbeth assures him, "what's done is done" (III.ii.12). In the sleepwalking scene this becomes "What's done cannot be undone" (V.i.64); finality has become entrapment. While the deed is done in the sense of committed quite early in the play, it is not done in the sense of finished.[8] Macbeth's fantasy that his hand would turn the sea red finds an equivalent in reality when the darkness he and Lady Macbeth have called for becomes literal in the outside world, as the light–dark reversal of *Romeo and Juliet* finally affects Verona: "by th' clock 'tis day, / And yet dark night strangles the travelling lamp" (II.iv.6–7). Others besides Macbeth have heard strange voices in the night (II.iii.55–62). As Macbeth's tyranny advances, Scotland itself becomes a wilderness of crying voices. At first we know who is crying: "Each new morn, / New widows howl, new orphans cry" (IV.iii.4–5). But eventually the source ceases to matter: "sighs, and groans, and shrieks that rent the air / Are made, not marked" (IV.iii.168–69). The passive voice has returned, and with it the horror of being no longer able to feel horror, no longer wanting to know who is crying.

In a crude way Macbeth has invaded other lives and other houses: "There's not a one of them, but in his house / I keep a servant fee'd" (III.iv.130–31). But he has invaded other lives more insidiously than that. The Lord who speaks with Lennox describes the present condition of Scotland by contrasting it with what he hopes for:

> we may again
> Give to our tables meat, sleep to our nights,
> Free from our feasts and banquets bloody knives,
> Do faithful homage, and receive free honours,
> All which we pine for now. (III.vi.33–37)

He is describing Macbeth's own condition: insomnia, lack of true fealty, feasts turned to horror. Scotland suffers not just because of Macbeth but along with him. The border between the private consciousness and the outside world, holding firm in Hamlet's distinction between the world as it seemed to him and the world as it really was, has become alarmingly porous. We may recall the way Lavinia's ordeal shadows the entire world of *Titus Andronicus*.

It is not just that physical violence has spread. The mental conditions that helped to breed that violence have also spread. Chief of these is the undoing of identity. *Troilus and Cressida* showed a world of unstable identities, theatrically centering on Cressida. *Macbeth* shows a similar world, not just theatrically centering on Macbeth but created by him. Macbeth, to know his deed, could not know himself; Rosse complains, "cruel are the times, when we are traitors, / And do not know ourselves" (IV.ii.18–19). Scotland is in the same condition, "Almost afraid to know itself" (IV.iii.165). Mass slaughter means identities no longer matter: "the dead man's knell / Is there scarce ask'd for who" (IV.iii.70–71). This is the horror of the death camp, of nameless bodies bulldozed into mass graves. Anonymity shows in small ways, in the recurring effect of unknown messengers entering. When Rosse arrives in England Malcolm does not at first recognize him (IV.iii.160). The messenger who warns Lady Macduff begins, "I am not to you known" (IV.ii.64). A more terrible non-recognition is Lady Macduff's question of the murderers, "What are these faces[?]" (IV.ii.78). She is looking at things that resemble the human face; but what are they really?

The deceptive appearance of loyalty and hospitality the Macbeths have presented to Duncan makes appearance itself seem untrustworthy. This mistrust shapes Malcolm's treatment of Macduff in IV.iii. The appearance of virtue, so powerful when Desdemona walked on stage and Othello's suspicions fell away, has now been rendered inoperative: "Though all things foul would wear the brows of grace, / Yet Grace must still look so" (IV.iii.23–24). Grace has no choice but to look like itself, but it is so easily imitated its appearance means nothing. Yet Malcolm finds a way of turning deception against itself. He paints a false portrait of himself as evil, to see if Macduff has a breaking point, if there is a degree of evil he will not tolerate. The experiment works, but it is a near thing. Macduff is willing to accept lust and avarice on a grand scale, and though Malcolm's unswearing of his own detraction finally restores confidence between the two men it leaves Macduff silent at first, then confused: "Such welcome and unwelcome things at once, / 'Tis hard to reconcile" (IV.iii.138–39). There is a touch of Macbeth-like equivocation here: Malcolm cannot be ill, cannot be good. Macduff speaks, however, not of contradiction but of reconciliation; and he calls reconciliation hard, not impossible.

RESISTING MACBETH

Up to a point, Macbeth's consciousness has spread outward and infected the world. Paradoxically, this sign of his power is also a sign of his failure. He has not closed off Duncan's murder with the act itself, as he wanted to; the act has taken on a life of its own, carrying him and everyone else along with it. In the scene in England Malcolm uses Macbeth's own instruments, equivocation and deception, against him. In another image of the body turning against itself (and with an echo of Hamlet forcing Claudius to drink his own poison) Macbeth has declared,

> this even-handed Justice
> Commends th'ingredience of our poison'd chalice
> To our own lips. (I.vii.10–12)

In the second half of the play Macbeth's actions both spread beyond him and turn against him.

We see this in the murder of Banquo. It seems a mirror image of the killing of Duncan. Banquo expresses duty and loyalty to his king, as Macbeth did (III.i.15–18) but we know his thoughts too are otherwise; this time, however, it is the king who after an exchange of courtesies kills the subject. Speaking to his wife Macbeth uses the old language, the passive voice that conceals agency: "there shall be done / A deed of dreadful note" (III.ii.43–44). Murder thrives on anonymity, and the hired killers are simply "those men" (III.i.45). (At a similar point Richard III hired Tyrrel, who hired Forrest and Dighton. They had names.) Macbeth has again called on darkness to cover the murder, keeping the killers nameless and unseen; but this time darkness works against him. When the third murderer asks "Who did strike out the light?" and the first replies, "Was't not the way?" (III.iii.19), it is clear there has been a blunder, and in the darkness Fleance escapes.

Banquo returns, like Hamlet's father, not as a disembodied ghost but as a walking corpse, covered with blood like Duncan, but not, this time, decently offstage to be described in decorative language. Like the ruined Lavinia, the blind Gloucester and the dead Cordelia, he is there on stage, and Macbeth has to look at him. The horror is focused by the fact that only Macbeth can see him, and sharpened for the audience by the fact that we can see him too. We could not literally see the copulating bodies Othello saw; but we have no such protection here. Breaking out of the grave like Hamlet's father, Banquo frustrates Macbeth's need for an ending:

> the time has been,
> That, when the brains were out, the man would die,
> And there an end. . . . (III.ii.77–79)

We might have thought Banquo's appearance at the banquet was dramatic enough, and need not be repeated. But as the Ghost reappears unexpectedly in Gertrude's closet, Banquo reappears unexpectedly in the cauldron scene to gloat over the procession of his descendants. This is another way in which Banquo denies closure: he has a son, whom Macbeth fails to kill, and the first of his descendants to appear leads Macbeth to cry in protest, "Thou art too like the spirit of Banquo:

down!" (IV.i.112). The cry of "down!" is Macbeth's vain attempt to stop the future.

If he cannot stop the future, perhaps he can gain a kind of control by knowing it. For that he turns to the witches. Up to a point they mimic the mental world he created in order to murder Duncan. In a grotesque literalizing of his images of the disconnected body, their brew consists of dismembered body parts: eye, toe, tongue, liver, gall, finger – nothing is put in whole. The riddling ambiguity of the last two prophecies (none of woman born can harm him, he cannot be vanquished till Birnam Wood comes to Dunsinane) reflects Macbeth's own equivocation, his own tendency to hide the truth in language. Yet the first prophecy is a plain and valid warning: "beware Macduff" (IV.i.71). Its speaker, an armed head, suggests a warrior in battle, and (being only a head) fore-shadows Macbeth's fate. It is the second apparition, whom the witches describe as "More potent than the first" (IV.i.76), who begins the equivo-cation. But while the words offer lying hope, the pictures, like the armed head, offer hidden warnings. The second, a bloody child, suggests violent, unnatural birth, the hidden meaning of "none of woman born" (IV.i.80). The third, holding a tree in its hand, shows how the trick of Birnam Wood will be done. The first two apparitions address Macbeth by name, three times; the third does not use his name. The effect is that as the future they foreshadow draws inexorably nearer, Macbeth's identity fades.

Whatever power the witches represent acts as the Porter says drink acts on the drinker: it "equivocates him in a sleep, and, giving him the lie, leaves him" (II.iii.35–37). As in the cauldron scene the two deceptive prophecies are grounded in the first prophecy's simple truth, in the subsequent action equivocations unravel into plain meaning – Macduff was born by Caesarean section, Malcolm and his soldiers carry boughs in their hands – leaving Macbeth nowhere to hide. Malcolm's command, "Now, near enough: your leavy screens throw down, / And show like those you are" (V.vi.1–2) signals a return to reality and an end to deception, even the deception he himself has practiced.

The countermovement establishes values that work against Macbeth's evil. The survival of Fleance, and the show of eight kings, confirm the fertility with which Banquo has been associated since he asked the witches which of the seeds of time would grow (I.iii.58–59) and saw the "pendent bed, and procreant cradle" where martlets "breed and haunt" (I.vi.8–9) even on Macbeth's castle. The majesty and sheer continuity of the show of kings, horrifying to Macbeth, proclaim the survival of the order his killing of Duncan violated. As he saw his own hands plucking out his eyes, now he finds himself blinded by the sight of majesty: "Thy crown does sear mine eye-balls" (IV.i.113). Young Macduff seems at first a cynical child, a fit inhabitant of the world Macbeth has created: there are enough liars and swearers to hang up the honest men, if his mother does not weep he will quickly have a new father. But though Lady Macduff has unequivocally called her husband a traitor (IV.ii.44–45) – which he is, to his family – when the murderer repeats the charge the boy cries, "Thou liest, thou shag-hair'd villain!" (IV.ii.82). Loyalty is one of the values Macbeth has violated; with an echo of Desdemona's denial of Othello's crime and Cordelia's "No cause, no cause," the boy's loyalty to his father wipes out his father's disloyalty to him.

The King of England is a kind of anti-Macbeth, healing his subjects with a touch of his hand, able to pass the gift to his successors, having "a heavenly gift of prophecy" (IV.iii.143–56). Macbeth has no successors, he is the plaything of devilish prophecies, and his hands are not exactly healing. At the end of the play, Malcolm's announcement that Thanes will now be Earls suggests a new language for a new era, and an Angliciz-ing of Scotland, with an implied hope that he will rule as the English king does. His declaration, "Cousins, I hope the days are near at hand, / That chambers will be safe" (IV.iv.1–2) counters the horror of violated space that has run through the play. "Cousins" restores the language of rela-tionship, a language Malcolm uses constantly:

> You, worthy uncle,
> Shall, with my cousin, your right noble son,
> Lead our first battle. . . . (V.vi.2–4)

Malcolm brings back to Scotland some of the values Macbeth has violated.

ENEMY ACTION

So far, the play seems to be generating images of restoration and healing like those we thought were at work in the final scenes of *Titus*. But Malcolm's order "Show like those you are" (V.vi.2) contains that treach-erous word, "like," the word that unsettled the identity of the Ghost in *Hamlet* even as it seemed to confirm it. Equivocation, the medium of the witches and of Macbeth himself, is still with us. Repeating an effect we have seen in *Titus*, *Hamlet* and *Lear*, Scotland is restored through an invasion by a traditional enemy, England. Macbeth makes some play with this: his taunt "Then fly, false Thanes, / And mingle with the English epicures" (V.iii.7–8) shows his contempt for the effete and decadent south. Malcolm's declaration that from now on Thanes will be Earls may make us wonder if he has come to save Scotland or to abolish it. The saintly English King remains offstage; England is represented onstage by Old Siward, whose refusal to mourn the death of his son has some of the inhumanity, the denial of relationship, we see in Macbeth. Malcolm politely refuses to accept it (V.ix.12–19), but we are left with a question: is the force coming in from the south all that different from the force it is dislodging?[9] In the opening scenes, with loyal generals fighting rebels, it was Macbeth and Banquo, fighting on the side of right, who seemed to "memorize another Golgotha" (I.ii.41), equating them with the killers of Christ. Is there similar ambiguity here?

Malcolm does not kill Macbeth; that is a task for Macduff, a more ambivalent figure. Macduff's first appearance in the play follows immediately upon the murder of Duncan; before that, we had no inkling of his existence. It is as though the murder itself has called him into being. Macbeth has created his own nemesis, with a name eerily like his own.[10] This similarity, as in the case of Edmund and Edgar, is a clue to a mirror-effect. Macduff is in some respects unnatural, like the man he kills.[11] His desertion of his family preserves him to help save Scotland, but it still registers as a betrayal. His wife calls him a traitor (IV.ii.3–4, 44–45) and complains "He wants the natural touch" (IV.ii.9). His disloyalty leaves his son in a Macbeth-like contradiction: "Father'd he is, and yet he's father-less" (IV.ii.27). It fuels Malcolm's suspicion: "Why in that rawness left you wife and child . . . Without leave-taking?" (IV.iii.26–28). Hearing of the slaughter, Macduff himself turns quickly from blaming heaven's desertion to blaming his own:

> Did Heaven look on,
> And would not take their part? Sinful Macduff!
> They were all struck for thee. (IV.iii.223–25)

When he declares that if anyone else kills Macbeth, "My wife and children's ghosts will haunt me still" (V.vii.16) it seems one haunted man is about to be killed by another.

While each man has in a sense made himself unnatural, Macduff, "from his mother's womb / Untimely ripp'd" (V.viii.15–16), was unnat-ural in his very birth. He speaks of his birth as the Macbeths speak of the murder, in the passive voice that conceals agency, making it an act that cannot be fully imagined – and with good reason. The language stresses the violation of the natural time of childbirth, and the damage to his mother's body. Caesarean section in this period was fatal to the mother; Macduff killed his mother by being born. The language-trick of the prophecy makes Macduff an uncanny contradiction: he is alive, but he was never born. The second apparition, the bloody child, conflates his own birth and his child's death. Though Macduff comes with the party of healing and restoration, there is something in him that comes from Macbeth's territory. As Othello must kill himself, Macbeth must be killed by something like himself. It is the ultimate consequence of the disappearance of the border that separates the self from the other.

MURDER, SEX AND GENDER

As a child, a husband and a father, Macduff is unnatural, and through his association with marriage, birth and parenthood, he takes us back for a closer look at the couple who kill Duncan. A central paradox of the play is that the murderers who try to keep their deed without a name and without an agent reveal themselves in the process with a detailed intimacy that makes this arguably one of the closest examinations of private life in English drama. It matters first of all that they are a couple. More is at stake here than the violation of kingship, loyalty and the host–guest relationship. The sexual preoccupations of earlier tragedies may seem at first to have little place in this play. But Macduff's violent origin adds to the blood of murder the blood of childbirth, and the other blood, the blood of the marriage bed that figures so prominently in *Romeo and Juliet* and *Othello* is, as we shall see, not so far away. Asserting his virtue, Malcolm declares he is a virgin, and a man who has not killed is a virgin.[12] That may be why his final dismissal of "this dead butcher, and his fiend-like Queen" (V.ix.35) has such an odd double effect: we see its theoretical justice, yet it seems chilling and priggish. The virginal Malcolm, "Unknown to woman" (IV.iii.126), cannot know what has passed between Macbeth and Lady Macbeth; he does not know them as we have. He has neither committed murder nor made love.

Though sexuality does not touch the language of violence in this play as pervasively as it does in *Romeo and Juliet* and *Troilus and Cressida*, it is there. Fortune is Macdonwald's whore, Macbeth is Valour's minion and Bellona's bridegroom (I.ii.14–15, 19, 55). The evil that seems to be in the air is also touched with the sexual. Banquo's prayer, "Restrain in me the cursed thoughts that nature / Gives way to in repose!" (II.i.8–9) suggests the Compline Hymn,[13] a charm against nocturnal emissions in which good Christian men try to protect themselves from succubi: "Tread under foot our ghostly foe, / That no pollution we may know." Macbeth and his wife regularly use forms of the verb "do" for murder, and, threatening the sailor whose wife refused her chestnuts, the first witch uses it without (at first) an apparent meaning: "I'll do, I'll do, and I'll do" (I.iii.10). But elsewhere in Shakespeare "to do" is to copulate,[14] and when the witch has found her victim, "I'll drain him dry as hay" (I.iii.18). That will finish his relations with the wife who has offended her.[15]

Sex and gender are key issues for Macbeth and his wife, and they intertwine. Romeo, Troilus and Lear felt their gender roles, their identities as men, destabilized. They feared and resisted the woman in themselves. The instability of gender affects both parties here. Which is the lord, and which is the lady? Lady Macbeth's telltale reference to "my battlements" (I.v.40) suggests she owns the castle. She accuses her husband of being "too full o'th'milk of human kindness" (I.v.17). When she urges him to come home "That I may pour my spirits in thine ear" (I.v.26) it sounds as though she is going to impregnate him as Mary was impregnated. Elsewhere in Shakespeare "spirit" can mean penis or semen.[16] In the next line "chastise with the valour of my tongue" (I.v.27) attributes what is conventionally a male virtue to what is (just as conventionally) a woman's weapon.

Her most powerful effort is to turn something like Lear's curse on Goneril's body against her own. This takes her beyond simple gender reversal, into a new sense of what it means for her to be a woman. In asking to be unsexed she is not just calling for sterility:

> Come, you Spirits
> That tend on mortal thoughts, unsex me here,
> And fill me, from the crown to the toe, top-full
> Of direst cruelty! make thick my blood,
> Stop up th'access and passage to remorse. . . . (I.v.40–44)

Remembering the sexual meaning of "spirit," she is asking, paradoxically, to be both unsexed and impregnated. She wants the spirits to fill her body, but in the process to block its passages. She is not asking for a male body, but for a female body that once the spirits have done their work will be impregnable, because it is already pregnant. Thickened blood recalls the curdled milk to which the Ghost compares its poisoned blood (I.v.68–70), and anticipates the thickening light of Macbeth's invocation of darkness (III.ii.50). Pregnant with cruelty (otherwise what milk would she have in a childless marriage?) she will breastfeed accordingly: "Come to my woman's breasts, / And take my milk for gall, you murth'ring ministers" (I.v.47–48). The ministers will either turn her milk to gall, or suckle on the gall that is her milk, or both.[17]

When she imagines – and not just imagines, remembers – breastfeeding a human infant, she turns the image around in what sounds like a denial of the nurturing capacity of her own body, a denial more shocking because it draws not on a latent inhumanity but on a genuine memory of maternal love:

> I have given suck, and know
> How tender 'tis to love the babe that milks me:
> I would, when it was smiling in my face,
> Have pluck'd my nipple from his boneless gums,
> And dash'd the brains out, had I so sworn
> As you have done to this. (I.vii.54–59)[18]

Promise-keeping is a male virtue, a warrior's virtue. Hector went to battle against the pleas of his family because he had promised the Greeks, and one of the most stinging battlefield taunts in *Coriolanus* is "I do hate thee / Worse than a promise-breaker" (I.viii.1–2). Macbeth has promised; and men, his wife argues, should keep their promises even if it means killing a child; she would. But if promise-keeping is a male virtue, she describes it in an image drawn from an experience only a woman can have. The bearded witches may inhabit a gender twilight zone, but Lady Macbeth is a woman. There is nothing that in Shakespeare's theatre would remind us of the male body beneath the costume; that is a trick for the comedies. Asking to be unsexed, she is asking not to be turned into a man, not even (as we might at first think) to be made asexual. She wants her sexuality transformed while remaining that of a woman. Language gives her no way to formulate this, and so she falls back on the negative, self-canceling word "unsex." The result is perhaps the most extraordinary of the attacks on the female body we have seen throughout these plays, an attack she conducts herself as she asks to be impregnated with cruelty and to breastfeed with gall, and talks of killing an infant she herself is nursing, and loves, as an act of integrity. The body is still female, but the values it exemplifies belong to a gender that, like the murder, has no name.

She wants Macbeth to be a man; but they have to debate what that means. To his protest, "I dare do all that may become a man; / Who dares do more, is none" she replies, "When you durst do it, then you were a man" (I.vii.46–49). Is it manly to kill, or manly not to kill? The issue as Lady Macbeth frames it is not man versus woman but man versus beast: "What beast was't then, / That made you break this enterprise to me?" (I.v.47–48). This cuts off the possibility that the restraint Macbeth wants to show is a female virtue and therefore a human one (it was the woman in Hector who wanted to end the war); she tries to present it as subhuman. But because this is a scene between a man and a woman, the question of gender is implicitly in play; and the notion of maleness becomes unstable as they give contradictory readings of it. As part of his mirroring of Macbeth, Macduff is similarly challenged. When he hears of the slaughter of his family, Malcolm tells him, "Dispute it like a man" and he replies "I shall do so; / But I must also feel it as a man" (IV.iii.220–21). Malcolm plays something like Lady Macbeth's role, seeing violent action as manly; Macduff, breaking convention, sees passionate grief as manly. A few lines later he will revert to stock thinking – "O! I could play the woman with my mine eyes" (IV.iii.230) – but just for a moment he extends, as Macbeth has tried to do, the idea of what it is to be a man. He needs a period of simple grief, which Malcolm, who wants him to turn straight to anger, does not seem to understand. Malcolm is a virgin, and has no children.

Lady Macbeth tries to transform her gender into something unnameable, while remaining sexually a woman; Macbeth and Macduff in different ways try, if not to work against gender, at least to rethink the gender stereotypes they are offered. Romeo and Troilus, challenged to act like men, do not question what that means. Macbeth and Macduff do. But if Macbeth is prepared to question gender, his sex, like his wife's, remains constant. Her challenge to him to be a man cannot be separated from the fact that this is a childless marriage. Since Lady Macbeth has breastfed, she must have had at least one child (the number does not matter), as her historical equivalent did from a previous marriage.[19] Here we enter into a set of questions, like the questions around Othello's wedding night, that the play provokes but does not directly answer. Did the Macbeths have children, who died? Daughters, whom they discount? Did Lady Macbeth have children only by another man? In the latter case, it would appear that the problem lies with Macbeth, not with her, and an implicit taunt in "I have given suck" might be, "It's not my fault that we can't have children." Is Macbeth impotent, or potent but sterile? Or was Lady Macbeth's body damaged in childbirth?[20] None of these questions can be answered directly, and we may think that Shakespeare's art has trapped us once again into taking his characters as real and prying into their private lives. Yet Macbeth makes one assumption that is worth noting: he accepts without question the implication of the witches' address to Banquo as "greater" and "happier" than himself (I.iii.65–66):

because Banquo's issue will succeed, that means his will not (III.i.60–63), though logically the future could leave room for both. Whatever medical speculations we may entertain, the point is that Macbeth sees himself as without issue. It is a condition, if not of his body, at least of his mind; at that level the witches have sterilized him as the first witch sterilized the sailor.

It is at that level, the mind and the imagination, that the sexuality in this play operates most powerfully. All we know about the Macbeths in bed is that neither of them can sleep properly. For the play's purpose the key event in their sex life is the murder of Duncan. Lady Macbeth's invocation of the spirits is at one level a masturbatory fantasy that arouses her sexuality even as it transforms it. She prepares Macbeth for the deed by challenging his manhood. The act itself, that seems for a while to have no identity, has in fact a double one, a linking of killing and sexual consummation that recalls *Romeo and Juliet* and *Othello*. The Porter's lecture on drink provides a gloss on Macbeth's hesitation to kill:

Lechery, Sir, it provokes, and unprovokes: it provokes the desire, but it takes away the performance. Therefore, much drink may be said to be an equivocator with lechery: it makes him, and it mars him; it sets him on, and it takes him off; it persuades him, and disheartens him; makes him stand to, and not stand to. . . . (II.iii.29–35)

The self-canceling of language becomes the body's own self-canceling, transposing into a different key Lady Macbeth's rebukes to her husband for having the desire but not the performance, and her accusation that the fitness of the occasion has unmade him. She asks him, "Was the hope drunk, / Wherein you dress'd yourself?" and continues, "From this time / Such I account thy love" (I.vii.35–39). Making the killing a test of his love as well as of his manhood, she challenges him sexually: is he too drunk on equivocation to do the deed?

Macbeth imagines withered murder moving "with Tarquin's ravishing strides" (II.i.55), making the killing of Duncan (who like Lucrece is in bed) a displaced sexual act.[21] In *Titus Andronicus* we have seen rape conflated with marriage. The Macbeth marriage as we have seen it has been about one thing: killing Duncan. In the early scenes that is all they ever talk about. It is by killing Duncan that Macbeth consummates his marriage. The blood on the bed makes this a wedding night, and when he emerges from the chamber Lady Macbeth addresses him for the first time as "my husband!" (II.ii.13).[22] The couple is then disturbed as Troilus and Cressida were after a night of sex (IV.ii.36–45) by a knocking at the door.

Shakespeare kept Romeo's killing of Tybalt separate from his taking of Juliet's virginity, even as he allowed an interplay between them. Here killing and consummating are folded into one, and we begin to realize why naming the deed is so difficult.

Naming the perpetrator has also been difficult. If we see the deed as the consummation of Macbeth and Lady Macbeth's marriage, then we can say that the doer of the deed is not Macbeth or Lady Macbeth but the marriage itself. The sheer difficulty, the straining of the normal sense of agency, involved in putting it that way suggests why the agent is so hard to identify, why the characters so often retreat to the passive voice. But if we can think in these terms, we can see a link with other plays in which the agent of violation unravels, undone by the deed itself.

Macbeth kills Duncan; there is blood on the bed. To that extent the consummation succeeds. But as Romeo and Juliet saw in their consummation only death, a death they not only accepted but desired, so the Macbeths breed no new life. The difference is that Romeo and Juliet, wanting only to "die" together, have no interest in the future; but the Macbeths do. Resolved on the deed, Macbeth tells his wife, "Bring forth men-children only!" (I.vii.73), as though once he has done it she will conceive at last. But Rosse's tribute to his conduct on the battlefield, "Nothing afeard of what thyself didst make,/Strange images of death" (I.iii.96–97), suggests that Macbeth as procreator can only make one thing. The result of the consummation is not a new-born babe, naked or bloody, but a dead old man, and by the end of the play Macbeth is killing children. When the murderer taunts Macduff's son, "What, you egg!" (IV.ii.82), the killing seems to extend earlier than birth. Scotland has become an infertile body in which life dies before it can be born. The consummation has failed and it seems – the reservation is important – that the marriage fails along with it, the agent undone, as were Othello and Lear, by the deed it committed.

PORTRAIT OF A MARRIAGE

Other marriages in the tragedies we have examined – Lavinia and Bassianus, Juliet and Romeo, Desdemona and Othello – are brief and end violently. Violence is the heart of the Macbeths' marriage, its consummation. But it is the central event in a long story, not the culmination of a brief one. Unlike the other couples they are established when the play begins, and we have glimpses of a shared history. Their marriage also undergoes not a quick, violent end, a wedding night that is also a death, but a slow unraveling through time. Once consummated, it falls apart for reasons Cressida would understand: things won are done. The Macbeths are like a couple who were brought together by sex and draw apart when their sex life fades, or whose only mutual interest was their children, and who draw apart when the children leave home. They end the play as far apart as Troilus and Cressida, in contrast to the close final relationships of other couples, sexual and familial: Romeo and Juliet, Othello and Desdemona, Titus and Lavinia, Lear and Cordelia. The murder of Duncan broke the bonds of loyalty, severed the ties of king and subject, father and son, disconnected words from their meanings, and one sense from another. Now it seems to have broken the marriage bond of the couple who perpetrated it, as though the violent consummation of their marriage at once fulfilled it and destroyed it.

Yet, just as there is an Othello who can say, "That's he that was Othello; here I am" and a Lear who can say "This is not Lear," so to say that the marriage of Macbeth and Lady Macbeth is simply finished may not be the whole truth. We need to take account, first of all, of the uncanny strength of their relationship as we see it in the early scenes. Their initial bonding is remarkable. Lady Macbeth first enters reading aloud a letter from her husband, and the inseparable blending of his words and her voice melds them together. Even before he arrives she addresses him urgently, in the second person, as though he were on stage with her. They both, in different scenes, call for the coming of darkness (I.iv.50–51, I.v.50–54): their minds operate together, over a great distance, as Romeo's and Juliet's do after Romeo's banishment.

After the murder that bond seems to be broken. There are overtones of sexual disappointment in Lady Macbeth's "Nought's had, all's spent, / Where our desire is got without content" (III.ii.4–5).[23] She complains, as Portia and Lady Percy did, that her husband is keeping alone, not sharing his griefs with her (III.ii.8–9). His attempt to open out to her, "O! full of scorpions is my mind, dear wife!" (III.ii.36) involves a split in language between a natural endearment that now sounds incongruous and an image of private torment. He has told her about the air-drawn dagger, and she sounds skeptical about it (III.iv.61–62); but the most striking dramatization of the split between them is that he can see Banquo and she cannot. The more urgently he tells her to look – "Pr'ythee, see there! / Behold! look! lo!" (III.iv.67–68) – the clearer it becomes that she cannot see as he does: "You look but on a stool" (III.iv.67). Theatrically the authority belongs to Macbeth; it is part of the play's horror that we have begun to see with his eyes, to sense what it is like to *be* Macbeth.

In the process, Lady Macbeth draws away from him, and from us; she has only one more appearance, and they are never seen together again. He misreads her inability to see the ghost as courage in not reacting to it, and pays tribute: "You make me strange / Even to the disposition that I owe" (III.iv.111–12). The wording of the tribute implies two kinds of estrangement: setting his fear against her courage, he feels estranged from himself; but there is also a suggestion of his growing estrangement from her. Simply put, they no longer understand each other.

Yet he is also, up to a point, drawing on her. He begins to play something like her old role, urging her to put on false courtesy to Banquo as she urged him to deceive Duncan (III.ii.29–35) and challenging the murderers' sense of their own manhood (III.i.90–102). Playing her role, he both makes her redundant and shows how much he has learned from her. He hides from her his intention to kill Banquo, saying in effect, I can do this without you. Yet he still needs other voices to encourage him, to tell him to be "bloody, bold, and resolute" (IV.i.79), and so he turns to the witches. Their instruction to him to say nothing to the apparitions, only listen to them (IV.i.69–70, 89), shows how unlike his new source of courage is to his old one. Even when they were in conflict, Lady Macbeth was always prepared to hear him out before she counterattacked. Now he is dealing with strange powers whose relation to him is unclear, and there is no real dialogue. In the process we sense anew how much he needed her, and how much he has lost in his estrangement from her.

For all his vacillations she could steady him enough to make him do the deed. Now he alternates between flat despair and reckless defiance, going in a few lines from "I have liv'd long enough" to "I'll fight, till from my bones my flesh be hack'd" (V.iii.22, 32). Menteth describes Macbeth as a man radically at war with himself: "all that is within him does condemn / Itself, for being there" (V.ii.24–25). The self-canceling of language now becomes the self-canceling of Macbeth himself as he goes alone into a private hell – whose effect, paradoxically, is so public that even a minor character viewing him from a distance can see what is happening. Lady Macbeth could urge him to action, to a sense of himself, and to concealment. In the banquet scene she tried to stop him from going to pieces in public and when she failed did her best to cover for him; her influence gone, going to pieces in public becomes his mode of life, and he is totally exposed to his enemies. The more alone he is, the more we feel his original dependence on her.

She too is alone; but in the strange border country of the sleepwalking scene, in which she is asleep yet moving and speaking, she carries on a one-sided conversation with him, a ghostly echo of their early relationship. In her first scene she talked to her absent husband as though he were there. Now she talks to him again. The difference is that this time he will not come on to the stage and join her. She talks to someone who cannot hear, and is heard by people she does not know are listening. The Gentlewoman reports, "Since his Majesty went into the field, I have seen her rise from her bed, throw her night-gown upon her, unlock her closet, take forth paper, fold it, write upon't, read it, afterwards seal it, and again return to bed; all this while in a most fast sleep" (V.i.4–8). We think back to that first letter, the sign of their bonding, whose words we heard. This is a letter, like Cressida's, whose words we never hear and whose purpose is unknown. Again language has disappeared. Is she writing to him or to herself? Is she writing over again the letter he wrote to her? In any case she has been doing this since he went to war; it is in some way an attempt to deal with his absence.

Her only relationship has been with him; she has no Nurse, no Pandarus, no Emilia. The Gentlewoman is a horrified watcher who can do nothing but watch; her mistress shows no awareness of her. Just once her imagination reaches out to another woman: "The Thane of Fife had a wife: where is she now?" (V.i.41–42). This is the one point where she strays beyond what we have seen of her early in the play, and the one killing she seems to think of with remorse. As Macbeth has drawn away from her, has she come to think of herself, for the first time, as a woman who might have links with other women?[24] Her death is marked by an offstage cry of women, as though there is a whole female community that mourns her, a community we have never seen or even known about. As though to highlight the separation of men and women, the cue for the cry is one of Macbeth's most masculine images, "We might have met them dareful, beard to beard, / And beat them backward home. What is that noise?" (V.v.6–7). He does not seem to recognize the sound of female voices.

Yet whatever unseen life that cry may suggest, Lady Macbeth has shown no awareness of it, any more than she does of the Gentlewoman. In the sleepwalking scene, the only time she is on stage with another woman, the only person she talks to is Macbeth. Most of her lines are explicitly addressed to him, and all of them could be. Like Lear's last conversation with Cordelia, it is one half of a dialogue with someone who does not respond, and it may be that lack of response that keeps drawing her back to him, refighting the old arguments, reissuing the old commands. Though she scrambles different murders together (V.ii.59–61), her

memories center on the murder of Duncan, the night of their consummation, the blood on her own body she cannot wipe away. She ends with
an attempt to restore their broken bonds, saying as Edgar says to
Gloucester, "give me your hand," telling him their loss of virginity is
forever, "What's done cannot be undone," and leading him off with the
threefold command, "To bed, to bed, to bed" (V.ii.63–65) as though for
another encounter, like Juliet and Cressida urging their lovers not to
leave. Through all this she is in her nightgown, carrying a candle that
evokes a bedchamber. It is their most intimate scene.[25]

Does he reach out to her as she does to him? It is the cry of women that
leads him to observe how dead his senses are (V.v.9–15). He asks the
Doctor about "your patient" (V.iii.37), not "my wife." But he does ask,
and he seems to know without being told that her memory is her affliction
(V.iii.40–45). When he asks the doctor if he can cure the kingdom (V.
iii.50–56) he may simply be turning back to business; but the implied
equation of her sickness and Scotland's (like the equation of Lavinia's
violation and Rome's) makes a link between public and private life,
Macbeth as king and Macbeth as husband. His first response to her death,
"She should have died hereafter: / There would have been a time for such
a word" (V.v.17–18), sounds like the indifference of a busy man. But the
word "hereafter" triggers the word "to-morrow" and Macbeth's fullest,
most terrible vision of the wasteland he now inhabits. By one reading, he
has forgotten her already and turns to philosophizing and self-centered
despair. By another and I think a truer one, "To-morrow and to-morrow
and to-morrow" is a depth-charge of grief that goes off after a small delay.
She is not mentioned in it because she is everywhere in it, pervading all
its ideas. Elsewhere Macbeth's despair has indeed been focused on
himself:

> I have liv'd long enough: my way of life
> Is fall'n into the sere, the yellow leaf;
> And that which should accompany old age,
> As honour, love, obedience, troops of friends,
> I must not look to have. . . . (V.iii.22–26)

Here and in his other moments of despair it is his own particular life that
is ruined. In 'To-morrow and to-morrow and to-morrow' it is life itself. If
we ask what makes the difference, the answer nearest to hand is that he has
just heard of the death of Lady Macbeth.[26]

In her eagerness for the murder of Duncan Lady Macbeth urged time
on so that it collapsed on itself:

> Thy letters have transported me beyond
> This ignorant present, and I feel now
> The future in the instant. (I.v.56–58)

For a brief moment, when a servant says "The King comes here tonight"
and she replies 'Thou'rt mad to say it" (I.v.31) Macbeth is already king in
her mind, and she is shocked that a servant knows the secret. At this point,
for her there is nothing but the future, as in the sleepwalking scene there is
nothing but the past. Now that she has gone time resumes its normal
course, trudging forward with no purpose at all:

> To-morrow, and to-morrow, and to-morrow,
> Creeps in this petty pace from day to day,
> To the last syllable of recorded time;
> And all our yesterdays have lighted fools
> The way to dusty death. Out, out, brief candle!
> Life's but a walking shadow; a poor player,
> That struts and frets his hour upon the stage,
> And then is heard no more: it is a tale
> Told by an idiot, full of sound and fury,
> Signifying nothing. (V.v.19–28)

Creation began with the Word; "the last syllable" implies that recorded
time is a language; and language, unstable and self-destructive for so
much of the play, will one day simply stop. When we look ahead we
see universal death, and when we look behind we see more deaths,
individual deaths. In the middle is the individual consciousness, the brief
candle. Perhaps Lady Macbeth appears in the speech after all, the candle
of the sleepwalking scene become the candle of her life, and Macbeth's,
and (like the grave in *Hamlet*) anybody's.

Macbeth is in it too, a player who has done a lot of strutting and
fretting in the last few scenes, whose part will end, like Hamlet's, in
silence, not just because he has stopped speaking but because he is no
longer heard. In his isolation Macbeth feels like an actor without an
audience. The idea touched on in earlier plays, that we see ourselves only
in the eyes of others, is taken deeper here. The actor exists only in the
perception of the audience, and when there is no audience to hear him
there is nothing of him left. At the personal level, Macbeth's speeches (and
therefore Macbeth) have been meaningless without Lady Macbeth to hear
and reply. Finally, he is not even an actor, with the freedom and the
initiative an actor has to conduct his own performance. Everyone is a
character in a story, with no existence outside the voice of the narrator;
the story's language is meaningless noise, and the narrator is an idiot. But

if life is a tale told by an idiot, who is the idiot? Iago mischievously imagined God as a peeping Tom; Macbeth's blasphemy cuts far deeper. With Lady Macbeth he took part in a dialogue, a drama, in which each had a voice. Now there is only one voice, neither hers nor his, but the voice of a cosmic idiot telling a story that means nothing.

UNSETTLING THE ENDING

At this point a messenger enters and Macbeth commands, "Thou com'st to use thy tongue; thy story quickly" (V.v.29). Life, we might think, goes on after all, as it does in *The Tempest* when Prospero, having imagined the vanishing of all life, turns with brisk energy to disposing of Caliban. Language resumes, and storytelling has an immediate purpose. But the story the messenger tells, that Birnam Wood is on the move, seems to make all action meaningless: "If this which he avouches does appear, / There is nor flying hence, nor tarrying here" (V.v.47–48). The messenger's tale may be colored after all by its existence in that other story, the tale told by an idiot.

It may even be that we take this awareness through the rest of the play. Perhaps, amid the triumph of good and Macbeth's own heroic resistance, including the last grand gesture when he frees himself from the prophecies and fights to the end, this vision of absurdity is never quite shaken. There are many local reasons for misgivings about the ending. Is Donalbain's absence, to which the dialogue calls our attention (V.ii.7–8), a sign of future trouble?[27] In Siward's inhuman stoicism, we have noted, there may be a touch of Macbeth. Malcolm ends as Duncan began, thanking his followers, and the repeated cries of 'Hail!' echo the witches.[28] We are back to the beginning of the play, and this is not reassuring. According to Naomi Conn Liebler, "Malcolm's and Macduff's combination of unusual birth, childlessness, and virginity suggest no potential for procreative renewal."[29]

But there may be misgivings that cut deeper than this. The play began with confused narrative and murky language. It steadied itself after the murder of Duncan – once done, that deed registers clearly as an act of horror – and the contrast between Macbeth's tyranny and the saintly English king gives a sharp moral clarity. Yet we never see that king, and the journey we take through the play is largely Macbeth's journey. "Nothing" is a key word in *King Lear*, but we can draw meaning and value out of Cordelia, even – we might say, particularly – in the agony caused by her death. But the last scenes of *Macbeth*, even more noisy and violent than the first since battles are now enacted, not just described, are shadowed by the possibility that all this sound and fury is a tale told by an idiot, signifying nothing. If we see it that way, and if we take it that this sense of absurdity comes into the play as Macbeth's reaction to the death of his wife, it may be a last grim tribute to the Macbeths and the power of their marriage.

We could never enter the mind of Lavinia; but as we have seen, her experience of being violated echoed in various ways through the play, which was haunted by her rape. The world of *Macbeth* is haunted by Duncan's murder in a similar way, but it is more deeply haunted still. There was no question of entering into the minds, if they had them, of Chiron and Demetrius, but the mood of post-coital exhaustion that hits the play might owe something to them. We do enter, with alarming intimacy, into the minds of Macbeth and Lady Macbeth, and into what we might call the mind of their marriage. Their attempt to deny agency is, ironically, part of a close examination of these particular agents. What looks like a noisy public play, beginning and ending with the clang of battle, has at its still, frightening center a murder in a domestic space, and turns out on closer inspection to be one of Shakespeare's most intimate dramas, his fullest examination of a marriage. It is a marriage sealed in blood, linking it with *Romeo* and *Othello,* and with the conflation of marriage and rape in *Titus.* While Troilus and Cressida worked to undo each other, Macbeth and Lady Macbeth work together to undo not just Duncan's life but life itself – along with language and meaning. In the process they seem to become estranged from each other; but if we look more closely at the scenes in which they are most alone, we can see them reaching out to each other, as Titus tries to reach Lavinia across the gap of silence and Lear tries to reach Cordelia across the gap of death. In Lavinia we see, from outside, what it looks like to be the target of violation, and that is hard enough to take. The whole play struggles to cope with it. In Macbeth and Lady Macbeth we are taken, with terrible authority and conviction, into the minds of two people who have centered their life together on doing a deed of violation, we watch those minds infecting each other and the world, and in their destruction, greeted by other characters with easy satisfaction, something of us is destroyed – because they themselves have exemplified so powerfully the very human bond they have violated.

Conclusion

We began with Lavinia dehumanized by violence; we end with Macbeth and Lady Macbeth, the perpetrators of violence, humanized. We began with Lavinia unable to name the crime because she has been physically deprived of language; we end with Macbeth and Lady Macbeth unable to name the crime because they are afraid of language. As the ideas of violation and identity develop through these seven tragedies we see a series of reactions and contradictions as one play ricochets against another; and we see an internalization of what in *Titus Andronicus* is physical and literal.

To begin with the contradictions: the physical assault on Lavinia includes taking her identity, which her father restores, claiming she is not just a ruined thing, she is still Lavinia. In the family, she gets her name back. The rape has been a parody of a love-encounter, beginning with conventional love-language. Romeo and Juliet come together in a genuine love-encounter which, if we put the plays together, seems to reverse and heal the violence of Lavinia's rape. While Lavinia's loss of identity is a horror, Romeo and Juliet long for a free space in which they would have no names. The involvement of their families, and of Romeo's friends, for whom their names matter, brings violence into the private world of their love and ends in a second wedding night in which Juliet's blood is shed as Lavinia's was. *Romeo and Juliet* begins by reacting against *Titus Andronicus*, cutting itself free; but as the Goths invade Rome, the horror of the first play finally infiltrates the romanticism of the second.

Both tragedies center on what is done to a woman, particularly to her body. *Hamlet* reverses this, beginning with the physical violation of a man, the late King Hamlet, and the dislocation of his identity in the form of the Ghost. This time it is a son who has to cope with a damaged father. *Troilus and Cressida* returns the focus to a woman, with an uneasy blending of the assault on Lavinia and the kissing of Juliet: Cressida is kissed not by one man who matters to her but by several men about whom her feelings are guarded and problematic. This time it is her former lover who declares her identity has been dislocated, her name taken from her like Lavinia's; only his focus is not on what has been done to her but on what has been done to him. In this, something of the unease we feel about Titus' tending of Lavinia, his focus on his own suffering, creeps back. In another reaction against *Hamlet*, the intense seriousness of the issues in the earlier play, where the state is rotten and the time is out of joint, has been replaced by at least the possibility of cynical comedy, a sense that a great fuss is made over nothing – like the Trojan War itself, which Thersites sees as a war over a placket.

Othello keeps the focus on a woman, but reacts against *Troilus* in two ways. The sexual jealousy is no longer trivial; it leads to Desdemona's murder. And while Cressida is surrounded by commentary whose effect is as ambiguous and uncertain as Cressida herself, Desdemona's clear chastity is surrounded by commentary that is just as clearly a destructive lie. The commentary on Lavinia is an attempt, sometimes well-meaning, sometimes tainted, to cope with her rape. The commentary on Desdemona leads directly to her murder. There is a simple reversal of structure: Lavinia is raped, then talked about; Desdemona is talked about, then murdered. Her identity is never in question for the audience; but Othello is made to question it, and when he realizes he has killed her for a lie, his own identity is broken apart. It takes Titus to kill Chiron and Demetrius, Hamlet to kill Claudius. (Troilus tries to kill Diomedes but fails and loses interest.) Othello gives a twist to the pattern by taking revenge on himself, his double identity issuing in a paradoxical fusion of murderer and avenger.

King Lear returns to *Titus Andronicus* and produces one of the most startling and disturbing reversals in the series. This time it is the father who assails the daughter, trying to annihilate her identity. For a while he appears to succeed: while Lavinia is a constant, troubling presence in the middle scenes of the play, Cordelia in the equivalent scenes disappears. When she goes missing, Lear's own identity goes missing. Even when she returns, their reunion is disturbed by memories of what he tried to do; and in her death his initial curse is fulfilled. *Titus* ends with a father killing the daughter he tried to keep alive; *Lear* ends with a father trying to bring life back to the daughter he tried to annihilate.

Macbeth returns to *Hamlet*, in that this time the assault is on a man (and a father, and a king) but reverses the focus on to the killers themselves, as though the earlier play were to concentrate on Claudius. And this time it is not the identity of the victim that is at stake; Duncan stays dead, provoking none of the questions the Ghost provokes. It is the identity of the deed, and it is the killers themselves who have the greatest difficulty naming what they are doing. Their difficulty is a clue to their own double natures: to do the deed they try to make themselves inhuman, but in their struggle to do so they reveal how human they are. As Othello internalizes revenge by killing himself, Lady Macbeth internalizes the assault on Lavinia's body by assaulting her own, violating her humanity as Chiron and Demetrius violate Lavinia's, turning herself into a thing that has no gender in order to do a deed that has no name. In a reversal of Lavinia's silence, we are taken into her mind to hear the fiercely articulate voicing of her thoughts.

The growth of internalization between the earliest play in this discussion and the latest is characteristic. Lavinia, Alarbus, Chiron and Demetrius are literally dismembered; Macbeth talks about the separation of one function from another, the eye from the hand. Literal dismemberment is saved for the witches' cauldron. The physical assault on Lavinia becomes a way of rethinking other, less literal forms of assault: her own marriage, the kissing (and rereading) of Cressida, Lear's banishment of Cordelia. In each case we see a violence that leaves no scars on the body, but raises disturbances equivalent to Lavinia's rape. The literal difficulty of recognizing her identity – physically, she is so changed when she returns to Rome that for a moment Titus genuinely does not know who she is – becomes a figurative dislocation of identity when Cressida becomes Diomed's Cressida, Desdemona that cunning whore of Venice, Othello he that was Othello, Lear something that is no longer Lear. In each case there is no literal change in appearance, but a profound change, real or imagined, within. The Ghost in *Hamlet* presents one variation: his literal appearance is that of the King, but that is just the problem; the King is dead, and anything that looks and talks like him is suspect. It is not physical change, but physical similarity, that calls his true nature into question. *Romeo and Juliet* presents another variation: to lose their names is just what the lovers want, and they talk about it as something they could literally do; their tragedy lies in the fact that they cannot.

The internalizing of the physical, as in the double rape of Lavinia, is bound up with another implication of the relationship between violation and identity. Identity means naming, knowing the true nature of things, and when identity is violated, the true nature of things becomes dislocated, uncertain. If a marriage and a rape can be so alike, the ground is prepared for seeing a murder as a wedding night, as in *Romeo and Juliet*, *Othello* and *Macbeth*. Troilus takes this to a more general level, seeing a collapse of meaning itself in the dislocated identity of Cressida. What may be fevered exaggeration in Troilus is explored more seriously throughout *Hamlet* as the reality of oneself, of other people, and of the world at large, becomes problematic. In *Lear* the structure of society collapses as though with the un-naming of the king all the ideas that hold society together have vanished. The boundary between self and other, a key to identity, breaks not only in the literal enemy invasions of Rome, Denmark, Britain and Scotland, but in the way Lavinia's experience spreads outward to color the whole action of the play; the way Scotland suffers not only under Macbeth but with him, sharing in the restless dread that torments his mind; the way Verona experiences as the lovers do a dawn that brings darkness.

With identity unfixed, meaning, social structure and the boundary between self and other are all shaken. It is no wonder that none of these tragedies has a truly settled, untroubled ending. Whatever the initial act of violation was, it can never finally be undone. We question Lavinia's silence in death as we did her silence in life, while Aaron goes on talking. Verona may seem healed, but it is haunted by the lovers as the lovers were haunted by it. Hamlet is given a funeral that seems meant for another man, his relation to his father (and therefore his own identity) remains problematic, and the enemy his father defeated has taken over. The ending of *Troilus* is so unsettled that the disturbance, like Pandarus' diseases, seems to spread to the audience. The initial misreading of Othello's marriage as an outrage has been validated by Othello himself, and Lodovico's order to hide the sight of the bodies on the bed means not that the disturbance is resolved, but that it cannot even be faced. *King Lear* ends not with order restored but with inconsolable suffering, and with terrible questions about the human bond that ought to be our greatest comfort. *Macbeth* ends not just with a restoration of order that leaves a chill in the air, but with a sense that its moral judgments of Macbeth and Lady Macbeth, though perfectly valid, have missed the point. Their humanity in the midst of everything they have done goes on to haunt us, even more than the voice of Aaron or the silence of Iago. They have exemplified the human bond, including the sexual bond and the closeness it entails, the very bond that Chiron and Demetrius violated when they raped Lavinia and tried to reduce her to a nameless thing.

The rape of Lavinia, and the subsequent questioning of her identity, come early in the play and early in Shakespeare's career. The way the act and the questions are replayed with continual variations, so that their significance keeps spreading, shows that even when he finished with *Titus*

Shakespeare, so long as he wrote tragedy, could never get Lavinia out of his mind, could never heal those wounds or silence that silence. To watch him at work on this theme is to be aware that no single, pat conclusion is possible. Even in the last plays the disturbance continues. The suggestions of incest when Titus makes Lavinia take her hand in his mouth, and when Lear makes his total demand on Cordelia, become literal at the beginning of *Pericles*, where Antiochus' nameless daughter is mother, wife and child, her identity blurred by her father's abuse. Pericles continues to be haunted by that first encounter, and begins his reunion with his own daughter by pushing her violently away, as though afraid (like Lear) of what her love could mean. Imogen wakes beside the headless body of Cloten, who wanted to rape her; she thinks it is her husband. We think of Lavinia's rape and her marriage; and of Chiron and Demetrius beheaded. The silent statue of Hermione moves, breathes and speaks: we think back on other silences that were never broken, other women who never spoke or breathed again.

The configuration of father, daughter and rapist returns in *The Tempest*, where Prospero prevents Caliban's assault on Miranda, heading off the damage Titus could neither prevent nor undo. He goes on to lecture Ferdinand on chastity, giving him Caliban's job of piling logs, as though to test the Caliban in him, aware of the conflation of husband and rapist and trying to separate the two. But the most disturbing echo is in the relations of Caliban and Miranda. Chiron and Demetrius took away Lavinia's language; Miranda taught Caliban how to speak. She taught him the names of things, the bigger light and the less. Though neither of them says so, it may be that, since he had no language of his own, she taught him his own name, gave him his identity. In return he tried to rape her. He describes his attempt as the procreative instinct at work, a desire to people the isle with Calibans. But he also claims that he uses the language she taught him in order to curse. Chiron and Demetrius rape Lavinia as an assault on her identity, as though that identity disturbs them, giving her power over them – the rape sequence begins with their squabbling over her – and this is the way to break it. Does Caliban try to rape Miranda because in giving him language she has given him his name, and thus has power over him – and this is a way to break that power? Is it because he finds the consciousness of himself that language bestows intolerable, and this is his revenge? It is characteristic that Shakespeare's last treatment of the intertwined themes of violation and identity provides not a final answer, a summing-up, but new and disturbing questions.

Notes

INTRODUCTION

1 Linda Woodbridge, *The Scythe of Saturn: Shakespeare and Magical Thinking* (Urbana and Chicago: University of Illinois Press 1994), pp. 45–85; Heather Dubrow, *Shakespeare and Domestic Loss* (Cambridge: Cambridge University Press 1999), pp. 18–77. Pascale Aebischer's brilliant and provocative *Shakespeare's Violated Bodies: Stage and Screen Performance* (Cambridge: Cambridge University Press 2004) arrived when the present study was virtually complete. We have a common starting point in the idea of violation, and our readings of *Titus Andronicus* in particular intersect at several points. But her primary concern, unlike mine, is with recent stage and screen productions, particularly their reflection of the cultural and sexual politics of our time.

2 References to *The Spanish Tragedy* are to the Revels edition, ed. Philip Edwards (London: Methuen 1959).

3 *Iter Boreale* (1618), quoted in Andrew Gurr, *Playgoing in Shakespeare's London* (Cambridge: Cambridge University Press 1987), p. 233.

4 Arden edition, p. 101.

5 *The Art of Loving: Female Subjectivity and Male Discursive Traditions in Shakespeare's Tragedies* (Newark: University of Delaware Press; London and Toronto: Associated University Presses 1992), p. 120.

6 Quoted in E. K. Chambers, *The Elizabethan Stage*, IV (Oxford: Clarendon Press repr. 1961), p. 256.

7 See my "The Death of John Talbot," *Shakespeare's Histories: A Quest for Form and Genre*, ed. John W. Velz (Binghamton, N Y: Medieval and Renaissance Texts and Studies 1996), pp. 17–18.

TITUS ANDRONICUS: THIS WAS THY DAUGHTER

1 I am grateful to Karen Bamford for her advice on this part of the argument.

2 See John Kerrigan, *Revenge Tragedy: Aeschylus to Armageddon* (Oxford: Clarendon Press 1996), p. 196; and David Willbern, "Rape and Revenge in *Titus Andronicus*," *English Literary Renaissance*, 8 (1978), p. 171.

3 See Michael Neill, *Issues of Death: Mortality and Identity in English Renaissance Tragedy* (Oxford: Clarendon Press 1997), pp. 290–91.

4 The link between the two events is explored by a number of critics, including Mary Laughlin Fawcett, "Arms/Words/Tears: Language and the Body in *Titus Andronicus*," *ELH*, 50 (1983), pp. 266–67; Bernice Harris, "Sexuality as a Signifier for Power Relations: Using Lavinia, of Shakespeare's *Titus Andronicus*," *Criticism*, 38 (1996), p. 388; Lorraine Helms, "'The High Roman Fashion': Sacrifice, Suicide, and the Shakespearean Stage," *PMLA*, 107 (1992), p. 557; and Willbern, "Rape," p. 163.

5 See Harris, "Sexuality," p. 390.

6 Marjorie Garber, *Coming of Age in Shakespeare* (London and New York: Methuen 1981), p. 152.

7 Willbern, "Rape," p. 161.

8 See Coppélia Kahn, *Roman Shakespeare: Warriors, Wounds and Women* (London and New York: Routledge 1997), p. 47; Naomi Conn Liebler, *Shakespeare's Festive Tragedy: The Ritual Foundations of Genre* (London and New York: Routledge 1995), pp. 142, 146; and Molly Easo Smith, "Spectacles of Torment in *Titus Andronicus*," *Studies in English Literature*, 36 (1996), p. 316.

9 Lucrece, attacked in her own home, in Rome itself, "Pleads in a wilderness where are no laws" (544).

10 According to the promptbook, in Deborah Warner's 1987 production for the Royal Shakespeare Company Chiron stopped Lavinia's mouth with a kiss, then spat out a piece of her tongue; the archive videotape shows him putting a hand over her mouth. See Christina Luckyj, "'A Moving Rhetoricke': Women's Silences and Renaissance Texts," *Renaissance Drama*, n.s.24 (1993), pp. 42, 53. Though Lucrece is not deprived of language in the same way, during the rape Tarquin muffles her cries by wrapping her head in "the nightly linen that she wears" (680).

11 This may be a development from *Henry VI Part Three*, II.vi, where the Yorkists taunt the dead body of their old enemy Clifford.

12 See Brian Gibbons, "The Human Body in *Titus Andronicus* and Other Early Shakespeare Plays," *Deutsche Shakespeare-Gesellschaft West Jahrbuch* (1989), pp. 219–20.

13 John Kerrigan suggests that "deflower" is a taunt at Bassianus for not consummating his marriage (*Revenge Tragedy*, p. 196).

14 On the raped wife as "decategorized," see Linda Woodbridge, *The Scythe of Saturn: Shakespeare and Magical Thinking* (Urbana and Chicago: University of Illinois Press 1994), p. 78.

15 This was the effect in the Warner production: see Jonathan Bate's note on this passage in the Arden edition. Bate adds at this point a stage direction, "*Lavinia opens her mouth.*"

16 See Geoffrey Bullough (ed.), *Narrative and Dramatic Sources of Shakespeare*, vol. 6 (London: Routledge and Kegan Paul; New York: Columbia University Press 1966), p. 43.

17 On the problematic relation between Marcus' linguistic artifice and the reality of Lavinia's body see Nicholas Brooke, *Shakespeare's Early Tragedies*

(London: Methuen 1968), p. 15; Gibbons, "Human Body," p. 18; Heather James, "Cultural Disintegration in *Titus Andronicus*: Mutilating Titus, Vergil and Rome," *Violence in Drama* (*Themes in Drama* 13), ed. James Redmond (Cambridge: Cambridge University Press 1991), p. 129; and Eugene M. Waith, "The Metamorphosis of Violence in *Titus Andronicus*," *Shakespeare Survey*, 10 (1957), pp. 47–48.

18 See Pascale Aebischer, *Shakespeare's Violated Bodies: Stage and Screen Performance* (Cambridge: Cambridge University Press 2004), p. 31. Julie Taymor's 1999 film *Titus* treats the passage very differently: Titus' speech is an accurate interpretation of a pantomime performed by Lavinia. In general the film, compared with other productions on record, makes Lavinia unusually articulate and her relationship with Titus unusually coherent.

19 The moment in Sam Shepard's *Buried Child* when Bradley puts his hand in Shelley's mouth recalls this moment in *Titus*, and again suggests a sexual assault. Fawcett reads Titus' command as an incestuous act conveying the patriarchal nature of language ("Arms," pp. 261–62).

20 At this point, according to Maurice Charney, "Titus is coming closer to understanding his daughter's grief by becoming like her": *Harvester New Critical Introductions to Shakespeare: Titus Andronicus* (New York: Harvester Wheatsheaf 1990), p. 56. Katherine A. Rowe denies this sympathy, claiming "Lavinia . . . represents to her family nothing more than their own experience": "Dismembering and Forgetting in *Titus Andronicus*," *Shakespeare Quarterly*, 45 (1994), p. 295.

21 The Arden edition presents the moment differently, having Lavinia kiss her brothers' severed heads. The original text will admit either possibility, and the basic effect of a freely offered sign of love that gets no response is the same.

22 According to Fawcett, "When she takes her uncle's staff into her mouth, she uses the language of the fathers, the cultural dominators" ("Arms," p. 269).

23 As she uses Latin to announce the rape, Demetrius used a couple of Latin tags while planning it (I.i.633–35). In Taymor's *Titus*, Lavinia reimagines the rape as she writes, and the experience is unbearably traumatic.

24 All references to *The Spanish Tragedy* are to the Revels edition, ed. Philip Edwards (London: Methuen 1959).

25 Alan C. Dessen, *Shakespeare in Performance: Titus Andronicus* (Manchester and New York: Manchester University Press 1989), p. 93. In the Warner production it was as though the act of writing had drained her: see Luckyj, "Moving Rhetoricke," p. 47.

26 See Emily Detmer-Goebel, "The Need for Lavinia's Voice: *Titus Andronicus* and the Telling of Rape," *Shakespeare Studies*, 29 (2001), p. 87.

27 Bullough, *Sources*, p. 44.

28 Dessen, *Performance*, pp. 94–96, and Aebischer, *Violated Bodies*, pp. 58–63. Aebischer stresses, and protests, the dominance of stagings in which Lavinia consents to her own death. Maurice Charney exemplifies the critical dilemma, variously describing the killing as "a loving act' and "murder" (*Harvester*, pp. 42, 98.) Aebischer calls it a "betrayal" (p. 57).

29 "'I can interpret all her martyr'd signs': *Titus Andronicus*, Feminism, and the Limits of Interpretation," *Sexuality and Politics in Renaissance Drama*, ed. Carole Levin and Karen Robertson (Lewiston, Queenston and Lampeter: The Edward Mellen Press 1991), p. 195.

30 In a Romanian production, directed by Silviu Pucarete, which toured Britain in 1997, Aaron broke through the ending. As the audience left the auditorium, "in the foyer Aaron, buried up to his neck under a brown plastic sheet, was jabbering in Romanian at the bewildered patrons, who stayed as far away from him as they could" (Aebischer, *Violated Bodies*, p. 119).

ROMEO AND JULIET: WHAT'S IN A NAME?

1 In the original texts there is no stage direction for Juliet's entrance in II.ii. At the opening of III.v the lovers appear "*at the window*" in the First Quarto, "*aloft*" in later Quartos and the Folio.

2 David Bevington, *Action is Eloquence: Shakespeare's Language of Gesture* (Cambridge, Mass., and London: Harvard University Press 1984), p. 112.

3 The irony is compounded by the accidental appropriateness of the ship image, recalling as it does a sonnet of Petrarch describing the state of a lover, Englished by Wyatt as "My galley chargèd with forgetfulness."

4 Thomas Moisan, "Rhetoric and the Rehearsal of Death: The 'Lamentations' Scene in *Romeo and Juliet*," *Shakespeare Quarterly*, 34 (1983), pp. 392, 394.

5 In the First Quarto version of the wedding scene, a much more cheerful and celebratory occasion than its counterpart in the familiar Second Quarto, the Friar tells the lovers, "Come wantons, come, the stealing houres do passe / Defer imbracements till some fitter time" (E_4v).

6 See Charles R. Forker, "The Green Underworld of Early Shakespearean Tragedy," *Shakespeare Studies*, 17 (1985), p. 28.

7 Forker, "Underworld," p. 31. Some editors kill the effect of Romeo's entrance by moving it to the end of the Friar's speech.

8 Geoffrey Bullough (ed.), *Narrative and Dramatic Sources of Shakespeare*, vol. 1 (London: Routledge and Kegan Paul; New York: Columbia University Press 1966), pp. 270, 292–3.

9 *Man's Estate: Masculine Identity in Shakespeare* (Berkeley, Los Angeles and London: University of California Press 1981), p. 87.

10 T. McAlindon, *Shakespeare's Tragic Cosmos* (Cambridge: Cambridge University Press, 1991), also sees the language as artificial, but his explanation is that we cannot believe in the reality of Juliet's love for Tybalt (p. 71).

11 Bullough, *Sources*, p. 286.

12 André Malraux, *La Condition Humaine*, quoted in Jan Kott, *Shakespeare our Contemporary*, trans. Boleslaw Taborski (London: Methuen 1964), p. 94.

13 Perhaps because the double standard is at work, the play is less explicit about Romeo's virginity than about Juliet's; but she imagines her wedding night as "a winning match / Play'd for a pair of stainless maidenhoods" (III.ii.12–13).

14　As Madelon Gohlke puts it, "sexual intercourse . . . comes to be described as a kind of murder": "'I wooed thee with my sword': Shakespeare's Tragic Paradigms," *The Woman's Part: Feminist Criticism of Shakespeare*, ed. Carolyn Ruth Swift Lenz, Gayle Greene and Carol Thomas Neely (Urbana, Chicago and London: University of Illinois Press 1980), p. 152.

15　Gayle Whittier, "The Sonnet's Body and the Body Sonnetized in *Romeo and Juliet*," *Shakespeare Quarterly*, 40 (1989), p. 35.

16　See Kahn, *Estate*, p. 85; and Michael Neill, *Issues of Death: Mortality and Identity in English Renaissance Tragedy* (Oxford: Clarendon Press 1997), p. 312.

17　See Michael Goldman, *Shakespeare and the Energies of Drama* (Princeton: Princeton University Press 1972), p. 41.

18　In the Second Quarto Romeo, just before taking the poison, tells Juliet, "come lye thou in my arme" (L₃r). (The Folio reads "armes" [p. 75].) The line, which editors normally cut, seems to be part of an earlier version of the speech, preserved by accident.

19　See Alan Macfarlane, *Marriage and Love in England: Modes of Reproduction 1300–1840* (Oxford: Basil Blackwell 1986), pp. 315–16.

20　Lynda E. Boose, "The Father and the Bride in Shakespeare," *PMLA*, 97 (1982), p. 329.

21　Whittier, "Body," p. 41.

HAMLET: A FIGURE LIKE YOUR FATHER

1　Adrian Poole, *Tragedy: Shakespeare and the Greek Example* (Oxford and New York: Basil Blackwell 1987), p. 116.

2　Michael Neill, *Issues of Death: Mortality and Identity in English Renaissance Tragedy* (Oxford: Clarendon Press 1997), p. 258.

3　Arthur Kirsch, *The Passions of Shakespeare's Tragic Heroes* (Charlottesville and London: University Press of Virginia 1990), p. 32.

4　The First Quarto and the Folio read "body," removing even this reference to the other characters. On the decorum considered proper to funerals in Shakespeare's society, see Roland Mushat Frye, *The Renaissance Hamlet: Issues and Responses in 1600* (Princeton: Princeton University Press 1984), pp. 144–45. David Bevington notes that at the end of the play the "military orderliness" of Hamlet's funeral seems to restore proper standards, but that "no obsequies at all are proposed" for Claudius: *Action is Eloquence: Shakespeare's Language of Gesture* (Cambridge, Mass., and London: Harvard University Press 1984), pp. 186–87. See also James V. Holleran, "Maimed Funeral Rites in *Hamlet*," *English Literary Renaissance*, 19 (1989), pp. 65–93.

5　*The Scythe of Saturn: Shakespeare and Magical Thinking* (Urbana and Chicago: University of Illinois Press 1994), p. 60.

6　John Barrymore used to motivate Hamlet's hatred of Claudius in the "rogue and peasant slave" soliloquy by thinking, "That bastard puts his prick in my mother's cunt every night!" Michael A. Morrison, *John Barrymore, Shakespearean Actor* (Cambridge: Cambridge University Press 1997), p. 131.

7 Maurice Charney, *Hamlet's Fictions* (New York and London: Routledge 1998), notes the tendency in Hamlet's imagination to "infinite regress" (p. 66). Edward Pechter notes one of the play's recurring devices, verbal repetition that delays an exit: "Remembering 'Hamlet': Or, How It Feels to Go Like a Crab Backwards," *Shakespeare Survey*, 39 (1987), pp. 136–38.

8 Peter Holland, "*Hamlet* and the Art of Acting," *Drama and the Actor (Themes in Drama 6)*, ed. James Redmond (Cambridge: Cambridge University Press 1984), p. 52.

9 See Marjorie Garber, *Coming of Age in Shakespeare* (London and New York: Methuen 1981), p. 237.

10 The First Quarto moderates the effect by putting the soliloquy near the beginning of its equivalent of II.ii.

11 See John Kerrigan, *Revenge Tragedy: Aeschylus to Armageddon* (Oxford: Clarendon Press 1996), p. 182.

12 On the possibility of taking Gertrude's viewpoint, see Alan L. Ackerman Jr., "Visualizing Hamlet's Ghost: The Spirit of Modern Subjectivity," *Theatre Journal*, 53 (2001), pp. 130–31.

13 *Suffocating Mothers: Fantasies of Maternal Origin in Shakespeare's Plays, Hamlet to The Tempest* (New York and London: Routledge 1992), p. 31.

14 I owe this suggestion to William Blissett, in conversation.

15 In the First Quarto the King reacts immediately to the poisoning. As in the earlier placing of "To be or not to be," this version produces a more conventional drama.

16 In Michael Almereyda's 2000 film the Ghost (Sam Shepard) seems to lose his voice for a moment on the word "mother."

17 The First Quarto differs from the other texts in presenting Gertrude quite explicitly as Hamlet's ally against Claudius.

18 *Suffocating*, p. 34. This is a reservation in Adelman's reading of Gertrude, which regards the question of her moral reclamation as impossible to settle. In the Olivier and Almereyda films it is clear that Gertrude knowingly drinks the poison to save Hamlet. In Svend Gade's fascinating revision of the story in his 1920 film Hamlet (a woman disguised as a man, played by Asta Nielsen) has already killed Claudius before the final scene; Gertrude plans to avenge her husband by having Hamlet drink the poisoned wine, but drinks it herself when the goblets are switched.

19 Charney, *Fictions*, p. 43.

20 See Susan Letzler Cole, *The Absent One: Mourning Ritual, Tragedy, and the Performance of Ambivalence* (University Park and London: The Pennsylvania State University Press 1985), pp. 56–58. Cole sees Ophelia's songs as the only example of proper ritual lamentation in the play.

21 See David Schalkwyk, *Speech and Performance in Shakespeare's Sonnets and Plays* (Cambridge: Cambridge University Press 2002), p. 125.

22 What looks to us a misinterpretation of accidental drowning as deliberate suicide was apparently endemic in Shakespeare's England; drowning was a common cause of accidental death, and in many such cases juries returned a verdict of *felo de se*. An Elizabethan jury would likely not have taken Ophelia's madness into account; the verdict of *non compos mentis* was used in only 1.6 per cent of recorded cases between 1478 and 1660. See Michael MacDonald, "Ophelia's Maimèd Rites," *Shakespeare Quarterly*, 37 (1986), pp. 310–11.

23 In Laurence Olivier's 1963 National Theatre production, the men not only fought in Ophelia's grave but tossed her body back and forth between them like children fighting over a rag doll.

24 As Alan Ackerman has pointed out to me, there is a link between the men's leaping into Ophelia's grave and the Ghost bursting from its tomb; in both cases a threshold is violated.

25 As R. A. Foakes observes, the male ethos "has no place for women other than as loyal and pure, subservient to men, breeders of more heroes": *Hamlet versus Lear: Cultural Politics and Shakespeare's Art* (Cambridge: Cambridge University Press 1993), p. 156.

26 As Avi Erlich puts it, "Hamlet worries that he and his father have been unmanned by women": *Hamlet's Absent Father* (Princeton: Princeton University Press 1977), p. 261.

27 That is the Arden reading. Compressed and cryptic, the Second Quarto's "of ought he leaves, knowes" has given editors trouble; but I think the meaning is the same.

28 See R. A. Foakes, *Shakespeare and Violence* (Cambridge: Cambridge University Press 2003), p. 107.

29 *Shakespeare's Tragic Cosmos* (Cambridge: Cambridge University Press 1991), p. 125.

30 The Roman entry into Cleopatra's monument at the end of *Antony and Cleopatra* is similarly noisy: "*Enter the guard, rustling in*"; "*Enter Caesar and all his train, marching*" (V.ii.318sd, 331sd).

31 In production the equation of the two characters has been made by a variety of means. In Laurence Olivier's 1948 film, Olivier himself plays both parts. At the Royal Court in 1980, Jonathan Pryce produced the Ghost's voice "from his own solar plexus as if possessed": see Robert Hapgood, *Shakespeare in Production: Hamlet Prince of Denmark* (Cambridge: Cambridge University Press 1999), p. 136. At the Toronto Free Theatre in 1986, the Ghost appeared behind a wall of glass, and as Hamlet pressed his face to his father's they seemed to mirror each other. Disturbed by the viciousness of Hamlet's attack on Gertrude, John Barrymore played part of the closet scene as though Hamlet was not speaking in his own person but possessed by the Ghost (Morrison, *Barrymore*, pp. 194, 197). In *Julius Caesar* the ghost of Caesar, asked its identity, replies, "Thy evil spirit, Brutus" (IV.iii.280).

32 See Stephen Greenblatt, *Hamlet in Purgatory* (Princeton and Oxford: Princeton University Press 2001), pp. 225–27.

33 Kerrigan, *Revenge Tragedy*, pp. 187–88.
34 *Young Hamlet: Essays on Shakespeare's Tragedies* (Oxford: Clarendon Press 1989), p. 126. Kirsh, *Passions*, claims Hamlet "partly exorcises and partly incorporates" the Ghost (p. 40).
35 Cole, *Absent*, pp. 44–45.
36 Everett, *Young Hamlet*, p. 126.
37 In the Almereyda film the Ghost appears in his own person for the last time as Hamlet prepares for death ("the readiness is all") and again as a video image as Hamlet dies.

TROILUS AND CRESSIDA: THIS IS AND IS NOT CRESSID

1 On the possibilities for defense in that position, see the Long Note in the Arden edition, p. 357.
2 In the 1987 production at Stratford, Ontario, directed by David William, Hector (in the previews) was not just killed but gang-raped by the Myrmidons. The effect proved too strong for some stomachs, and was cut.
3 "Shakespeare's Cressida: A Woman of Quick Sense," *Philological Quarterly*, 63 (1984), p. 357.
4 "The Text of Cressida and Every Ticklish Reader: *Troilus and Cressida*, the Greek Camp Scene," *Shakespeare Survey*, 41 (1989), p. 65.
5 As David Schalkwyk points out, she is playing the role of the inaccessible mistress in a Petrarchan sonnet: see *Speech and Performance in Shakespeare's Sonnets and Plays* (Cambridge: Cambridge University Press 2002), p. 177.
6 Ann Jennalie Cook, *Making a Match: Courtship in Shakespeare and his Society* (Princeton: Princeton University Press 1991), p. 224.
7 Linda Charnes, "'So Unsecret to Ourselves': Notorious Identity and the Material Subject in Shakespeare's *Troilus and Cressida*," *Shakespeare Quarterly*, 40 (1989), p. 418.
8 Richard Monette's production at Stratford, Ontario in 2003 settled the matter: as part of his mockery of Cressida, Pandarus displayed the bloodstained bedsheet.
9 Grace Tiffany sees Cressida as "choosing choicelessness": "Not saying No: Female Self-Erasure in *Troilus and Cressida*," *Texas Studies in Literature and Language*, 35 (1993), p. 54. Other critics note a disconnectedness in the characterization: see Gayle Greene, "Shakespeare's Cressida: 'A Kind of Self'," *The Woman's Part: Feminist Criticism of Shakespeare*, ed. Carolyn Ruth Swift Lenz, Gayle Greene and Carol Thomas Neely (Urbana, Chicago and London: University of Illinois Press 1980), p. 135; and Michael Hall, *The Structure of Love: Representative Patterns and Shakespeare's Love Tragedies* (Charlottesville: University Press of Virginia 1989), p. 135. The effect of withdrawing Cressida from view at certain crucial points, with a corresponding reduction in the sense of agency, can be paralleled in Hardy's *Tess of the d'Urbervilles*. Tess is withdrawn from the reader when Alec seduces her, when she murders Alec, and when she is executed.

10 Grace Tiffany uses moments like this to construct a reading of Cressida as having no self-esteem, and willing to believe anything she is told about herself: see "Not saying No," pp. 48–50.

11 Lynch, "Shakespeare's Cressida," p. 361.

12 Janet Adelman, *Suffocating Mothers: Fantasies of Maternal Origin in Shakespeare's Plays, Hamlet to The Tempest* (New York and London: Routledge 1992), p. 57.

13 Marjorie Garber, *Coming of Age in Shakespeare* (London and New York: Methuen 1981), p. 45.

14 Lynch, "Shakespeare's Cressida," observes, "Cressida is kissed five times before she says a word – a fact that makes it difficult to interpret her behavior as blatantly provocative" (p. 363).

15 Juliet Stevenson, in the 1985 Royal Shakespeare Company production, took the Quarto and Folio reading, "beg, then," "barked out, accompanied by a snap of the fingers and an imperious gesture toward the ground": Carol Rutter, "Shakespeare, His Designers, and the Politics of Costume: Handing Over Cressida's Glove," *Essays in Theatre*, 12 (1994), p. 119. (Though both original texts have "begge then," Arden and many other editions emend to preserve the rhyme. But Cressida's breaking of the rhyme may be deliberate.)

16 Tylee, "Text," points out that Pandarus and Troilus have been unable to read Cressida's thoughts (p. 69).

17 According to Janet Adelman, after the kissing scene "She seems suddenly to have passed beyond us as she has passed from Troilus to Diomed" (*Suffocating*, p. 51).

18 Howard C. Adams, "What Cressid is," *Sexuality and Politics in Renaissance Drama*, ed. Carole Levin and Karen Robertson (Lewiston, Queenston and Lampeter: The Edward Mellen Press 1991), p. 87.

19 In Lydgate's *The Historye Sege and Dystruccyon of Troye* Cressida's relationship with Diomedes is more clearly spelled out. At first she keeps him devoted to her by holding him off "cunnyngly and in full sleyghty wyse," but gives her heart to him out of pity after Troilus wounds him: Geoffrey Bullough (ed.), *Narrative and Dramatic Sources of Shakespeare*, vol. 6 (London: Routledge and Kegan Paul; New York: Columbia University Press 1966), pp. 174, 181.

20 The play may already have lent some credence to this conventional view: depending on how seriously we can take it, the court gossip of Pandarus in I.ii. suggests that Helen is getting tired of Paris and beginning to flirt with Troilus.

21 I borrow the phrasing from Clifford Leech, in conversation.

22 In Lydgate Achilles kills Troilus as he kills Hector in the play, having the Myrmidons gang up on him when he is exhausted, and finally dragging his body at his horse's tail. Outraged by this treachery, the narrator attacks Homer for presenting Achilles as a hero (Bullough, *Sources*, pp. 182–86).

23 On the textual question posed by the epilogue, and the possibility that it was at one point cut, see the Arden edition, pp. 416–21.

24 In a production directed by Jennifer Roberts-Smith at Hart House theatre, University of Toronto, in 2002, the armed figure Hector killed lay on stage through the last scenes of the play. Then he rose, took off his armor, and spoke the Epilogue. It was Pandarus.

OTHELLO: I TOOK YOU FOR THAT CUNNING WHORE OF VENICE

1 See Edward Pechter, *Othello and Interpretive Traditions* (Iowa City: University of Iowa Press 1999), pp. 30–33.

2 Ann Jennalie Cook, *Making a Match: Courtship in Shakespeare and his Society* (Princeton: Princeton University Press 1991), p. 206.

3 The Folio reads "storm" for "scorn," anticipating the storm through which Othello and Desdemona journey to Cyprus.

4 "Weaving and Writing in *Othello*," *Shakespeare Survey*, 46 (1994), p. 53.

5 T. G. A. Nelson and Charles Haines claim that Othello never consummates his marriage, and the disruption of the first night on Cyprus is an important part of their argument: "Othello's Unconsummated Marriage," *Essays in Criticism*, 33 (1983), p. 1.

6 Virginia Mason Vaughan, *Othello: A Contextual History* (Cambridge: Cambridge University Press 1994), pp. 46–47.

7 Stephen Greenblatt sees Iago as dealing in "the surfaces of social existence," constructing a stock comic plot about the infidelity of a young wife married to an old husband: *Renaissance Self-Fashioning: From More to Shakespeare* (Chicago and London: University of Chicago Press 1980), pp. 234–35. Barbara Everett calls Iago "the voice of the Mob" who cannot be killed because society, unlike the individual, always survives: *Young Hamlet: Essays on Shakespeare's Tragedies* (Oxford: Clarendon Press 1989), pp. 47–48. According to Jane Adamson his is "an essentially simple mind, for whom life is correspondingly simple"; his power over others stems from the fact that "moral simplicity is always seductive to those whose lives are complicated and anguished": *Othello as Tragedy: Some Problems of Judgement and Feeling* (Cambridge: Cambridge University Press 1980), pp. 76–77.

8 See Pechter, *Interpretive Traditions*, p. 67.

9 In Cinthio's version of the story, the relations between the Ensign and Disdemona are more straightforward. He loves her; she ignores him; his love turns to hatred, and he determines that if he cannot have her the Moor will not either. See Geoffrey Bullough (ed.), *Narrative and Dramatic Sources of Shakespeare*, vol. 7 (London: Routledge and Kegan Paul; New York: Columbia University Press 1973), p. 244.

10 In this period, according to Michael Neill, "any mixture of racial 'kinds' seems to have been popularly thought of as in some sense adulterous": "Unproper Beds: Race, Adultery, and the Hideous in *Othello*," *Shakespeare Quarterly*, 40 (1989), pp. 408–9.

11 The connection is drawn by Lawrence Danson, *Tragic Alphabet: Shakespeare's Drama of Language* (New Haven and London: Yale University Press 1974), p. 114. Danson points out that in both cases the questioner's own identity is at stake.

12 This is the argument of E. H. Gombrich's *Art and Illusion* (Princeton: Princeton University Press 1960).

13 Katharine Eisaman Maus, *Inwardness and Theater in the English Renaissance* (Chicago and London: University of Chicago Press 1995), p. 126.

14 Stanley Cavell, *Disowning Knowledge in Six Plays of Shakespeare* (Cambridge: Cambridge University Press 1987), pp. 131–32. Having proposed this reading, Cavell then sets it in play with other possibilities.

15 Lynda E. Boose, "Othello's Handkerchief: 'The Recognizance and Pledge of Love,'" *English Literary Renaissance*, 5 (1975), p. 368; Arthur Kirsch, *The Passions of Shakespeare's Tragic Heroes* (Charlottesville and London: University Press of Virginia 1990), p. 57.

16 Nelson and Haines, "Unconsummated," pp. 1–18; Graham Bradshaw, "Obeying the Time in *Othello*: a Myth and the Mess it Made," *English Studies*, 73 (1992), pp. 223–28. Bradshaw attacks the double-time theory, arguing that the marriage and the stay on Cyprus are both brief, and what concerns Othello is not what Desdemona and Cassio have done after the marriage, but what they did previously, during the courtship.

17 "Unproper," p. 396. Neill refers particularly to Nelson and Haines, but his comment could be applied to other critics who have tackled the question.

18 "Her name" is the Quarto reading. The Folio has "My name," making the entire speech about Othello himself. What both readings have in common is that Othello feels his own blackness as a disgrace, and Desdemona has triggered that feeling.

19 According to Janet Adelman, what Othello sees in Desdemona is "the reflection of his own contaminating and contaminated blackness": *Suffocating Mothers: Fantasies of Maternal Origin in Shakespeare's Plays, Hamlet to The Tempest* (New York and London: Routledge 1992), p. 67. As Edward Berry puts it, "In his diseased imagination she becomes, paradoxically, the stereotype of the Moor: cunning, 'black,' sexually depraved, and diabolic": "Othello's Alienation," *Studies in English Literature*, 30 (1990), p. 328.

20 In Orson Welles' 1952 film Othello not only pushes the handkerchief away but steps on it.

21 Elizabeth Hanson, "Brothers of the State: *Othello*, Bureaucracy and Epistemological Crisis," *The Elizabethan Theatre*, 14 (Toronto: P. D. Meany 1996), p. 42.

22 On the handkerchief as an image of concealment, see Philippa Berry, *Shakespeare's Feminine Endings: Disfiguring Death in the Tragedies* (London and New York: Routledge 1999), pp. 94–95.

23 Adelman, *Suffocating*, pp. 67–68; Boose, "Handkerchief," pp. 362, 368.

24 *Fashioning Femininity and English Renaissance Drama* (Chicago and London: University of Chicago Press 1991), pp. 90, 92.

25 *The Rape of the Lock* itself picks up the idea. Its comic analogies for Belinda's anger at the loss of her hair include: "Not fierce Othello in so loud a strain/ Roared for the handkerchief that caused his pain" (V.105–6).

26 *A Short View of Tragedy* (1693), in Brian Vickers (ed.), *Shakespeare: The Critical Heritage*, vol. 2 (London and Boston: Routledge and Kegan Paul 1974), pp. 28, 51.

27 Valerie Traub, *Desire and Anxiety: Circulations of Sexuality in Shakespearean Drama* (London and New York: Routledge 1992), p. 39.

28 Derek Cohen, *Shakespeare's Culture of Violence* (London: St. Martin's Press 1993), p. 121.

29 The eyewitness account of the 1610 performance, quoted in the Introduction, stresses the moving power of Desdemona's face, especially after her death.

30 Nelson and Haines, "Unconsummated," p. 9.

31 Hanson relates Iago's silence to that of victims (like Robert Southwell) who kept silence in Elizabethan torture chambers: "Brothers," pp. 31–32.

32 The Quarto has a comma after "Othello," the Folio a colon. Arden has a question mark, which I think weakens the statement.

33 "Unproper," p. 407.

KING LEAR: WE HAVE NO SUCH DAUGHTER

1 In quoting from the Arden edition I have omitted the superscript letters that identify Quarto-only and Folio-only readings. My discussion draws on both versions of the play, but I have called attention to significant differences as they arise.

2 See Jodi Mikalachki, *The Legacy of Boadicea: Gender and Nation in Early Modern England* (London and New York: Routledge 1998), p. 82.

3 The Folio reduces the count to twelve. To consider even more curiously, after her principal speeches Cordelia has two more lines in dialogue with Lear, bringing her total (in the Quarto) to fifteen, equal to the combined number of her sisters' lines. (The line-count is based on the lineation standard in modern editions; Quarto lineation differs, but not so as to affect the point about the overall length of speeches.) H. A. Mason calls Cordelia "not genuinely tongue-tied . . . but damnably explicit," and adds a sardonic twist: "She is scoring off her sisters rather than speaking sincerely": *Shakespeare's Tragedies of Love* (London: Chatto and Windus 1970), p. 174.

4 Jeffrey Stern, "*King Lear*: The Transference of the Kingdom," *Shakespeare Quarterly*, 41 (1990), p. 300.

5 *Identity in Shakespearean Drama* (Lewisburg: Bucknell University Press; London and Toronto: Associated University Presses 1983), p. 134.

6 "The Father and the Bride in Shakespeare," *PMLA*, 97 (1982), p. 333.

7 For a defense of Lear's initial scheme, see Ralph Berry, *Tragic Instance* (Newark: University of Delaware Press; London: Associated University Presses 1999), pp. 137–49.

 8 R. A. Foakes, "King Lear: Monarch or Senior Citizen?," *Elizabethan Theater: Essays in Honor of S. Schoenbaum*, ed. R. B. Parker and S. P. Zitner (Newark: University of Delaware Press; London: Associated University Presses 1996), p. 280.
 9 G. B. Shand, "Lear's Coronet: Playing the Moment," *Shakespeare Quarterly*, 38 (1987), p. 81.
10 This reflects the use of inversion in contemporary popular rebellion, as described by David Underdown, *Revel, Riot and Rebellion: Popular Politics and Culture in England 1603–1660* (Oxford and New York: Oxford University Press 1985), p. 111.
11 The Folio cuts Lear's next speech ("I would learn that . . .") in which the Quarto, characteristically more discursive and explicit, spells the idea out.
12 William C. Carroll, "'The Base Shall Top Th'Legitimate'; The Bedlam Beggar and the Role of Edgar in *King Lear*," *Shakespeare Quarterly*, 38 (1987), p. 436.
13 Janet Adelman, *Suffocating Mothers: Fantasies of Maternal Origin in Shakespeare's Plays, Hamlet to The Tempest* (New York and London: Routledge 1992), pp. 113–14; Arden note, pp. 241–42.
14 Arden note, p. 158.
15 Jay Halio, "Gloucester's Blinding," *Shakespeare Quarterly*, 43 (1992), pp. 221–23.
16 In Peter Brook's 1962 stage production Cornwall wore spurs.
17 Lawrence Danson, *Tragic Alphabet: Shakespeare's Drama of Language* (New Haven and London: Yale University Press 1974), p. 181; Jonathan Dollimore, *Radical Tragedy* (Chicago: University of Chicago Press 1984), p. 193.
18 Lynne Magnusson notes that Cordelia addresses Lear as her father while he sleeps, but as her king when he awakes. She goes on to note that Cordelia restores the traditional language of hierarchy. Writing from a contemporary feminist perspective, she finds this "disappointing." See *Shakespeare and Social Dialogue: Dramatic Language and Elizabethan Letters* (Cambridge: Cambridge University Press 1999), pp. 149–50.
19 Adelman, *Suffocating*, pp. 121, 124.
20 Alan Somerset has suggested to me an alternate reading: Lear shrinks from being told he is in his own kingdom because he has given up his fantasies of power.
21 *The Wheel of Fire* (London: Methuen repr. 1960; first published Oxford University Press 1930), p. 178.
22 C. F. Williamson, "The Hanging of Cordelia," *Review of English Studies*, 34 (1983), pp. 414–18.
23 Talbot cradling the body of his dead son John in *Henry VI Part One* anticipates the ending of *King Lear*; as John's body is brought on stage, a servant conflates birth and death in the line," O dear my lord, lo, where your son is borne!" (IV.iv.129).

MACBETH: A DEED WITHOUT A NAME

1 See Arthur F. Kinney, *Lies Like Truth: Shakespeare, Macbeth, and the Cultural Moment* (Detroit: Wayne State University Press 2001), p. 200.

2 To Marion Lomax it sounds as though Duncan is wearing a masque costume: *Stage Images and Traditions: Shakespeare to Ford* (Cambridge: Cambridge University Press 1987), p. 57. Marjorie Garber points to the error in heraldry of placing metal against metal: *Coming of Age in Shakespeare* (London and New York: Methuen 1981), p. 107.

3 On the narrative confusion of the opening scenes, see Barbara Everett, *Young Hamlet: Essays on Shakespeare's Tragedies* (Oxford: Clarendon Press 1989), p. 99. There is a cinematic equivalent in Akira Kurosawa's *Throne of Blood* (1957) in the confusing journey of Washizu and Miki (the equivalents of Macbeth and Banquo) through the Cobweb Forest.

4 Lawrence Danson, *Tragic Alphabet: Shakespeare's Drama of Language* (New Haven and London: Yale University Press 1974), p. 123.

5 Geoffrey Bullough (ed.), *Narrative and Dramatic Sources of Shakespeare*, vol. 7 (London: Routledge and Kegan Paul; New York: Columbia University Press 1973), pp. 494–95, 495, 513, 519. Stephen Greenblatt writes of Shakespeare's witches, "it is . . . extremely difficult to specify what if anything they do, or even what, if anything, they are": "Shakespeare Bewitched," *Shakespeare and Cultural Traditions*, ed. Tetsuo Kishi, Roger Pringle and Stanley Wells (Newark: University of Delaware Press; London and Toronto: Associated University Presses 1994), p. 31.

6 Adrian Poole reads the passage in similar terms, and sees an equivalent effect in "if th'assassination/Could trammel up the consequence" (I.vii.2–3), where it is "assassination," not Macbeth, that does the deed: *Tragedy: Shakespeare and the Greek Example* (Oxford and New York: Basil Blackwell 1987), p. 46.

7 James L. Calderwood, *If It Were Done: Macbeth and Tragic Action* (Amherst: University of Massachusetts Press 1986), p. 39.

8 On the lack of finality in the play, see Stephen Booth, *King Lear, Macbeth, Indefinition, and Tragedy* (New Haven and London: Yale University Press 1983), pp. 93–94.

9 David Margolies, *Monsters of the Deep: Social Dissolution in Shakespeare's Tragedies* (Manchester and New York: Manchester University Press 1992), p. 102.

10 There is a similar effect in *Richard III*, where Richmond enters the play's consciousness for the first time when Richard becomes king; again the names are similar.

11 In the 1979 Thames television production, based on Trevor Nunn's 1976 stage production for the Royal Shakespeare Company, Macduff, after killing Macbeth, enters holding two daggers in his bloodstained hands, exactly as Macbeth did after killing Duncan.

12 See Chapter 2, n.12.

13 Arden note, p. 46.

14 Gordon Williams, *A Glossary of Shakespeare's Sexual Language* (London and Atlantic Highlands, NJ: Athone 1997), pp. 101–2.

15 Dennis Biggins, "Sexuality, Witchcraft, and Violence in *Macbeth*," *Shakespeare Studies*, 8 (1975), pp. 257–60.

16 Williams, *Glossary*, pp. 284–85.

17 This speech is examined in terms of Elizabethan medical theory by Jenijoy La Belle, "'A Strange Infirmity': Lady Macbeth's Amenorrhea," *Shakespeare Quarterly*, 31 (1980), pp. 381–86. The blocked passage implies a stopping of menstrual blood, and breast milk was menstrual blood turned white (382–83). A woman whose periods had stopped could, like the witches, grow a beard (384).

18 Holinshed's account of the manners of the Scots, taken from Hector Boece, includes the detail that Scottish women took breastfeeding as a serious responsibility and were particularly insistent on nursing their own children (Bullough, *Sources*, p. 506).

19 Bullough, *Sources*, p. 433.

20 In *Shakespeare: A Life* (Oxford: Oxford University Press 1998) Park Honan speculates that Anne Shakespeare's reproductive system was damaged when she had twins, and this would explain the subsequent childlessness of the marriage (p. 231).

21 On the sexual connotations of the murder, see Calderwood, *If It Were Done*, pp. 42–47, and Ralph Berry, *Tragic Instance: The Sequence of Shakespeare's Tragedies* (Newark: University of Delaware Press; London: Associated University Presses 1999), pp. 150–63. As Karen Bamford has pointed out to me, Macduff's reference to the Gorgon carries associations of rape: Medusa was transformed to a Gorgon after Neptune raped her.

22 Arthur Kirsch, *The Passions of Shakespeare's Tragic Heroes* (Charlottesville and London: University Press of Virginia 1990), p. 81.

23 Biggins, "Sexuality," pp. 260–61.

24 William Davenant's Restoration adaptation and Orson Welles' 1948 film both construct a relationship between Lady Macbeth and Lady Macduff, Davenant by writing new dialogue, Welles by having Lady Macduff reside in Macbeth's castle and reassigning speeches to create conversations between the women.

25 As Arthur F. Kinney points out, there is a public dimension to this scene: Lady Macbeth "in a nightdress, carrying a candle . . . enacts a popular shaming ritual for shrews, but one often employed also for witches" (*Lies Like Truth*, p. 171). However, unlike the victim of an actual shaming ritual, Lady Macbeth has no awareness whatever of being watched and judged.

26 In Diana Leblanc's 1999 production at Stratford, Ontario Macbeth delivered the speech over the body of his wife, which had been brought on stage. The effect was moving, and of course settled the question of the speech's relation

to her death. But it required new business that changed the effect of the text, and it may be more powerful to let the audience make the connection itself, making us responsible for it rather than having it forced on us.

27 Donald W. Forster, "*Macbeth*'s War on Time," *English Literary Renaissance,* 16 (1986), p. 321. Roman Polanski's 1971 film version ends with Donalbain on his way to consult the witches.

28 Booth, *Indefinition,* pp. 91, 92.

29 *Shakespeare's Festive Tragedy: The Ritual Foundations of Genre* (London and New York: Routledge 1995), p. 222.

Index